The Segess

The Segesser Hide Paintings

Masterpieces Depicting Spanish Colonial New Mexico

By Gottfried Hotz

Translation by Johannes Malthaner

Revised Edition with a new foreword by
Thomas E. Chávez

Museum of New Mexico Press

To Martha

who assisted me in visiting dozens of tribes in North America and in building a collection relating to the cultures of the North American Indians.

 Originally published as *Indian Skin Paintings from the American Southwest.*

Manufactured in the United States of America.
10 9 8 7 6 5 4 3 2 1

Library of Congress Cataloging-in-Publication number: 91-60818
ISBN 0-89013-222-4 (paperbound).

Cover design by GLYPHICS/Terry Duffy Design.

Museum of New Mexico Press
P.O. Box 2087
Santa Fe, NM 87504

Contents

List of Plates

Foreword

"It was quite casual that at the end of the Second World War I was informed of the existence of two large hide paintings," wrote Swiss scholar Gottfried Hotz. The discovery came while Hotz was studying Plains Indian art. The hides, he learned, hung in an estate in Lucerne, in the possession of the von Segessers, whose ancestor, an eighteenth-century Jesuit missionary to the Spanish province of Sonora, Mexico, had commissioned the works and bestowed them as gifts to his family. For Hotz, the happenstance discovery of the works launched him on a twenty-five year study of their origins, meanings, and significance. The public unveiling of the hides in 1986, at the Museum of New Mexico's Palace of the Governors, brought to view the finest and best-preserved examples of documentary skin painting that the world had known.

Trained at the Seminary of Kusnacht in Zurich and a lifelong teacher, Hotz was, at the time of his discovery, the Curator of Ethnology of the Indian Museum in Zurich. From there he traveled to Lucerne to view the paintings, then in the possession of Hans Ulrich von Segesser and his mother Mrs. Josefine von Segesser. He conducted related research in libraries, archives, and through correspondence, and in the process he journeyed by Volkswagen through the United States and parts of Sonora to study American geography and North American Indian cultures.

Hotz's work culminated in a book written in German titled *Indianische Ledermalereienm Figurenreiche Darstellungen von Grenzkonflikten zwichen Mexiko und dem Missouri un 1720*, which translates to *Indian Leather Paintings Showing Border Conflicts Between Mexico and the Missouri in 1720*. The book caught the attention of George E. Hyde, an ethnologist at the Smithsonian Institution, who recommended the book to the University of Oklahoma Press to be published as part of its prestigious "Civilization of the American Indian" series. Despite criticism, some of which incorrectly postulated that Hotz had never been to the United States and that his work was "an armchair theory in typically prolix German form," the English translation was published in 1970 as Volume 94 of the series. Though the book's publication was met with praise, its popular success was doubtless hampered by the fact that the hides were still in their remote Swiss lodgings.

Research and events subsequent to Gottfried Hotz's study have borne out his enthusiasm for the paintings he named "Segesser I" and "Segesser II." But beyond confirming his work, the reception to Hotz's book inspired a field of investigation that has resulted in much additional knowledge of the early eighteenth century in northern Mexico and the American Southwest. In the process, the Segesser hide paintings have come full circle, provoking a study whose publication stimulated scholars to more fully answer questions the paintings raise.

The time came for a public viewing. In 1986 Dr. Segesser loaned the paintings to the Palace of the Governors. By then they had been absent from the North American continent for more than two centuries. After extensive negotiations, the State of New Mexico purchased the works, and they were accessioned into the permanent collections of the Palace. When not traveling to other museums, the hide paintings are viewed at home by some one hundred thousand annually. They continue to be the subject of much study.

In the course of his research, Hotz concluded that the paintings had been created in New Mexico and that they depicted events related to New Mexico history. Hotz was solid in his facts, though some of his conclusions regarding Segesser I remain debatable. The reader should note that the exact identity of the subject depicted in Segesser I remains a mystery. Nevertheless, scholars continue to marvel at Hotz's ability to uncover sources and draw conclusions. This abiding respect is particularly intriguing in view of the work's early critics.

Hotz's conclusions, and the fact that he refused to share his photographs of the paintings until his work was published, incurred the wrath of some scholars, especially New Mexicans, who labeled him an autodidact. Among many broad doubts was the assertion that such paintings could not have been executed in New Mexico due to the fact that all known hide paintings up to that point depicted religious topics. The possibility that the paintings represented previously unreported events, or that they were unique, apparently occurred to Hotz alone.

Criticism of the work reached impressive rhetorical heights. New Mexico's renowned Spanish colonial specialist, E. Boyd, complained of Hotz's "Teutonic think patterns" and his "bombastic and preposterous interpretations." She summarily dismissed his correct identification of the subject matter in Segesser II as a premise he adopted "like an obedient hunting dog . . ., alternately following the scent and giving tongue," and described the book as a "plethora of Teutonic mass mystic." Eleanor Adams, scholar and editor of the *New Mexico Historical Review*, approved of Boyd's "appraisal of Hotz's horror," adding that somebody should give "this nonsense the business," which Boyd gladly did with a book review of uncommon bile and length in the July 1971 edition of Adams' journal. But the test of time and subsequent research by others has justified Hotz's diligence and confirmed his "big picture" view. His backers, especially George E. Hyde and Savoie Lottinville, the editor at the University of Oklahoma Press, deserve credit for their unwavering support.

Somewhere in the great archives of the heavens, Gottfried Hotz has got to be pleased.

THOMAS E. CHÁVEZ, DIRECTOR
PALACE OF THE GOVERNORS

Preface

It was in 1945, through Alfred Steinmann, of Zurich, and Edmund Mueller, M.D., of Beromuenster, that I first learned of the existence of the two skin paintings that are the subject of this book. For a number of years I had been engaged in a study of Plains Indian skin paintings, and these gentlemen hoped that I might be able to cast some light on the setting and subject matter of the paintings.

The present owners of the paintings, Hans Ulrich von Segesser and his mother, Mrs. Josefine von Segesser, of Lucerne, made it possible for me to make a careful examination of the paintings and of the writings about them. For their kind cooperation I express my sincere appreciation.

GOTTFRIED HOTZ

Zurich, Switzerland
January 15, 1970

The Segesser Hide Paintings

I
The Origin of the Skin Paintings

In the possession of the von Segesser von Brunegg family of Lucerne, Switzerland, are two large skin paintings of North American origin. Each painting consists of three large, rectangular pieces of leather sewed together with sinew. Each painting is about 4 feet 6 inches high and 18 feet 10 inches wide. For the purposes of this book, the paintings have been designated Segesser I and Segesser II.

The first painting, Segesser I, depicts an attack of Indian raiders, partly armed with European equipment, on unmounted inhabitants of a small tipi camp in a wooded, mountainous region. Segesser II shows an attack of soldiers dressed in typical eighteenth-century grenadier uniforms on a camp of unmounted European soldiers. Uniforms as well as weapons resemble those of the seventeenth, and even of the sixteenth, century and are adapted to frontier Indian warfare. In Segesser II the many Indian allies of the attacking soldiers have cropped hair and are naked; the few Indian allies of the defenders are clothed similarly to their white masters. Neither of the Indian parties in Segesser II bears firearms.

For almost two hundred years efforts have been made to determine the locale of the paintings, the nationalities of both white and red men who appear in them, and the battles in which they were engaged. Before proceeding to a detailed description of the paintings, it seems appropriate to summarize the history of the paintings themselves.

According to a tradition in the von Segesser von Brunegg family, one of its members, Father Philipp, a Jesuit missionary in the Spanish province of Sonora, sent the skin paintings to relatives in Switzerland about the middle of the eighteenth century. According to *Genealogisches Handbuch zur Schweizergeschichte*, Philipp was born in 1689, the son of Heinrich Ludwig Segesser von Brunegg II and his wife, Catharina Rusconi. In 1717, Philipp became a member of the Society of Jesus, and from 1731 until 1762, the year of his death, he served as a missionary in Mexico.[1]

Philipp was the third of seventeen children. One brother, Jost Ranutius (1686–1740), was a clergyman and from 1723 to 1734 was chaplain at Hochdorf. Another brother, Ulrich Franz Josef (1698–1767), became mayor and banneret of Lucerne. It was to Ulrich Franz Josef that Philipp was to send the skin paintings.

Philipp probably started his studies in the Jesuit college in Lucerne. In 1708 he journeyed to Landsberg, in Bavaria, to enter the Jesuit order. Evidently he was not admitted until 1717; on April 1 of that year his father deposited an inheritance settlement of 900 guilders for him with the college in Lucerne.[2]

Additional information about Philipp's life is revealed in his letters[3] to his father, his brother Jost Ranutius in Hochdorf, and his brother Ulrich Franz Josef during the years 1719 to 1761. From 1719 to 1721 he was in Ingolstadt. In 1721 he celebrated his ordination as a priest. From 1722 to 1723 he was in Oettingen and later taught in Straubing. On May 4, 1726, he wrote from Neuburg, Bavaria, that he hoped God would fulfill his wish to become a missionary, but it was not until 1729 that he received his appointment. In April, 1729, he traveled from Munich by way of Genoa to Cádiz, a forty-day trip. In the mission home of the Jesuits in Seville he spent over a year preparing himself for his new vocation. During this time he kept up a regular correspondence with his family.

In the fall of 1730 he sailed for America and reached Havana after a voyage of seventy-eight days. There, with more than one hundred other missionaries, he had to wait for repairs to be made to the ships from Veracruz. In June, 1731, he arrived in Mexico,

[1] Compiled by H. A. von Segesser von Brunegg (Zurich, 1908–16), III, Table IV, 148–49, 201.

[2] Philipp A. von Segesser, *Die Segesser in Luzern und im deutschen* Reiche (Berne, 1855), Part II, 158–59; Philipp Segesser, *Die Berichte des P. Philipp Segesser aud der Gesellschaft Jesu ueber seine Mission in Sonora, 1731–1761* (ed. by Philipp A. von Segesser), (Lucerne, 1886), 8–24.

[3] In the family archives, Segesser Palace, Lucerne, Switzerland.

where after a brief illness he was assigned to a new mission in Sonora. In June 17, 1731, he and two German missionaries started for Durango by way of Zacatecas with an escort of soldiers to protect them from hostile Indians. On December 15 he reached San Ignazio de Pimería Alta, where he remained as vicar for six months. There he learned the Pima language.

Finally, on June 8, 1732, he wrote from his own mission, San Xavier del Bac en Pimería de Sonora. He was the first missionary to serve in the region, except for Father Eusebio Kino of Trento, who had founded a church there in 1700.[4] Russell calls Father Philipp Segesser and Father Juan Bautista Grashoffer the first permanent white residents in Arizona.[5]

In a letter to his family Father Philipp wrote about the Indians of this region (extending north to the Gila River):

> They do not practice idolatry, but there are a few who have nightly conversations with the devil, who is said to appear to them in various forms. The devil is supposed to give them a poison which they blow with deadly effect into the bodies of their victims. One must win them gradually with patience and love. The missionary has to provide everything; otherwise, the Indians would go hungry and would return to the mountains to the pagans, from whom the villages of the converted Indians suffer greatly, especially from the Apaches.[6]

It should be noted here how the Jesuit missions in Sonora supported themselves. The task of colonizing the land with native Indians had been assigned to the Jesuits under the Bishop of Durango, whose diocese included the entire northwestern region of the

[4] The town of Tubac, which belonged to this mission, was located about fifty kilometers north of the present Arizona-Mexico border. The first Church of San Xavier del Bac, nine miles south of Tucson, was built by Father Kino about 1700. In 1783 the construction of a new church was begun near the site of Father Kino's church. It has been called the most beautiful church in Sonora. It stands in what is now the Papago reservation. Frederick Webb Hodge (ed.), *Handbook of American Indians North of Mexico*, Bureau of American Ethnology *Bulletin No. 30* (Washington, 1912), II, 28.

[5] Frank Russell, *The Pima Indians*, Bureau of American Ethnology *Twenty-sixth Annual Report* (Washington, 1908), 28.

[6] In the family archives, Segesser Palace, Lucerne, Switzerland.

territory of Mexico. The bishop appointed to the new missions in Sonora, not Spanish Jesuits, but preferably Jesuits from the German, Austrian, and Bohemian branches of the order. The missionaries received direct support from the king of Spain for the founding of the missions. Their primary tasks were to gather the nomadic Indians into villages, to encourage them to till the ground, and to Christianize them.

Father Philipp wrote about the income of his mission: "The Pimas of the Tecoripa mission are well dressed in cloth and linen. The missionaries buy the material for three to five thousand thalers a year and distribute it among them. This money they receive for the farm produce which they sell to the Spanish miners." He made it clear that the Indians were not dependent, wretched beings who could not provide for themselves: "The Pimas, like all Indians, love red clothes, ribbons, and bows; some dress in red velvet, which they obtain by trading horses, mules, or deerskins or by working."[7]

After 1733, in addition to serving the San Xavier mission, Father Philipp also had to supply the Guebavi de los Angeles mission. In 1735, because of illness, he was transferred to the Tecoripa mission in the Pimería Baja, where he remained until 1743.

Father Philipp's "Relación," dealing with the land and the people in the missions of Pimería Alta and Pimería Baja, which he wrote at the request of an uncle, bears the date July 31, 1737. At the end of the account Father Philipp reported about the Indian uprisings of that and the preceding years. The revolts had been quelled but were only the beginning of the general rebellion that broke out in the following years and lasted until 1761 (the year in which Father Philipp wrote his last letter), bringing devastation to the missions.

In a letter dated July 15, 1738, he expressed the fear that a plague might spread through his mission, which had already suffered greatly from smallpox, drought, and Indian uprisings. He also reported that he had asked for soldiers for his own protection.

There were no further reports until August 13, 1741, after three years of very troubled times. On that date he wrote from

[7] Philipp Segesser, "Relación," 27.

Tecoripa that the Indians of the Pimería Baja had "rebelled against the Catholic faith" on three occasions and that he had subdued them with great difficulty and had publicly burned their gods. Then a flood had severely damaged his church and his home, a catastrophe that a witch doctor had seized upon to create a new unrest. Father Philipp, together with a few Spaniards and soldiers, had been besieged in his home by two thousand Yaqui Indians but had been able to repel them. He was still in danger, he added, for the Apaches were also on the move and had slain his good friend Captain Juan de Ansa.

On August 27, 1742, he gave more details about the Yaqui uprising of the previous year. After the Pimas had been subdued, there was a rebellion of Yaquis who lived nearer the coast. They regained their land, destroyed all the missions there, and then invaded Tecoripa and laid siege to Father Philipp's house, not with the intention of killing him, they said, but to make a captive of him and to use him as an instructor in the art of war. For three months, Father Philipp reported, he had had to feed eighteen to twenty soldiers and about fifty other persons, and they had consumed more than six hundred head of cattle.[8] He added that he had asked for transfer to another mission to rest from the many hardships he had undergone and had received orders to leave for Ures, a mission station on the Sonora River, two days' journey south of Tecoripa.

On November 18, 1744, he arrived in Ures, where he stayed until his death. Even there the Indian threat was constant, with Apaches on one side and the Seris, who lived on the coast and on Tiburón Island in the Gulf of California, on the other. On September 2, 1750, he was appointed inspector, a dangerous office, for he had to travel through the territories of the rebellious Indians.

In a letter from Ures dated September 18, 1750, Father Phil-

[8] Father Eusebio Francisco Kino, apostle of the Pimas and founder of the mission of San Xavier del Bac (April, 1700), was born in 1644 in the Tyrol. Arriving in Mexico in 1681, he brought with him the livestock that started the herds which were scattered around some twenty missions in Sonora and present southern Arizona nearly half a century later, in Father Philipp's time. See *Kino's Historical Memoir of Pimería Alta, 1683–1711* (ed. by Herbert Eugene Bolton), (Cleveland, 1919).

ipp reported that the Indians had not yet been subdued. Almost all the soldiers had left for Tiburón Island, and the Indians were making raids on villages around Ures. By 1752 he still could give no encouraging reports about the mission; soldiers were stationed in his house constantly for protection against the marauding Seris. The Pimas in the Pimería Alta had again rebelled and had destroyed all the missionary work of eighty years.

On April 28, 1754, Father Philipp reported that he had become rector of San Xavier de Ures. Ures, he said, was crowded with civil and military officers, servants, and others, for all of whom he had to provide lodging and food. Conditions continued to be difficult; the Spanish guards could not prevent the raids of the Apaches, the Seris, and the Pimas.

The last letter from Father Philipp, written to his brother Ulrich Franz Josef on April 11, 1761, was composed in the fortress at San Miguel de Horcasitas, the headquarters of the captain-general of the province. Father Philipp reported that he had been summoned to the fortress to serve as administrator of the estate of the governor, Juan de Mendoza, who had been killed in an Indian attack. The governor, a nobleman from Estremadura and a close friend of Father Philipp's, had amassed a fortune of $100,000 during the five years he had served in the province. The paintings cannot have been part of the governor's estate, for in the April 11 letter Father Philipp referred to a box containing three "colored skins" which he had sent to Ulrich three years before Mendoza's death.

Father Philipp's reference to the paintings as "colored skins" is odd. He seems to have had little understanding of the character, customs, and beliefs of the Indians, as his letters and the "Relación" indicate. Yet in his old age he evidently gained some awareness of the value of these products of his charges, for he expressed concern about the safety of the box "in which my heart has been shipped." He had repeatedly received boxes from home from which some of the contents had been removed, and he was afraid that the paintings might have been stolen during the customs inspection. He had reason to be concerned, for the box containing the paintings was more than a year en route to Veracruz, where it was futher delayed before finally being shipped to Europe.

Because of their significance in the story of the paintings, passages from the 1761 letter are quoted below:

> It has worried me somewhat that I have not received a letter from my dear brother for a long time. In his last letter he sent me the desired news and expressed his concern that the heavy work might make me ill. I have in the meantime sent several letters and also the box in which my heart has been shipped and about which I have received good and bad news. It has been delayed in Mexico for more than a year. Later it was delivered to Mr. B. Thomas Apodáca (who has arrived with the mercury and is a merchant from Cádiz, as I mentioned in other letters). I have his receipt and letter, in which he writes that it will be necessary to open the box to find out what is being shipped in it and what duty might have to be paid for the things to the King, although I sent him a list of the contents and declared that actually all that is in the box is not worth four pennies except the three colored skins, which can be considered curios and of little value. He promised me to see to its safe delivery. If they open the box, I am afraid they will not repack it as carefully as it was packed when it was dispatched from here and therefore will be delivered badly damaged. In a previous letter I have listed what is to be found in the box. God grant that it arrive.

The 1761 letter is the third extant letter mentioning the box. In 1759, Father Philipp had written that in the previous year he had sent to his family a box in which he had enclosed a list of contents.[9] Still another list had been enclosed in a separate letter in which he had expressed his concern about the box, "which has been filled with my good will and 'atención.'" Below are two passages from the 1759 letter:

> Ures, the eighteenth of January, 1759:
>
> I sent some news a year ago about the happenings in this country and sent a box by the driver of the wagon which comes by here every year. The box contains a few unimportant things as can be seen by the two lists of contents, one in the box, the other in a

[9] Philipp A. von Segesser, *Die Berichte des P. Philipp Segesser*, 22.

> separate letter. I do not know whether the box was dispatched with the *Gloten,* because it seems that the driver did not reach Mexico in time. If the box did not get there in time before the *Gloten* started the return journey, I hope there will be another opportunity to deliver it to Mr. Thomas Apodáca in Cádiz, because I went to a great deal of trouble in this matter. Although there are no particularly important things in it, I would not want that the box be dispatched differently from the way I packed it since I did it with the greatest of care.
>
> For more than ten years I have experienced great hardships here. Three months ago the enemies (the painted Seris and recently also the unbearable Apaches, who have never invaded our mission territories up to now), raided our mission four times and took much cattle and many horses and mules. They put my mission and the neighboring settlers into such miserable condition that I had to provide clothing for some who did not even have shirts to cover themselves. To get food, it is necessary for my Indians, like the hunters in the mountains, to hunt a few wild cows or oxen. There has never been such misery since the missions have been established. In addition, the roads are so dangerous to travel that nobody is secure, and all are in great danger of falling into the hands of the enemy or of being killed by poisoned arrows and spears.

Perhaps the most significant of the letters regarding the box is the one dated 1758, the year the box was dispatched. The first double page of this letter is missing. On the second page (which would have been the fourth page of the original letter) Father Philipp briefly referred to the box, after saying that he was enclosing (probably in the letter) the plan of the mission home he was building and commenting that it was hard to find capable builders. Then he added:

> In the box will be found the description of the material and another inventory indicating for each item its purpose, use, and property [characteristics]. May my brother receive everything in the spirit in which it was sent, with my best wishes, although the things are not worth anything. *Affectum non affectum aspice!*

Later in the letter he again mentioned the box. Obviously the contents were important to him, although he repeated the comment that the items had no monetary value.

It is not difficult to guess why the first portion of the 1758 letter and the inventory enclosed in the box have been lost. They were no doubt either kept separate from the other letters or removed to serve as guides in explaining the paintings to acquaintances, and in time went astray.

The contents of the three letters seem to be clear evidence that the Segesser family tradition is correct—the skin paintings were indeed sent to Switzerland by Father Philipp.

The expulsion of the Jesuits from Mexico in 1767 destroyed the missions in Sonora. Names of church stations not connected with Spanish settlements, producing mines, or forts soon disappeared from the maps. But Father Philipp did not live to see the final destruction of his lifework and that of his colleagues; he died at San Miguel on September 18, 1762.

The skin paintings remained in the possession of the Segesser family. In 1890 they were in the possession of Heinrich Viktor von Segesser-Crivelli (1843–1900), in Lucerne. About 1894 he sold them to Paul von Segesser (1847–1900), trustee of the Segesser Palace in the Ruetligasse and financial director of the city of Lucerne. Paul left them to his son, Joseph Leopold, who in turn left them to his son, Hans Ulrich von Segesser, their present owner.

A piece of Segesser I, about forty inches wide, showing an Indian tent village, belongs to the architect August am Rhyn, who bought it some time before 1908 from the painter Benz, who had received it as a gift from Heinrich Viktor von Segesser-Crivelli.

Of the third of the three paintings Father Philipp mentioned in the 1761 letter nothing has survived, nor could any report concerning it be found.

In 1946, Mrs. Auf der Mauer, daughter of Paul von Segesser, mentioned to me that the skin paintings were at one time kept in the Huenenberg Castle, a Segesser family home near Ebikon, outside Lucerne. She did not know whether the paintings were hung there or whether one of them was cut to fit a section of wall in the castle.

There is a section of wall on the second floor of the castle where Segesser I may have hung; the measurements of the wall space and of the painting very closely correspond. Of course, it is also possible that Segesser I was cut in Sonora, where it may have served as a wall hanging in a mission house. It is certain that at some time it was used as a wall covering; the colors at the edges of the left side are much stronger and deeper than those on the remaining surface, indicating that they were covered with a molding or frame.

SEGESSER I

II
The Setting

In spite of the fact that Father Philipp sent the skins from Sonora, various experts have ventured the opinion that the skins originated in South America, perhaps in Paraguay in the system of missions established among the Guaranís in the seventeenth century.

A close examination of the paintings disproves this theory. In addition to bows and arrows, the Guaranís used the macana, a four-cornered or slightly curved club. No weapon resembling the macana appears on Segesser I. The Guaranís carried wooden shields covered with tapir skins.[1] The round large shields in Segesser I are so big that they would be extremely heavy and could not be flexible which they seem to be.

The Guaranís painted their bodies with vivid colors, and they were naked except for feather aprons. Though the Indians of Segesser II have multicolored and elaborate body paintings, those of Segesser I do not. The Guaranís were small of build but robust. This description fits the Indians of Segesser I but not those of Segesser II.

In 1640 the Guaranís under the control of the Jesuits[2] were given permission to bear firearms against their enemies. The Indians in Segesser I have no firearms. Moreover, the Indians under attack in Segesser I have typically North American conical tents that bear no resemblance to the huts of the Guaranís.

A further indication of the locale of Segesser I is to be found in the animals that appear in the painting. The pronghorns (*Antilocapra americana*) argue for a North American locale. Of particular significance are the five buffaloes running to the right out of the

[1] Maria Fassbind, *Der Jesuitenstaat in Paraguay* (1926), 14–19.
[2] *Ibid.*, 26.

picture, and a sixth buffalo below (behind the woman with the waterskin).

The animal figures, though somewhat primitive, are more nearly accurate than the first European drawings of this species—for example, the buffalo of Gómara (1554),[3] that of Thevet (1558),[4] or even that of De Bry (1595).[5] The horns of the lower buffalo might indicate the somewhat larger mountain or forest buffalo (*Bison bison athabascae*), but this animal lived only in latitudes 63 to 55 degrees north, and the landscape of Segesser I does not indicate such a latitude. It must therefore be assumed that the buffaloes are meant to represent the common American bison (*B. bison bison*), which at the time of the first European settlements in America were spread over a region extending almost from the Atlantic Coast to Arizona and north to the present borders of Nevada and Oregon, in latitudes 25 to 65 degrees north.[6] Buffaloes were reported by Cabeza de Vaca in Texas about 1530. Nuño de Guzmán and Coronado confirmed the existence of these animals and gave additional information about them.[7]

Father Philipp does not mention the buffalo in his "Relación," although he gives a long list of the animals of Sonora and their

[3] George Parker Winship, *The Coronado Expedition*, Bureau of American Ethnology *Fourteenth Annual Report* (Washington, 1896), Part I, 512.

[4] *Ibid.*, 516.

[5] *Ibid.*, 520.

[6] Brehm, *Saeugetiere* (Leipzig and Vienna, 1916), IV, 372.

[7] Juan de Torquemada, *Monarquia* (Madrid, 1725), I, 678.

Sketch of Segesser I

descriptions. The absence of buffaloes from his list supports the view that the setting of Segesser I is east or northeast of Sonora.

Until late in the eighteenth century the grazing region of the buffaloes extended much farther than is generally realized. For example, J. A. Allen cited many reports of observations of buffaloes in South Carolina during the first half of the eighteenth century.[8] Francis Moore, in his *Voyage Through Georgia*, testified to their presence even farther south and closer to the Atlantic: "The island [St. Simon's] has an abundance of red deer and rabbits. No buffaloes live on the island, although there are large herds on the mainland."[9]

Cortes saw buffaloes in the menageries of Montezuma in 1521, and it is obvious that the animals must have been captured near Mexico City. In 1602 the Franciscan monks of Nuevo León encountered many herds of buffaloes, which were also abundant in Nueva Vizcaya (later the states of Chihuahua and Durango) and sometimes ranged far south of that region. It is my belief that in their summer migrations northward the buffaloes passed across the gently rising prairies of Chihuahua and roamed at least as far west as the southwest corner of the present state of New Mexico (one possible setting for Segesser I). J. T. Allen extends the buffaloes' range to the west side of the Río Grande River.

Small numbers of buffaloes once roamed in northeastern Utah

[8] J. A. Allen, "The American Bison," Museum of Comparative Zoology *Memoirs* (Cambridge, 1876).

[9] Georgia Historical Society *Collections*, I, 117.

and probably also in the present state of Idaho. Fremont saw buffaloes in "immense numbers" in 1824 in the Bear River and Green River (Colorado) valleys and throughout the region from the Green River to the Lewis Fork of the Columbia (the present Snake River). They were found in the northwest corner of New Mexico as late as 1850.

The mountain sheep shown in Segesser I belong to one of two southern descendants of the Rocky Mountain sheep (*Ovis canadensis*), either Mexican mountain sheep (*Ovis mexicanus*) or Nelson's sheep (*Ovis nelsoni*), both of which lived in the mountains and deserts of the Southwest, from Nevada to Chihuahua. These varieties were at one time so numerous that entire tribes of Indians lived off their meat and used their skins for clothing. The strikingly terraced mountain on which the sheep are shown in the painting reminds one of the formations of the Grand Canyon or the mesas in the Río Grande basin.

The other animals shown in Segesser I are not of much assistance in determining the locale of the painting. Most of them belong to species widespread in America or to indeterminable subspecies.

III

Material, Measurements, and Colors

The three skins of Segesser I are buffalo- or cowhide, tanned Indian-fashion and stitched together with sinew. The over-all height of the painting is about 4 feet 6 inches. The length is about 1 foot 6 inches to the missing piece, then 9½ inches to the seam joining the first skin to the second, which is about 5 feet 2 inches wide. Then, after a gap of about 4 inches, is the fragment belonging to August am Rhyn.

There are two strips, one 8¼ inches wide and the other 1 foot 4 inches wide, with two small pieces that were at some time cut out, probably to allow for a door knob and a lock, and were later glued back in place (see Plate 4). The right edge of this strip, 8/10 inch wide, was at one time covered with a molding, for the colors on the strip are deeper than those of the rest of the painting.

There are incomplete figures of animals at both edges. The border at the right, which is a fraction over 6 inches wide, and the outer edges of the corners are stitched on with sinew. At the right edge of the passe-partout strip (which is ¾ inch wide), where a bush and a tree are cut off, traces of greenish-blue color and the continuation of the outline can be seen. The two dark tendrils of the border at the bottom almost exactly meet the tendrils of the rosette at the lower right corner, all of which indicate that the buffalo head at the bottom that seems to be peering out of the wings, as well as the hindquarters of the buffalo disappearing into the wings, were added with a humorous intent. A comparison of the border from the edge of the painting to the passe-partout of the border at the right shows that a vertical strip a little more than 1 inch wide is missing.

The length of the three stitched-together skins, of the extant and missing pieces, and of the probable total is as follows:

	*Length, Inches**
First skin: To the cutout	18½
Cutout	48
Length at the right of the cut, to the first seam (uncut)	9½
	76
Second skin: 72 inches beyond the cutout, less about 9½ inches to the seam	62½
(If the first and second skin were of the same length, then about 5 inches would be missing at the left of the "Am Rhyn" piece. A comparison of the borders, however, shows a missing piece of about 4 inches)	4
"Am Rhyn" piece up to the seam	8¼
	74¾
Third skin: "Am Rhyn" piece belonging to the third skin	31
Missing (according to a comparison of the borders)	11½
Section showing guard of water carriers, buffaloes, and mountain	9½
Section showing water carriers and buffalo	15¾
Missing narrow strip of the horizontal border	1
The top border, at the right side	6
	74¾
Approximate total length of the original painting	19½ feet

*Translator's note: The original measurements of both paintings were taken in centimeters. The equivalents shown here are close approximations.

The paint used in Segesser I is evidently of mineral origin, doubtless made by Indians. On the narrow strips which were once covered with moldings one can discern the following colors: level terrain, light yellow; slopes, dark green; trees and bushes, greenish-blue; tree trunks and border background, deep reddish-brown, with mountaintops and rosettes a somewhat deeper shade of brown. The outlines of animals, people, leaves, manes, hair, tree trunks, and the palisades of the refugium, or stronghold, are dark brown. The large, three-lobed leaves of the border were originally a dark steel blue, which faded to a yellowish color. There are two alternating designs on the borders: one unit is made up of an eight-pointed brown rosette with a yellow center and edged with yellow (which may originally have been white), with blue leaves on yellow tendrils and brown lateral blooms at the end; next to this design is one of blue tendrils extending from a rosette with a blue center surrounded by small yellow leaves which are encircled by a brown eight-pointed round rosette, which is bordered with white or left uncolored. In the latter unit the leaves of the tendrils are yellow, as are the four crown leaves of the lateral flowers enclosing the center.

The spearheads, swords, and bridle bits and the head feathers worn by the two mounted Indians are blue. The attacking foot soldiers' spearheads and the stripes on their shields are also blue; their arrowheads are brown.

The best-preserved colors are the bluish-green of the trees, the blue of the mountains or boulders at the left of the stronghold, and the brown of the mountaintops, rocks, horses' manes, warriors' hair, and outlines of people, animals, and foliage. The original dark brown of the bodies of people and animals has faded to a lead gray. A narrow strip of the chest of the horse at one time covered by molding is pale blue.

The once-yellow color of the ground and of the rose petals is least well preserved. Today these sections have faded to the skin color. Almost equally faded is the green of the mesa above the layers of rocks and of the ground of the stronghold and the slope beneath the palisade.

IV

People, Landscape, and Animals

At the right side of Segesser I stands a camp of eight conical tipis, at the right of which appears either a larger tipi or a shelter of some sort (Plate 3). One flap of each tipi is open, revealing bundles lying inside the tipi or propped against the wall and clay pots or woven baskets. Among the tents are armed warriors, most of them hurrying to the left. A small dog trips with them. Behind the warriors are women hastening through a narrow pass to a palisaded stronghold on a mesa. The top of the palisade appears to be piled with large stones or log ends.

At the far right of the scene two villagers hurry from a brook carrying on their shoulders water bags made of animal skins or buffalo stomachs[1] (Plate 4). The figure wearing the longer skin covering is probably a woman. The man is holding a bow and arrows in his left hand. Both figures are carrying shoulder-high sticks such as those used by the Indians to dig edible roots from the ground.[2] Above them a small herd of buffaloes are clumsily running up a mountain to the right out of the picture. In front of and slightly above the water carriers is a hunter with a quiver on his back and a bow and arrow in his left hand, running to the left toward the village. He may be guarding the water carriers, or he may simply be a hunter. The implications of the scene are obvious: the stronghold is to be provided with water in case the men of the village cannot repel the attack and must retreat to it. In front of the rise which forms the narrow cut leading to the stronghold, defenders, some armed with bows, others with tomahawks, hurry to the battle-

[1] George Bird Grinnell, *Blackfeet Indian Stories* (New York, 1945), 192; Johann J. Baegert, *Kalifornien*, 362.

[2] George Bird Grinnell, *The Cheyenne Indians* (New Haven, 1923), II, 66, 96.

field. Four feathers hang from the leather handle of one of the tomahawks. Its owner has turned back toward the tents, probably to cover the retreat of the women, most of whom are wrapped in blankets. Those already inside the barricade are watching the battle over the wall (Plate 7).

Four men armed with bows, three of whom also carry large round shields, are close behind the four leaders, who are engaged in battle with the two foremost enemies on horseback.

One of the four leading defenders is drawing his bow (Plate 6). The bow is more than an arm long; he is drawing his elbow back forcibly. His comrade is drawing a lance from behind his shield. A third defender is swinging a short stick over his shield, aiming at the rider galloping toward him with leveled lance. Behind him stands another defender with drawn bow. The attackers' horses wear neck protectors, like the collars worn by horses in jousting contests, and rawhide armor reaching almost to the ground. (Plate 5.)

The bridle of the horse in front consists of a neckstrap to which is attached a curb bit and a halter. The bits to which the reins are connected are curved in baroque style. In spite of the cumbersome armor, the horse of the second rider is apparently guided only by a strap tied around the jaw; there is no evidence of a bridle.

One of the riders wears a fur cap decorated with eagle feathers; the other wears a small cap with blue feathers. In the left hand of each rider is an unwieldy shield.

Both of these riders, confined in the long horse armor, remind one of Eskimos in their kayaks.

Behind the leading riders gallop seven more attackers, no doubt part of a larger troop that appeared on the cutout portion of the painting which has disappeared. The third rider, the one nearest the leaders, holds in his left hand his shield and a bow and arrow and in his right hand a large arrow. He wears a short coat, and his legs are bare. His horse, like those of the riders behind him is not armored but is covered only with a saddlecloth that widens at the bottom. The animal seems to be guided by a chin strap and reins. There is no headstall.

The fourth rider carries, instead of a lance, a short sword held with the point upward. Apparently the weapon has no cross guard. From the rider's headgear (probably small feathers woven into a base made of bast) extend six clipped blue feathers. A stiff, wide coat covers his knees. He holds himself erect in his stirrups. His shield and bow are in his left hand. The steed wears a curb bit and noseband. The blue-colored (and therefore iron) snaffle bar is curbed at the edge.

The fifth rider, above and behind the fourth rider, holds a shield in his left hand and a broad sword with large guard and cross guard in his right hand. His head is covered with a flat, helmet-like hat, which is decorated with what appear to be horns or short tufts of hair. His coat appears to have epaulets. These decorations and the headgear, as well as the absence of Indian weapons, indicate that he is perhaps the Spanish officer leading the troop.

The sixth rider, bareheaded and wearing a long coat with a high, stiff collar, is apparently holding bow and arrows in front of his quiver. He also carries a tomahawk but has no shield. The seventh rider, at his left, is adorned with a feather headdress of the kind later worn by Indians of the Northern Plains. In his left hand he carries shield and bow; his quiver is drawn across his chest. In his right hand he holds a sword with cross guard. His horse is guided merely by a halter. An ornamental disk of leather or metal hangs from the crupper over the hindquarters of the animal.

From the cap of the eighth rider (Plate 6) towers an eagle feather. His coat collar is turned up high. In his right hand he holds a pole. Shield, bow, and arrow complete his equipment. Each rider, as well as defender, seems to be carrying his shield on a strap around the neck and holding it by a handle near the edge of the shield.

Of the ninth attacker, who appears at the edge of the scene, only his left hand is visible. In his hand he holds a bow and arrow and a shield. The arrowheads shown in the scene are painted either brown or dark gray, brown probably representing flint and gray representing obsidian, which was commonly used in Mexico and some regions north of Mexico.

On the left side of the missing section is a large wall of rock with a stratification that indicates a fault (Plate 7). Under the fault one of the defenders, carrying his shield like a cape on his back, hurries to the left, away from the attackers. Why he is leaving the battle cannot, of course, be determined.

The fir, pine, and cedar-like trees, as well as what appear to be deciduous trees, and the shrubs are distributed in a certain free regularity throughout the painting, even in the stronghold. In places they overlap human figures, horses, tents, boulders, walls, and mountains. The trees themselves are but rarely overlapped, in one case by a tent, in another by the row of rocks, four times by animals, one by the narrow pass, twice by the plateau of the mesa, once by the back wall of the refugium, and once by a woman; a small part of one bush is covered by a tree. This makes only 12 of a total of 110 trees and bushes (68 in the main section, 21 in the tent section, and 21 in the brook section). These plants were used to define the limits of the different terrains; therefore, in fifty instances they overlap other objects (not counting insignificant instances), while at the left edge a tree, at the upper edge three trees, and at the lower and the right edge of the picture a tree and a bush continue under the border, evidently a deliberate effort on the part of the painter to emphasize the function of the edge of the border.

It is a different case with the wild animals, which are included as "space filler." They are entirely unconnected with the story and are without specific function, as, for example, the animal standing in the tent section on the farthest mountain peak above the pass depression (at the left of the animal is a bush). If animal and bush had been there before it was planned to draw in the pass and the mountains, then they do not have any particular meaning.

The fact that the deciduous trees, such as those along the stream, still have their foliage indicates that the season is early fall.

The soil of the foreground is yellow. The slopes inside and below the stronghold are green, as are the short, steep deposits of scree from the rocky cliff on the left side of the picture and the mesa above. The area between the rock wall and the stronghold, covered with brown and blue boulders, appears to be a depression; the lower edge of the entire chain of conical peaks is cut off toward the foreground by a single line representing a pass. Such rock formations, created by erosion and wind, are, of course, characteristic phenomena of the American Southwest and northern Mexico.

The terrain of the upper portion of the painting, from the border to the right of the stronghold above the tent village, is painted yellow. The gap is filled almost to the top with mountains, similar in shape to the boulders in the center but with steeper peaks. The section obviously represents a large mountain range behind a pass. Because of the absence of depth perspective, this section appears to have been added to the painting later.

On the mesa at the left edge of the picture are two conical formations, either rock formations or hills that have been rounded and smoothed by wind erosion (Plate 1). Such strange formations caught the attention of a people especially close to nature and were commonly looked upon as endowed with special powers.

In general the people, animals, mountains, and trees are about the same size. The central point of interest is the battle and its participants. The stronghold towers above the foreground to the left of the tipis, which are the largest objects in the painting except for the rocky wall. The tipis are in proportion to the human figures moving among them, but the trees in the area are small, an indication of their mainly decorative function in this section of the picture.

There is no perspective in the relationship of the foreground to the background. Trees and animals in the foreground and background are the same size. The artist placed the main scene at the bottom to emphasize its importance.

The attitudes of the people are somewhat stiff, but simple and unposed. The faces of the warriors are remarkably calm and composed. The heads dominate the figures, and the eyes, noses, mouths, and chins are accentuated, while the heads are foreshortened. Their legs are strong, with thick ankles.

Despite the simplicity of the presentation and the absence of perspective, the painting displays remarkable artistic talent and confidence. There is little distortion, and only a few of the animals are difficult to identify. In spite of a certain schematic treatment given to the participants in the battle, it must be assumed that the artist was well acquainted with the details of the event he reproduced in the painting.

The border, a baroque ornamentation, does not fit the simple style of the painting itself or the dynamic human figures, which are so reminiscent of those in Mexican codices. Since the border was painted in the same colors and has faded to the same degree as the painting itself, there is no question that both were executed at the same time. Moreover, it is the border which gives unity to the foreground and the upper part of the painting. Yet the border art is clearly a reflection of European influence. It appears likely that the painting was the work of a gifted Indian artist who had come under the influence of the Church and had received instruction in European artistic methods and techniques. The battle scene itself shows much less European influence. For example, the trees are so highly stylized that it is difficult to identify them. The rigidity, flatness, and absence of perspective must be understood as reflecting an early cultural period. The fauna, as well as the mountains, are not so much projections of something seen as the expression of something imagined. In other words, the artist painted from imagination, not from nature, producing "signs" which have a pictographic character.

In addition to the horses there are thirty-nine animals in the painting, eight on the mesa, two behind it, sixteen in the main section, three in the tipi section, and ten on the two strips at the right. At first glance they appear lifelike and well characterized, but when one tries to identify them, it becomes clear that some of them are stereotyped and undifferentiated in posture and movement. All the animals are shown in profile and the positions of their legs in motion are unnatural.

On the band of the mesa which slants down to the left are seven bighorn sheep of varying ages. Both in this painting and in Segesser II the eyes of human beings and animals generally appear as an arched line. The eyes of the mountain sheep, however, are drawn as circles with dots in the centers.

At the left edge of the painting is a large female elk moving out of the picture behind another animal, presumably also an elk, of which only the rump and the hind legs are visible (Plate 1). These animals were obviously added to fill space. They appear to be behind, not on, the mesa. At the right edge of the mesa lies an animal which appears to be either a jaguar or a puma.

At the top of the picture, moving to the left, is a herd of deer (Plate 2). From their large size, the forked horns of the male in the center of the herd, the shape of the ears, and the dark-tipped tails, it is apparent that the animals are mule deer. (In front of the herd is another jaguar or puma.)

These deer are probably the animals to which Father Philipp was referring when he wrote:

> They can be tamed like domestic animals. I have some that follow me everywhere like dogs, even into the garden, without doing any damage, and when I sit down, they lie at my feet. They are as big as deer; in my opinion this animal is the so-called elk.[3] I often use these animals to show the Indians how the dumb animals acknowledge their benefactors.[4]

Evidently Father Philipp had more success with animals than with his converts.

At the right of the edge of the mesa is another herd of deer. These deer are smaller than the herd above, and their antlers are thin and not forked. They appear to be Arizona white-tailed deer (*Odocoileus couesi*), small graceful animals found in the wooded mountains of central and southern Arizona, in southern New Mexico, western Texas, and the Sierra Madres of Chihuahua and Sonora —the old home of the Apaches. The composition of both deer herds makes it likely that the season of the year is fall, when the bucks gather their females for the mating season.

Below and to the right of the Arizona deer is a slender animal, perhaps a puma or a wolf, pursuing a fleeing rabbit, which, judging by the black ear tips, is the common western jackrabbit. Above the rabbit, facing the deer, is another puma. In the upper left corner is

[3] Here Father Philipp was mistaken; obviously he was describing an unusually large species of deer.

[4] Brehm, *Saeugetiere*, IV, 97.

a black bear with short ears, a heavy body, and handlike feet on thick legs.

Perched on a peak in the mountain range is a small unidentifiable animal (Plate 3, upper right corner). There are few animals in the tipi section. Between two tipis trots a small dog. Below him is faintly discernible the faded outline of an animal with a long tail, perhaps a wolflike dog.

In contrast to the scene at the left, the right-hand section of the painting has a pastoral, peaceful quality (Plate 4). In the lower right-hand corner a small animal frolics near the brook. The fairly long tail and heavy paws indicate that it is a beast of prey, probably an American gray wolf, or perhaps a dog. In the nearby tree is another animal, possibly a lynx, pursuing a small squirrel perched on top of the tree. At the right edge of the painting is the head of a buffalo with its tongue protruding. The portion of the head that was covered with a molding is a strong reddish-brown.

Toward the upper right corner of the picture are five large, humped animals running uphill; at the edge of the painting are the tail and rump of a sixth animal. These animals can only be buffaloes, as indicated by the hair on the chins and forelegs and the mane. The heads are not in proportion, the tails are rather long, and the horns are not sufficiently curved, indicating that the painter was probably not a Plains Indian and therefore not overly familiar with the animal.

This fact, together with the other species of animals shown in the painting, fixes the southern limits of the territory. The species and the nature of the terrain seem to confirm the assumption that the setting of the painting is the western Sierra Madre mountains of northern Sonora. From the appearance of the trees and shrubbery, as well as the composition of the deer herds, the time would appear to be early fall, before punitive expeditions against marauding nomads became risky ventures because of threatening snowfalls.

V
The People of the Tipis

The defenders shown in Segesser I are not readily identifiable; the characteristics of their homes, dress, and weaponry are not sufficiently distinctive to make positive identification easy. Perhaps it is more fruitful to say, first, who they were not and then to make some tentative judgments about their tribal affiliation.

In his writings Father Philipp often reported on the depredations of the Seris, who occupied Tiburón Island and the mainland coastal regions of Sonora. The Seris lived in huts made of branches, never in skin tipis, which were virtually unknown in Sonora. Moreover, the land of the Seris is barren and almost totally without trees.

It is clear from the symbolic disks, stripes, and other ornaments on the tipis that these homes were more to their inhabitants than mere temporary shelters from rain, wind, and sun. We must therefore take into consideration tribes who lived in tipis and whose homes were not far from Sonora. Among them were the southern Cheyennes. Beals places the southern Cheyennes northeast of the Jicarilla Apaches,[1] northeast of the source of the Río Grande. This region is somewhat too remote for raids into Sonora. Moreover, as late as 1804, Lewis and Clark found the Cheyennes, who had been driven from Minnesota by the Sioux and other tribes after about 1700, still living in the Black Hills. About 1826, not long before the construction of Bent's Fort on the upper Arkansas in Colorado, a large segment of the tribe moved southward to establish permanent quarters on the Arkansas River. These were the Sowonia, or Southern Cheyennes. They were preceded by the Arapahos, who came south as early as 1819. They did not undertake their first raid into Mexico

[1] Ralph L. Beals, *Comparative Ethnology of Northern Mexico Before 1750* (Berkeley, 1932), 159.

until 1835 (with disastrous results—in an engagement with Mexican cavalry all but three of the war party were slain). It seems, therefore, that the defenders shown in Segesser I cannot be Cheyennes.

Similarly, we can dismiss the Kiowas from consideration, for although they were mentioned in Spanish documents as early as 1732, they did not invade Sonora in force until about 1795.

The Tiwas, east of Sonora along the Río Grande, and the Zuñis, who lived 250 miles north of Sonora, lived in pueblos and must also be eliminated from consideration as the defenders in Segesser I.

East of the pueblo-dwelling Indians and the nomadic Comanches were the warlike Tonkawas, the buffalo-hunting nomads who lived in tipis. They, too, can be eliminated from consideration, for their home, in central Texas, was too far from Sonora.

Nearer Sonora were the Wichitas, of Caddoan stock. In keeping with their more settled mode of living as a farming people, they lived in large conical huts framed with poles and covered with grass. When the Wichitas were traveling or on hunting expeditions, they used the plains tipi of their nomadic neighbors. At one time they settled along the middle Arkansas and Kansas, and were later pushed south by Comanche, Kiowa, Mescalero, and Sioux tribes. They came in contact with the Spaniards in 1541, when Coronado entered their territory.

In 1758 the Spanish mission and presidio of San Saba, located on a tributary of the upper Colorado in Texas, was attacked and the mission destroyed by the combined forces of the Comanches and several Wichita tribes. In 1759, General Parilla, the Spanish commander, led a punitive expedition against the capital city of the Wichitas near the junction of the Wichita and Red rivers, but he and his Lipan Apache allies were put to flight by a superior Indian force.

Some details of the 1759 battle are worthy of attention. First, the Lipan Apaches were allied with the Spaniards in the battle, which occurred at a time when Father Philipp was referring to the Lipans as enemies. Second, in addition to regular troops and militia, Tlascala Indians and others from the mission also participated, which indicates that Indian allies and converts were regularly employed on military expeditions. It was also reported that in anticipation of this battle the Wichitas had fortified the town of the Tawehash Indians by digging deep ditches at the east and west ends of the town. The main fortification consisted of a palisade about four feet high, similar to that shown in Segesser I. Both the ditches and the palisade were designed particularly as defenses against attackers on horseback. The similarity of fortifications makes it possible, though not probable, that the defenders in Segesser I were Wichitas.

Among other tribes who lived in skin tipis were the Comanches. Wissler says that their home was the western part of Texas but that after 1714, by which time they had horses, they were able to roam over a wide region.[2] Hodge states that the Comanches were living in western Kansas at this time but roamed as far as the Platte River and the Bolsón de Mapimí in Chihuahua.[3] But the territory under their domination did not extend that far.

In 1744 Fray Miguel de Menchero wrote in a report about a new settlement of Genisaro Indians:

> This settlement is an exception, for the Indians come from different nations who had been robbed by the Comanches, a nation which is so bellicose and brave that they dominate all the other tribes in the interior of the country. They travel in the course of a year more than a thousand leagues from New Mexico. This was confirmed to me by an Indian who had been brought in 1731 for sale or exchange for a very white, four-year-old Indian girl who was so beautiful that she might have been taken for a Flemish child. When I asked him to which tribe he belonged and how far it was from here to his country, he counted to 110 suns, or days, which would amount to 1,100 leagues, traveling an average of 10 leagues a day. He said he belonged to the nation of the Ponnas.[4]

[2] Clark Wissler, *North American Indians of the Plains*, American Museum of Natural History *Handbook Series No. I* (New York, 1934), 13.

[3] Frederick W. Hodge (ed.), *Handbook of American Indians North of Mexico*, Bureau of American Ethnology *Bulletin No. 30* (2 vols., Washington, 1907, 1910), I, 327.

[4] Adolph F. A. Bandelier and Fanny R. Bandelier, *Historical Documents Relating to New Mexico, Nueva Vizcaya, and Approaches Thereto, to 1773* (trans. and ed. by Charles Wilson Hackett), (Washington, 1937), III, 401.

This would amount to 3,300 miles—a nice exaggeration since the distance from Santa Fe to the Pawnee villages on the Platte River was only about 625 miles. And the location of this human trade was Santa Fe, as we learn from a stirring complaint made by Fray Pedro Serrano to the viceroy of Mexico in 1761. According to his report, deplorable conditions existed in New Mexico. In the most brutal manner officials robbed dozens of villages of Indians who carried on agriculture and raised cattle. But they did not lift a finger to protect the Indians against nomadic hordes. According to the view of the missionaries, if there had not been constant warfare among the Indian farmers themselves, it would have been easy for them to exterminate the Spaniards, including the missionaries. Everywhere, said the priest, Spanish officials ordered: "Let the Indians come"; "let the Indians carry that." The Indians had to sleep in their fields. Cattle, fruit, grain, wool, pots, plates, jugs, stockings and blankets they had woven were taken away. The Indians even had to carry the goods on their backs eight, twenty, forty —the Zuñis even seventy—leagues to the governor's palace. If they broke anything or failed to carry out orders, they were beaten with whips and sticks. And if a missionary tried to protect his wards, the alcaldes simply laughed at them, for they had the favor of the governor, especially those who occupied the highest offices and oppressed the Indians the most severely.

The worst oppression of all took place when Comanches or other nomads arrived and pitched their tents, in groups of fifty to two hundred, according to Fray Serrano. Then the governor, the alcaldes, and the other officials hurried to gather as many horses as possible and all the hardware they could find: axes, hoes, wedges, pickaxes, bridles, machetes, belduques (large Mexican knives), and regular knives. These items were traded to the Indians for deer and buffalo skins and, worst of all, for Indian slaves, men and women, young and old, for they were

> gold and silver and the richest treasure for the governors who stuff themselves at their tables while the rest have to be satisfied with the crumbs. . . . When these barbarians bring a certain number of women for sale, many of them maidens and girls, then they

rape them if they are ten years old or more in the presence of numberless gathered barbarians and Catholics before handing them over to the Christians, who buy them, without any consideration but their unbridled lust and brutal shamelessness, and say to those who buy them with pagan insolence: "Now you can take her; now she is good."[5]

In 1706, Juan de Ulibarri mentioned in his report to Francisco Cuerbo, governor of New Mexico, a planned attack on Taos by Utes and Comanches. In the same year these tribes attacked the villages of the Jicarilla Apaches, among them those of the Carlanas, in northeastern New Mexico. From 1707 to 1717 the Comanches made several forays into New Mexico, ostensibly to ask for peace, but more often to obtain goods and animals. In 1716 they raided Taos and other settlements. Again two years later other Comanches appeared in northeastern New Mexico and forced the Jicarillas living there to flee to the Spaniards. A few months later they returned and murdered the inhabitants of Taos and Cochiti. In 1719 the Spaniards launched an unsuccessful military expedition against them. In 1720 the Comanches were living about three hundred miles north of Santa Fe, moving about a great deal on horseback and carrying with them tents made of buffalo skins.[6] Thus by that time they had already descended from the eastern chain of the Rocky Mountains and had settled down at the foot of the mountains and from there carried out hunting and marauding expeditions onto the plains, as well as into the mountains. The Comanches drove the Apaches out of southeastern Colorado about 1730. Then they turned against their own relatives, the Utes. About 1740 they made war on the Apaches on the upper course of the Canadian, east of Taos. By then they had established their reputation as the finest horsemen of the Plains.

Yet it seems improbable that the Indians in Segesser I were Comanches. In the first place, the scene of action would be more than six hundred miles northeast of Sonora, in the northeast corner

[5] *Ibid.*, 501.

[6] Alfred B. Thomas (trans. and ed.), *After Coronado: Spanish Exploration Northeast of New Mexico, 1696–1727* (Norman, 1935), 171.

of New Mexico or even in Colorado. Moreover, it is unlikely that the Spanish soldiers were at this time opposing the Comanches in the kind of open warfare shown in the painting, for by the time the painting was executed the Spaniards were carrying on a thriving trade in Taos and other towns in New Mexico for the Comanches' animal furs and skins. At that time the Comanches' enemies were, not Spaniards, but other Indian tribes.[7]

It is obvious that the defenders shown in Segesser I are not on the warpath. They have their women with them, and they have apparently been taken by surprise in their own country, or at least in a familiar refuge. The fact that the tipis are near the stronghold also indicates that the tribe is not on a hunting expedition.

A tribe that had at its disposal a fortified refuge on an easily defended mesa and yet did not erect its homes there, as Pueblo Indians would have done, must be considered at least a seminomadic tribe that followed the buffalo at certain times of the year—for example, after the sowing or before the harvest. Such tribal habits were characteristic of the Apaches.

True, most Apache tribes lived in wickiups, primitive shelters made first of mats and later of canvas wrapped around branches and poles bent together on top. The White Mountain and San Carlos Apaches made their shelters with blankets, and sometimes adopted the shape of the Navaho hogan with forked beams which were covered with branches instead of earth.[8]

At first it seems strange that Indians living in tipis and forced to a more or less nomadic life because of their dependence on the buffalo should use a well-protected refuge. But such nomads had favorite places to which they retreated in times of greater danger. These refuges were generally the steep-sided mesas scattered all over the southwestern United States.[9] The idea of constructing barricades

[7] Bandelier and Bandelier, *Historical Documents Relating to New Mexico, Nueva Vizcaya, and Approaches Thereto, to 1773*, III, 401, 479–501.

[8] Aleš Hrdlička, *Physiological and Medical Observations Among the Indians of Southwestern United States and Northern Mexico*, Bureau of American Ethnology *Bulletin No. 34* (Washington, 1908), Plate 2.

[9] See Walter Hough, *Antiquities of the Upper Gila and Salt River Valleys in*

may well have been suggested to the nomadic tribes by the elaborate Pueblo strongholds, and they adapted the practice by strengthening mesas with stone walls or wooden palisades. A large number of circular stone walls have been found in the old Apache territory, mainly in the mountainous regions of Colorado, south of the Arkansas River, and it is assumed that these are remnants of Apache strongholds.

Evidence from Father Philipp's correspondence quoted earlier also strongly points to the likelihood that the defenders in Segesser I are Apaches. He reported that his mission was threatened primarily by Seris, Pimas, and Apaches. Only one of these, the Apaches, lived northeast of Sonora. His "Relación" contains many accounts of their ferocity and cunning, and he tells about Fort Fronteras, which the king of Spain ordered constructed between Pimería Alta and Pimería Baja (near the present border between Sonora and Arizona) to discourage the Apaches' forays into Sonora. Other Spanish documents of the period report frequent incursions by the Apaches into the Pimería, as well as attacks on settlements in the neighboring regions of present Arizona and New Mexico. These accounts offer abundant corroboration of Father Philipp's reports of Apache raids, which had been occurring long before his arrival in Sonora. Because the Apaches were the only Indians who regularly moved in from the Plains, the conclusion seems inescapable that the people of the tipis are, indeed, Apaches.

Even after the middle of the nineteenth century the Apaches played the part of bandits and pillagers. They had a sarcastic proverb: "The Mexicans are our vaqueros, who provide us with horses and cattle, while the Americans are our wagoners and craftsmen, because they bring us goods and furnish us weapons."

J. Ross Browne, in *Adventures in the Apache Country: A Tour Through Arizona and Sonora*, wrote that the inhabitants of Sonora were poor in horses, because the best ones were in the possession of the Apaches and that the renowned chief of the Pinals rode the most beautiful horse in the country. The Apaches were respected

---

Arizona and New Mexico, Bureau of American Ethnology *Bulletin No. 35* (Washington, 1907), 66–78, Figs. 32–48.

Philipp von Segesser von Brunegg, S.J.

PLATE 1. The top of the mesa (Segesser I). Photo: Blair Clark.

PLATE 2. The battle scene (Segesser I). Mexican Indian militia (left); Apache defenders (right). Photo: Blair Clark.

PLATE 3. The camp of the Apache defenders (Segesser I).

PLATE 4. Apache water carriers (Segesser I). Photo: Blair Clark.

PLATE 5. Detail of Mexican Indian Militia (Segesser I). Photo: Blair Clark.

PLATE 6. Detail of militia horsemen, armor-clad horses, and Apache defenders (Segesser I). Photo: Blair Clark.

PLATE 7. Apache women watching battle from refugium (Segesser I). Photo: Blair Clark.

and feared in Sonora; they terrorized the region to such a degree that the American traveling party of which Browne was a member was escorted by thirty American soldiers. The Mexican officials objected only mildly, for they well knew how dangerous it was to travel in Sonora. The traveling party would have liked only too well to pillage every place, if not burn it down, especially Fronteras, the main trading center of the Apaches.

The Apaches were among the first tribes in the present United States to acquire horses. Therefore, it is surprising to find no horses in the tipi village or the stronghold shown in the painting. It is possible that the horses had been put out to pasture or perhaps driven off by the attackers.

The defenders in Segesser I carry their shields in a manner characteristic of Plains Indian warriors—on the left side and, in battle, across the chest. The warrior hurrying away from the battle at the left edge of the picture (Plate 1) carries his shield across his back. Concerning the Plains tribes, Mooney says: "The shield was carried upon the left arm by means of a belt passing over the shoulder, in such a way as to permit the free use of the left hand to grasp the bow, or could be slung around to the back in a retreat."[10] The attackers carry their shields in a different manner—by means of a strap held in the left hand (Plate 6).

The defenders with drawn bows (Plate 7) have no shields, either because they were attacked without warning or because shields would interfere with their shooting. Bancroft described a typical Comanche shield as follows: "The frame of the shield is made of light basketwork, covered with two or three thicknesses of buffalo hide, thus rendering them almost bullet proof."[11] This description even more accurately characterizes many Apache shields. Such a shield, filled with straw was displayed in the Grassi Museum in Leipzig, and another is in my possession. Both have been positively identified as of Apache origin.

One defender's shield is decorated with five golden-eagle tail

[10] In Hodge, *Handbook of American Indians*, II, 547.

[11] Hubert Howe Bancroft, *The Native Races of the Pacific States* (5 vols., San Francisco, 1882–86).

feathers hanging from the center, flanked by short red or black stripes, which are probably cloth (Plate 2, far right). Weygold found this type of decoration on shield models and sketches in the Hamburg Museum. Behind this defender another warrior hurries to the battle bearing a shield with an interesting decoration (Plate 3, far left). It appears to consist of strips of leather extending around the upper half of the shield and hanging down across the center. The ends of the strips are fringed. This is a common design among Plains Indians, including the Dakotas and, more importantly, the Pawnees,[12] who lived near the Plains Apaches.

Some of the shields shown in Segesser I are decorated either with colored disks at the center, symbolizing the sun, or with four smaller colored disks grouped around a central disk, symbolizing the sun and the four winds. The edge of one shield is decorated with a series of equilateral triangles painted in alternating light and dark colors (Plate 6). The dark triangles may represent the tips of the eagle feathers. Hall describes an Apache shield with a similar series of triangles at the edge.[13]

The shield of the warrior with the tomahawk (Plate 3) is decorated with a central blue disk surrounded by a light ring and on the outside a sharp-pointed ring of rays, giving a sunburst effect. This decoration, like those on the other shields, was widely used among the Apaches. Bourke reproduced Apache medicine shirts with such decorations, adding that they could also be found on medicine hats and wooden amulets. He interpreted them as representing large suns.[14]

At first glance the large size of the defenders' shields seems to be an inconsistency; the Plains horsemen generally carried small shields, while those tribes who fought on foot generally used the larger ones. It is possible that the painter simply distorted the size

[12] Frederick Weygold, "Die Hunkazeremonie," *Archiv fuer Anthropologie*, Vol. XI, No. 1/2, 147, 152.

[13] H. U. Hall, "Some Shields of the Plains and the Southwest," *University of Pennsylvania Museum Journal*, Vol. XXVII, No. 1 (1926), Fig. 7.

[14] John G. Bourke, *The Medicine Men of the Apache*, Bureau of American Ethnology *Ninth Annual Report* (Washington, 1887–88), 503, Fig. 434; 589, Plate 6; 590, Plate 7; 592, Plate 8.

of the shields, as he did the heads of the warriors, which are out of proportion to their bodies. A more likely explanation, however, is that the painter, who it is almost certain did not belong to a mounted tribe, reproduced shields in a size familiar to him, such as those carried by Pimas, Navahos, and Pueblos.[15]

The care that one must exercise in determining the accuracy of pictorial reproductions is illustrated in the paintings of George Catlin, who made almost no distinction in the sizes and shapes of the bows of various tribes, even those widely separated in area and culture. The painter of Segesser I, on the other hand, was careful to make such distinctions. The bows of attackers and defenders are quite dissimilar. The bows of the defenders have a pronounced double curve. The bows are the very short ones used by the Apaches, perhaps because their early bows were made of animal horns.

The types of arrows, as well as the tipis, shown in Segesser I probably eliminate the Mountain Apaches from consideration. The arrows of the mountain people consisted of thin hardwood front shafts protruding from thicker, weakly pennated cane shafts. Their flint arrowheads were smaller than those in Segesser I. One of the defenders holds an arrow with a black-colored point, probably indicating black obsidian, a favorite material among the Plains Apaches.

The quivers of nearly all the western and Plains tribes had bow casings. Probably the only exceptions were the quivers of the Apaches, short, narrow quivers without casings, like those shown in Segesser I.

The tomahawks carried by the defenders are not of much assistance in identifying the tribe. The heads of the weapons are made of iron. The handle of the tomahawk held by the warrior at the right of the tipi nearest the viewer (Plate 3) protrudes beyond the blade. At the rear end of the handle is a leather disk to which four eagle feathers are fastened. The number of feathers indicates that this weapon is a sacred one. Such feathered disks were adornments widely used on tomahawks and spears by the Southern Plains tribes until the end of the nineteenth century.

[15] In Hodge, *Handbook of American Indians*, II, 547.

The warrior bearing the shield decorated with triangles wields a short stick which appears to be the handle of a tomahawk or, less likely, the shaft of a stone club (Plate 6). The artist evidently neglected to paint the blade of the tomahawk.

Still other elements in the painting indicate that the defenders are Apaches. The two large jug-shaped drums in the tipis and the flower design painted on one of the tipis are genuine Apache elements, according to Arthur Woodward and Ralph Beals. Even today the Apaches use drums with a similar shape.

Some ethnologists question whether the Apaches used tipis in this early period and are inclined to believe that the Apaches took over the custom from neighboring Plains tribes in comparatively recent times. However, Thomas, among others, includes a report of a Spanish expedition of 1696 whose members came across an abandoned Apache tipi camp somewhere north of Taos, in the territory of the Jicarilla Apaches.[16]

Morris Edward Opler describes Mescalero tipis constructed with three main poles, and there are also a few other reports from the early eighteenth century about Plains Apaches living in tipis.[17] In 1599, along the Canadian River, Saldevar, a member of the expedition of the treasure hunter Oñate, found Apaches living in fifty large skin tipis painted bright red and white.[18]

In the foreword to *Death in the Desert*, Wellman presents a short survey of the migrations and the ultimate fate of the Apache people:

> Centuries ago, out of the bleak wastes of the arctic snowlands a people began its southward march. It was a poor people, schooled by rigid adversity, used to the pang of hunger, the bite of the elements, the constant struggle for existence. Though lacking every form of material wealth, it was rich in courage and pride, a pride which found expression in its name for itself—*Tinde, Tinneh, Dine*

[16] Thomas, *After Coronado*, 15.

[17] Morris Edward Opler, *An Analysis of Mescalero and Chiricahua Apache Social Organization in the Light of Their Systems of Relationship* (Chicago, 1936).

[18] George P. Hammond, *Juan de Oñate and the Founding of New Mexico* (Santa Fe, 1927).

or *N'de* in various dialects—which has always the same meaning wherever it is found today, *The People.*

Filtering slowly southward, the People debouched at last upon the great plains. Here for the first time they found plenty and some surcease from the pitiless fight for life. Bison, in limitless herds, were ready at hand for meat and shelter. There was other game in plenty, and the killing frost, far behind them, was forgotten. Gradually, through the years, the People moved farther and farther southward. And when the first precursors of the white race reached the plains they found the former children of the tundras living in a farflung territory, ranging from the Black Hills almost to the Sierra Madre. These first white explorers called the Tinde by various names, Vaqueros, Escanjacques, Faraons and Padoucas,[19] among others.

Then new forces began to be felt. The Sioux, impelled by pressure from the east where the Paleface was forcing the Chippewas westward, emerged with teeming numbers into the flat country. From the west came another people, a hungry people, the Shoshoni race, out of the barren desert lands in the high reaches of the Rocky Mountain plateaus.

The impact of these two vast migrations occurred in the regions at that time north of the habitat of the People, but its repercussions were soon felt. Invincible in war, the Sioux smashed the Shoshoni back to their mountains—all but one branch, a numerous, wily, lethal division which history was to call the Comanches.

These last moved southward to make room for the Siouan

[19] The Apaches occupied the Western Plains from the eastern border of the Rocky Mountains to the Missouri. In the middle of the eighteenth century the Kansas River was still called the Padouca, and until 1805 the North Platte was known as Padouca Fork. By mistake the Eastern Apaches, whom the French called Padoucas, were later taken for Comanches, who, until the beginning of the eighteenth century did not in fact undertake raids out of the mountains of Colorado into northern New Mexico and far to the east to the Pawnees, as is clearly evident from the Spanish sources which Thomas published. They did not come down into the Plains permanently until later, about 1730 or 1740, after they had obtained guns. Then, with the help of the Caddoes and the Sioux, they gradually destroyed the various groups of Plains Apaches or drove them westward into the mountains. In lengthy correspondence George E. Hyde and I discussed the question of the identity of the East Apaches with the Padoucas. French and earlier Spanish accounts as well as the conflicts among the Plains tribes led convincingly to the conclusion that the Padoucas and the East Apaches were the same tribe.

hordes, and where they went they drove the Tinde out. An epic story might be written on the wars of that slow invasion, but no chronicler was present. We only know that some time, within the last three hundred years, this race which once called the arctic tundras its home, found itself forced farther and farther into the equally barren, though this time torrid deserts of our Southwest.

And now a strange thing happened. In some manner, from the very ferocity of their surroundings, the People attained a ferocity of their own. The enervation of the sun which subdued the Pueblos, the Pimas and the Diggers, failed to tame the Tinde. Their warriors became lean, sun-baked, imbued with shocking cruelty and vitality, endowed with deadliness and malice beyond all other tribes of American Indians. So it was that, after centuries of wandering, they were named from their one outstanding trait, *Apache—Enemy*.

The white man found the Apache after the Mexican War, when the surging migrations across the continent reached the Southwest. And there, backed up at last in the least desirable of all the corners of the continent, the Apache made his final stand. Other desert tribes fought also. But the Apache was ever the great opponent.[20]

[20] Paul I. Wellman, *Death in the Desert* (New York, 1935).

VI
Locale of the Battle

The Apache defenders shown in Segesser I had probably learned the defensive value of the refugium from various tribes of Pueblo Indians, whose wooden-palisaded pueblos were observed by Antonio de Espejo on his 1582–83 expedition into New Mexico.[1]

The Opatas, a Piman group who lived in the upper part of Sonora, also built defensive works on volcanic rocks where the inhabitants of a village or several allied villages could find refuge in case of war with other Opatas or during attacks by Janos, Jocomes, and Sumas, warlike tribes who are believed to have been absorbed later by the Apaches. A number of Opata villages close to the Sonora-Chihuahua border were abandoned by their inhabitants as a result of such invasions, which were not, however, as lasting in their effects as those by Apaches in later years.

The Janos inhabited the region between Casas Grandes, in Chihuahua, and the town of Fronteras, in Sonora. The Jocomes roamed over the same region, as did the Sumas, who traveled as far as the region around the present El Paso. These three tribes were, however, seminomadic like the Apaches, and it is unlikely that they built fortifications like the one shown in Segesser I. It is much more likely that the stronghold in the painting was one built by a Tanoan tribe.

One of the Tano nations, the Tiwa Pueblos, who lived as far south as 32 degrees north latitude, were identified in the valley of the Río Grande but may have settled even farther west, perhaps in the valley of the Santa Maria River or in the valley of the Casas Grandes River, for neither the western Apaches nor the Tara-

[1] Bandelier and Bandelier, *Historical Documents Relating to New Mexico, Nueva Vizcaya, and Approaches Thereto, to 1773*, II, 50–51.

humares, a tribe of Uto-Aztecan linguistic stock who lived in the region, seem to have constructed palisades, though the Apaches used them. The Tiwas early came in conflict with the Spaniards, who demanded from them material for their soldiers' clothes, and they were robbed of robes and blankets by Coronado's men in 1540. The resulting resistance led to cruelties by the Spaniards, and when the Spaniards later violated an armistice and massacred prisoners, the Tiwas abandoned all but two of their villages and fled. Not until the seventeenth century did missionaries have some success among them, gathering the inhabitants of twelve scattered villages into eight, not only to have a better opportunity to convert them but also to provide more effective protection for them from marauding Apaches.

Another tribe of Tanoan Pueblos, who lived somewhat farther south than their close relatives the Tiwas, were the Piros. Today their villages, about sixteen in number, are deserted ruins.[2] The eastern Piros and Tiwas lived in desert-like salt lagoons southeast of present El Paso, as did a group of seminomadic Jumanos, whom Cabeza de Vaca located north of the Concho River on the Río Grande in 1636. Although the Jumanos belonged to the Caddoan or Uto-Aztecan stock, they seem also to have lived in pueblos. Moreover, they had become Christians by 1622 and by the early eighteenth century there was no reason for a punitive expedition against them like that shown in Segesser I.

Thus it seems likely that the refuge shown in Segesser I was the remains of a pueblo or a fortification constructed by Piros, Tiwas, or some other Pueblo people. The inclination of the slopes, as well as their green color and the trees growing on them, and the narrow pass in front at the right of the stronghold suggest that the elevation on which it stands is a natural formation, perhaps a mesa.

The scene of the battle probably lies not far from the main ridge of the Sierra Madre Occidental Mountains, which appear at the top of the painting, behind the passlike depression, as steep-sided rounded peaks representing a continuous series of very high eleva-

[2] Another forty-two villages may have been occupied by Piros, as well as twenty more that may have belonged to Piros or to Tiwas.

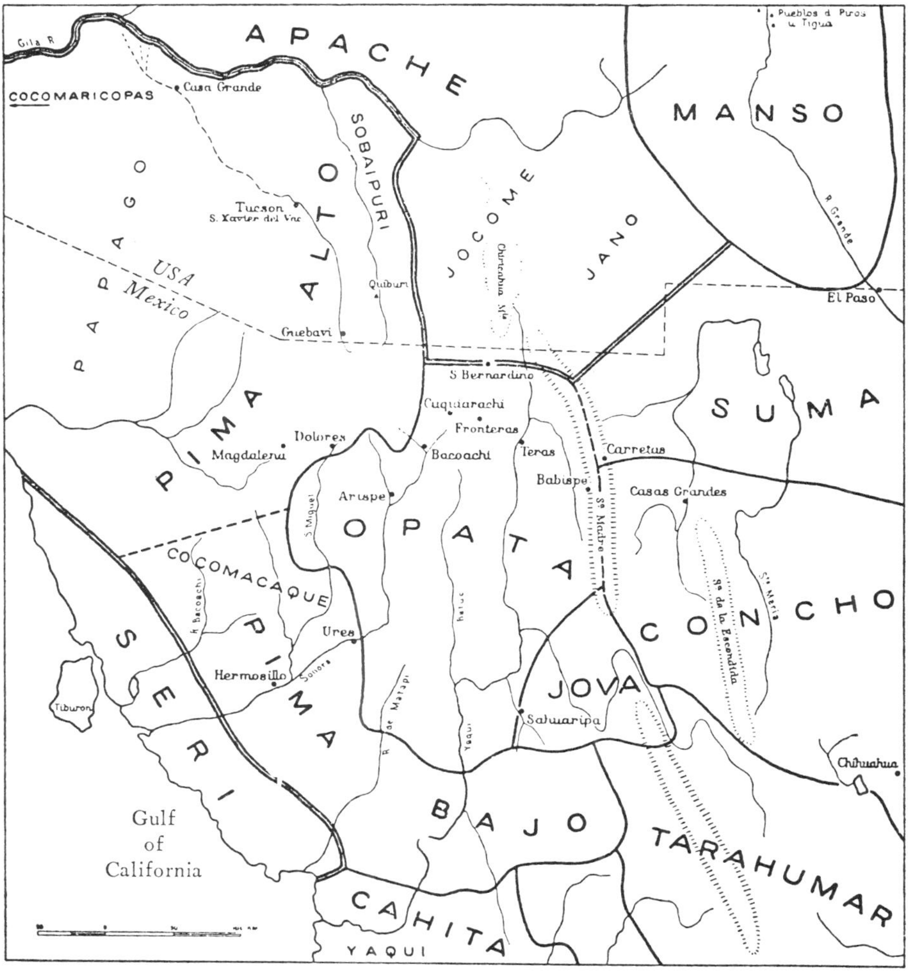

Tribal territories in Northwest Mexico about 1700 (according to Sauer).

———	Boundaries of the Pima Indians.
- - - -	Approximate boundary between the Pimería Alta and Pimería Baja.
═══	Boundary between language families (the membership of Mansos, Sumas, and Conchos is disputed).
⫼⫼⫼	The Continental Divide.
▲	Towns.
●	Indian settlements.

tions. This conclusion makes it necessary to determine the point at which the defenders crossed the Sierra Madres to enter Sonora or the point at which the attackers left.

The investigations of Sauer prove useful to this end, for he traced the routes of the Spanish explorers in the sixteenth century which led into Sonora and out to the north, to the legendary Cíbola of the Zuñis on the Colorado High Plateau. Almost all these explorers took the same route, which soon became the Camino Real as far as Tucson. Cortes traveled the route (1524–25), as did Nuño de Guzmán (1530–31), neither of whom entered Sonora. The route was also followed by Diego de Guzmán (1533), who did reach Sonora, and Cabeza de Vaca (1535–36), who traveled up the Río Grande and was the first to go north of the Sierra by traveling westward around it and then turned into the earlier route and followed it on his way back.[3]

The Franciscan friar Marcos de Niza crossed the present Arizona border (1538–39) but did not reach the Colorado Plateau. Coronado moved east of the region where Tucson is now located to Cíbola and apparently reached the Arkansas River.[4] An expedition led by De Soto crossed the Mississippi River. On that expedition he encountered trouble with the Opatas in Sonora Basin, in the canyons of Ures below present Arispe. He lost eighteen men to the poisoned arrows of the Opatas and was forced to move his base from their territory. (Their territory, by the way, was described as the most fertile and best cultivated in northern Sonora, a fact which makes it possible that the Opatas probably had a predisposition—and the time—for jewelrymaking and art.)

In 1562–63 an expedition led by Francisco de Ibarra crossed Sonora. This expedition was in search of not legendary cities but precious ores, especially silver. After Ibarra's death, which evidently occurred at the end of the expedition, Sonora was left in peace for a quarter of a century, until the Jesuits began setting up their theocratic-secular state and inaugurated a period of intensive exploration.

Sauer devoted himself to retracing the route followed by

[3] Carl O. Sauer, *The Road to Cíbola, Ibero-Americana*, Vol. III (1932), 15–16.
[4] Winship, *The Coronado Expedition.*

Ibarra, who crossed the Sierra Madres at the upper course of the Sonora River into Chihuahua and then moved southward again into Sonora after suffering great hardship and hunger.[5]

From Arispe, a compact, orderly Opata pueblo, Ibarra and his people followed the eastern tributary of the Sonora River, the Bacoachi, and at its upper end climbed through high, rough, hot mountain country to a place called Zaguaripa by Obregón, a member of the expedition, situated in a valley "surrounded by high sierras, deep gulches, crags, and large rock masses. . . . This valley and town of Zaguaripa is on the frontier of the Plains Indians. . . . [It is] a defensive site surrounded on two sides by a rough and deep barranca [gorge]." This description fits to a certain degree the locale of Segesser I. At the time Ibarra arrived, the town was peopled by a few half-blood descendants of the massacred garrison of Diego de Alcaraz, Coronado's third base.

Historians such as Mecham and Hammond believed that Zaguaripa was the modern Sahuaripa; the latter, however, is located at the southern end of the Opata country in a level basin which does not fit the description of the region Ibarra visited. Moreover, Sauer said that it would have been impossible to cross the mountains at this point to the territory of the Casas Grandes, a statement which gives us an idea of the nature of the western side of the Sierra Madres.

The description of the rest of Ibarra's probable route, as described by Obregón, fits even more closely the landscape in Segesser I. Ibarra left the Cíbola route in the upper Bacoachi Valley and, swinging eastward, followed for some distance the route by which Cabeza de Vaca had, from the opposite direction, penetrated into the territory of the Opatas. It was the trail from Bacoachi across the Sierra de los Ajos into the Fronteras basin.

Sauer added this sketch of an Opata village in the region: ". . . Cuquiárachi is nestled against the eastern base of the Ajos range, built on a dissected apron of the old gravel fill which gives rise to deep, narrow gulches and castellated promontories rising above an

[5] Quotations on this and succeeding pages from Sauer, *The Road to Cíbola*, 42–50.

ample flood plain." The foreground of Segesser I and the stratified mesa rising out of it agree somewhat with this description. To the northeast lie the Terrenos de Camón, which are part of the high, grassy plains that were within the range of Plains Indians at that time, presumably Sumas.

According to Sauer, Ibarra continued his journey east across the Fronteras basin, proceeding with great circumspection and using scouts through unusually high sierras. The party passed through country so broken and craggy that some of the horses gave out. After two days' journey they reached a pueblo of two hundred houses (probably at the upper Bavispe River). Here they left the lands of the Opatas and entered that of the Querechos (the Spaniards' name for buffalo-hunting tribes, mostly detachments of Mescalero Apaches). By following one of the streams in the region, the party could find a sufficiently easy route east to the upper Bavispe basin and thus directly to the great pass leading into Chihuahua.

The crossing into Chihuahua was quoted by Sauer:

> The expedition having marched two days from the last settlement of the provinces and confines of the valleys and dependencies of the Valle de Sonora, . . . the party ascended the northern last chains of the sierra, on whose crest we beheld large and beautiful and fertile valleys composed of and adorned by the most beautiful plains, meadows, springs, rivers, and creeks of pure and clear water, and lands of agreeable temperature, better than ever I [Obregón] have seen. This beautiful and fertile land is adorned and accompanied by five mountain ridges. . . .

The foreground of Segesser I has less rugged terrain than that of the steep peaks behind the pass. The presence of buffaloes in the painting makes it probable that the setting of the painting is east of the pass, facing westward, not between two of the western chains. There were no buffaloes west of the Sierra.

Donald Brand, who investigated the ruins of Casas Grandes, reported to Sauer that Pulpit Pass and upper Las Varas Creek, a tributary of the Carretas, matched Obregón's description of Ibarra's route. That route was the easiest one between northeastern Sonora and the valley of the Casas Grandes, having the easiest pass and being well provided with water, grass, and wood. The change from the rugged narrow pass to the open llanos is abrupt and would be more likely to inspire Obregón's description than the gradual transition by way of the Carretas pass, farther south:

> The pine-clad Sierra Hachitahueca, south of the pass, joins the Sierra del Oso, and the entire range is still noted for the bears Obregón mentions. Walnut trees in groves and as isolated trees are most common in the mountain valleys, but extend also to the plains. The madrone a wild grape, and a wild plum are common in the mountains. The plains of Carretas are one of the finest natural pasture grounds in Chihuahua, and at present, in spite of heavy grazing, one may see deer in the foothills, and antelope [probably pronghorns] in the open llanos. Doves, quail, and water fowl still abound, as described by Obregón.

The great difference between the eastern and the western slopes of the Sierra Madres is pointed out by Vidal:

> The western Sierra Madre, with its deep gorges, high plateaus, and mountain ridges, with its green meadows and forests, reveals a different type of landscape from that of the rest of Sonora. The mountainous land, located between deserts, reminds one of the Moroccan Atlas. Its higher peaks, Cumbre and Cerro Pimal (both south of Sonora) rise about 10,500 feet and 11,320 feet, respectively.
>
> Starting from the eastern prairies, one climbs gradually to the higher levels, while the descent to the Pacific plains follows the bottom of deep gorges between slopes sometimes interrupted by terraces.
>
> The peculiarities of the hydrographical net and the combination of *cumbres*, mesas, longitudinal valleys, and cross canyons will not be surprising to one who is familiar with Mexican relief. The eastward-flowing creeks run into basins that have no outlet (significantly, they are called "suicidal rivers" by the Americans), and the Sonora River disappears in the ground before it reaches the Gulf of California, and the cattle may have to do without water for weeks and even months in the Sonora lowlands.
>
> To this must be added the difference in precipitation. The

> middle slopes which face toward the Pacific receive a considerable amount of rain owing to the moisture carried up by the southwest winds. The zone of the *quebrados* (mountain gorges) of Durango, between 1,640 and 5,900 feet, is well watered, considerably better than the rest of the slope.
>
> Here only rarely and at widely spaced intervals one sees agaves or a few smaller cacti, the characteristic plants of the dry tropical plains of Mexico. . . .
>
> The mesas and *cumbres* are sometimes covered with tall grass, more often with forests of oaks and firs, mixed with juniper trees which grow even on the driest ridges. The oak groves growing in thickets in the middle of dry plains remind one of a heath.[6]

In contrast to the forests of northwestern United States, the forests on the high plateau of Sonora, Chihuahua, Arizona, and New Mexico, which are often surrounded by deserts, have more of a parklike appearance and are often broken by rather large treeless expanses. In these coniferous forests may be found the Douglas fir, the balsam fir, the ponderosa pine, and the piñon pine. Also widely distributed in the forests of the high plateau are two species of juniper.

Among the conifers may be found some deciduous trees, including cottowoods and oaks. Such true forest regions, which are relatively rare, may be found in the Tierra Amarilla in northern New Mexico, on the plateau of the Sierra Zuñi, on the Sierra de San Francisco in Arizona, and on the high plateau of Chihuahua. Though the trees in Segesser I have yellowish-red barks, because of their formalized conifer-like shape they are most likely the yellow pines (*Pinus ponderosa* Douglas) typical of the region.

Additional evidence supports the conclusion that the refuge shown in the painting stands on a natural elevation. In the valleys on the eastern slope of the Sierra Madre are many prehistoric ruins, particularly along Las Varas Creek to its confluence with the Carretas River and even farther across the plains. Some of the larger ruins may have been two or three stories high at the time of Ibarra's expedition.

[6] P. Vidal de La Blache, *Geographie Universelle* (1928), XIV, 36.

The ruins of Casas Grandes stand on the left bank of the river of the same name, 4,833 feet above sea level, in exactly such surroundings as Obregón describes. There is nothing to indicate that the hill on which the refuge stands was such a ruin. The outline of the structure also seems to preclude such a possibility. In his investigations of the ruins, Brand failed to find wood among the materials used in the walls. It seems astonishing that a tent people would have used tree trunks for palisades, but such cases are known. On the Upper Missouri, a Mandan village, Mituttahangkush (Metytahanke), was protected by strong palisades at least as early as the first half of the nineteenth century.[7] However, the palisades surrounded a settlement of earth lodges like those of the Pawnees and other tribes, and in the painting the tents stand outside the palisades. The villages of the Hidatsas[8] and the Arikaras[9] were enclosed by palisades ten and a-half feet high; those of the Pawnees were not, evidently owing to the lack of suitable trees in their territory. In 1759, while on a punitive expedition, the Spanish commandant Parilla found the main village of the Wichitas on the Red River fortified in a similar manner. All these tribes were to some degree nomadic.

From the available evidence it appears probable that the battle shown in Segesser I took place either on the Sierra Madre Plateau near Sonora, perhaps at Pulpit Pass or Carretas Pass, against Gila Apaches, traditional enemies of the Sonora Indians and of the Spaniards, or in the southeastern part of New Mexico, west of the Pecos River, against Faraon Apaches (later called Mescalero Apaches).

On June 18 and 19, 1968, I passed through the beautiful and impressive rock wilderness near Dragoon, fifty-two miles east of Tucson in the southwest corner of Arizona, near Coronado National Forest. Beyond this granitic wilderness of rocks, ranging in size from small ones to house-sized boulders, to the east are the Dos Cabezas

[7] Maximilian, Prince of Wied, *Travels in the Interior of North America, 1833–1834*, I, 342–44.

[8] Thaddeus A. Culbertson, "Journal of an Expedition to the Mauvaises Terres and the Upper Missouri in 1850," *Fifth Annual Report of the Smithsonian Institution* (Washington, 1851), 118–19.

[9] Charles Le Raye, "Journal," *A Topographical Description of the State of Ohio, Indiana Territory and Louisiana* (ed. by Jervis Cutler), (Boston, 1812).

Mountains, leading out to Simon Valley. These strange landscapes at once suggested to me the setting of Segesser I. If the boulders in the painting were not meant to represent mountains, it is understandable why the trees behind the boulders are of about the same size as the rock towers, as are a bush on top of one boulder and an animal at the summit of another. To the east of the Arizona wilderness the road leads toward the Continental Divide in New Mexico. Is it possible that I chanced to come upon the "stage" of Segesser I? At any event, the region would have been an ideal hiding place for a predatory band.

On the other hand, there also exist bizarre formations in New Mexico, as, for instance, in the region east of San Ildefonso Pueblo at Highway 4 leading to Interstate 25, only thirteen miles north of Santa Fe. There one finds rocks of soft material modeled by wind erosion and standing not far from classic mesas. But it must be added that these rock forms resemble the boulders of Segesser I much less than those in the Dragoon region, mentioned above.

VII
The Attackers

Starting from Sonora and passing through the territory of the Opatas, one enters the territories of Plains tribes that lived in tents, toward the northeast and east. Since Lower Pimas and Opatas roamed as far from their lands as northeastern New Mexico to trade buffalo hides and often accompanied the Spaniards northward, presumably it is members of one of these tribes, most likely Opatas, who make up the party of attacking horsemen. Their attire and equipment help confirm this assumption. Their stiff, short-sleeved coats bear a striking resemblance to those of the Spaniards and their Indian companions in Segesser II, as do their spears and sabers. Father Philipp gives us the explanation for the Indians' Spanish attire. Speaking of the confusion and the hard work involved in preparing for a trip to a missionary station, he adds: "Often we need an escort, and then we have to ask the captain for it, but sometimes they dress Pimas and other Indians as soldiers; frequently they show greater courage than the Spanish soldiers themselves."[1]

Philipp also describes the soldiers' equipment:

> The clothing of the soldiers in this country consists, instead of a cuirass, a coat made of deerskins, five or six sewed on top of each other, thick and heavy, so that arrows will not penetrate. They also have shields made of thick paper with which they catch flying arrows; they also have rifles and sabers and lances, of which the Indians are very much afraid.[2]

This description fits the equipment shown in Segesser II and also Segesser I, except that the riders do not have rifles. From the

[1] "Relación," 52. Italics added.

[2] *Ibid.*, 53.

beginning Spain strictly forbade her merchants and colonists to trade arms with the natives, under threat of severe punishment. But Spain could not prevent certain Frenchmen, Dutchmen, and Englishmen from providing the natives with firearms, much to the endangerment of the peace of the colonial empire.[3]

The shields of the riders in Segesser I are round, as are those of most of the North American Indians, in contrast to those of Segesser II, where only the white men of the Spanish party have shields, which are of a Hispano-Moresque design, flattened at the sides and turned inward at the top and at the bottom. What Father Philipp meant by the "thick paper" of which the shields were made is not clear; perhaps he was referring to rawhide.

It is clear that the coat sleeves were short to permit easy arm movements. Only the third and the fifth rider wear long-sleeved jackets. The latter may be the white leader, for he is not armed with bow and arrow, although he carries a round shield as the others do; he appears to be wearing epaulets and wears a helmet-like hat.

The clothing and equipment of the Indian riders thus corresponds to those of the Pimas who wore soldiers' dress and were employed in Sonora as auxiliary soldiers. The Indians' headgear however, seems to vary from that generally ascribed to natives of Sonora. Four of the riders have small feathers inserted into their cap, which are probably made of fibers; the whole resembles a pompom. Two of the riders wear caps with feather fans in them. Two others have caps with one large feather each. The cap of the foremost spearman is large and is decorated with the tail feathers of an eagle. The cap may be woven of bast, but is more likely made of leather. This rider may be the chief of the Indians, for only he and the helmeted rider are equipped with regular swords. The sword carried by the Indian, which is larger and has more detail, is of seventeenth-century design. The other swords are of eighteenth-century design, as are the long leather coats with high collars to protect the back of the head from arrows. The long covers on the two horses nearest the Apache defenders are an early form

[3] Georg Friederici, *Skalpieren und aehnliche Kriegsgebraeuche* (Braunschweig, 1906), 31–32.

of protection for the legs, from which were developed the chaparajos worn by American cowboys. They are a later version of the medieval covers worn by horses used in jousting contests. Such coverings for horses were common in seventeenth- and eighteenth-century America and served as protection both from enemies and from thick underbrush and cactus. They are shown in Spanish drawings on the walls of Canyon de Chelly, in Arizona. The Plains Apaches are supposed to have adopted them and to have glued sand on the outsides for reinforcement.[4]

The origin of the painting indicates that the riders could hardly have been Pueblo Indians or members of one of the more southerly tribes such as the Yaquis. More likely they were members of a Sonoran nation, either the Lower Pimas or their relatives the Opatas. Yet, as Father Philipp wrote: "The Pimas take special care of their hair; most of them wear it so long that it covers more than half their bodies. One can inflict no harsher punishment on them than to cut off their hair. They would rather die."[5] This statement makes it virtually impossible for the riders to be Lower Pimas, for their hair is cut strikingly short.

It is also possible that the riders are Opatas, through whose land lay the route from Sonora to the north and east. The border of the Opatería in the northeast Sonora coincided approximately with the present border between the United States and Mexico. Opata names are still used for the rivers, mountains, and valleys in this and nearby regions; for example, the name of the Chiricahua Mountains in Arizona comes from an Opata name. Although the region was not part of the territory of the Opatas, their influence evidently extended beyond their boundaries.

The Opatas were converted by Jesuits in the seventeenth century, but the salvation of their souls did not always benefit their earthly life, for the efforts of the missionaries to settle them in compact pueblos so as to gather them regularly for church services, instruction, and common work exposed them to European diseases.

[4] Alice C. Fletcher and Francis La Flesche, *The Omaha Tribe*, Bureau of American Ethnology *Twenty-Seventh Annual Report* (Washington, 1911), 79.

[5] "Relación," 26.

The protective isolation of the native mode of living gave way to an ideal condition for spreading disease. One European sickness after the other took a heavy toll of a people who lacked immunity, hygienic measures, and medicine.

The epidemics were usually followed by famine, probably because the Indians, weakened and decimated by illness, were unable to cultivate their fields and used up their supply of seed corn. Survivors of depopulated villages were moved to other villages, and the abandoned settlements usually fell into the hands of Spanish officials who used them as breeding stations for horses, mules, and cattle, the most salable products of the country. This policy of land sequestration constantly narrowed the Indians' bases of existence. Although the missionaries protected the Indians from attacks by hostile tribes, in territories to the south, their coming inevitably resulted in the reduction of the tribes. According to a Jesuit census taken in 1730, there were seven thousand Opatas in the region.[6] In 1635 it had been estimated that sixty thousand Indians lived in Opatería.

In the central region of Opatería mines were opened almost simultaneously with the Jesuit missions. Soon Spanish ranches and haciendas were crowded among the mission villages. The Indians were driven into the mines and were lost to all missionary supervision. Beginning with the first commandant, Pedro de Perea, the history of Sonora is filled with accounts of constant encroachment by Spaniards on the Indians' land and freedom, an encroachment the Jesuits bravely, but vainly, opposed.

The early reports (that is, of 1653) about the valleys of Sonora, Huásabas, Batuc, and Mátapé mention just as large population numbers as modern counts—an estimate of sixty thousand for the native Opatas, the same number as the modern rural population of the Opatería. It might be mentioned that in that part of Sonora a rather widespread destruction of the alluvial land through flood erosion has taken place during recent years and that the living

[6] Hubert Howe Bancroft, *North American States and Texas* (San Francisco, 1883), I, 513-14.

space has shrunk considerably compared with that of the colonial period.[7]

Because the Opatas were generally submissive toward the Spaniards, it would not be surprising that they comparatively early adopted partial European dress and European arms as well as hair styles. Nor would it be surprising that use was made of them as auxiliary troops. Both Pimas and Opatas, as well as other inhabitants of the region through which the expeditions moved, accompanied the Spaniards on their trade and war expeditions to the north.

One argument against identifying the riders as Opatas is their hair styles, which are typical not of Sonora Indians but of Tarascan Indians, who lived far south of Sonora at the southern border of the Mexican highlands, in Michoacán. Doubts that the riders came from Sonora are increased by a passage from one of Father Philipp's letters in which he wrote that the Pimas refused to take part in a punitive expedition against the Apaches, so greatly did they fear them. Moreover, the Spaniards preferred to enlist as soldiers the Tarascans and other southern tribes, primarily because of their greater efficiency in battle.

However, the decisive evidence which makes this seemingly farfetched conclusion almost a certainty is the headdress of the riders, which is clearly of southern Mexican origin. In Mexican codices, in the Lienzo de Tlaxcala, and on reliefs and statues may be found the same types of headdress. The feather bonnet is also found occasionally.

If short hair and headdresses are considered to be decisive evidence, it appears that the riders must be members of a southern nation—most likely Tarascans or Tarascan half-bloods. It is logical that they would be equipped with Spanish weapons and uniforms. That Indian forces from such a remote territory were employed in the north can be explained by the fact that the Spaniards themselves started from there. A later incident serves as an example of such troop movements. In 1758, Comanches and Wichita tribes

[7] Carl O. Sauer, *Aboriginal Population of Northwestern Mexico*, *Ibero-Americana*, No. 10 (1935), 29.

destroyed the mission station established among the Lipan Apaches at San Saba. In revenge an army consisting of regular Spanish troops and militia, mission Indians, and Tlascalans was equipped for a four-month campaign.

Tlascalans in Texas; Tarascans in Sonora or elsewhere in northwestern Mexico or even New Mexico—both possibilities exist.

There are other possibilities as well. In 1630 the Franciscan Alonso Bonavides noted that the Mansos, who lived in the vicinity of present Las Cruces, New Mexico, wore their hair cut so short that it resembled a skullcap. Diego Perez de Luxán, a member of the Antonio Espejo expedition to New Mexico in 1582, reported that the Jumanos wore their hair cut short in a scalp lock twisted together on top in a kind of cap. The Sumas, a western group of Jumanos, were restless wanderers and known as troublemakers and seem unlikely to have been military allies of the Spaniard, particularly against the Apaches, by whom they were later absorbed.

In this connection should be mentioned some discoveries made in the course of investigating Segesser II. The second painting presents the climax of an expedition which started from Santa Fe and in which Pueblo Indians supposedly took part. The size of the paintings, the baroque borders, and the presentation of individual actions that took place simultaneously, including a large number of figures, make it obvious that the two paintings belong together and must have come into the possession of Father Philipp at the same time. If Segesser II presents an actual expedition, then Segesser I very likely also does so.

Against whom were punitive actions in the extreme north of Mexico directed? It seems obvious that Apaches must have been involved. Now the ring can be drawn closer, because enemies of the Pueblo nations of New Mexico were involved. Such punitive expeditions began taking place in 1696, the year of the second Pueblo uprising, when the reconqueror of the province, Diego de Vargas, pursued fleeing Pueblo Indians from Taos and Picuris. On October 23 he found an abandoned Apache camp of thirty-one tents. The road taken by the fleeing Apaches and Pueblos was littered with abandoned tent poles. The pursuers overtook the Indians in a canyon, and Vargas' men captured a chief and several of his followers. They also took as booty forty loaded pack horses. Some of the Indians were killed, but others escaped. In the next two days, men, women, and children straggled into the Spaniards' camp to surrender. Vargas ordered his soldiers to share their supplies with the Indians. From them he learned that the chief of the Picuris and a few others had fled eastward with the Apaches. In commemoration of the victory the Spaniards erected a tall cross, after which they started their journey back to Pecos, then the capital of the province. Not until November 7, 1696, did Vargas arrive in Pecos, after encountering severe snowstorms and violent winds in which he lost more than two hundred horses and mules. His Indian auxiliary forces, the Pecos and Tiwas from Tesuque, suffered even greater losses. The friendly reception Vargas gave Taos Indians who had surrendered did not prevent him from distributing them with their children as "servants" among his men.[8] The more resolute rebels were enslaved by the Apaches of El Cuartelejo.

It is unlikely that Segesser I presents this engagement, since the tipis are in place, not abandoned or torn down. The riders could not have been Pueblo Indians from Pecos or Tiwa, but must have been a unit of "cavalry" from the south.

I know of only one punitive expedition of the early eighteenth century in which it is reported that the Indian defenders sought refuge on a mountain. In the early 1700's the Navahos tried to outdo the Apaches in raids on the Río Grande Pueblos. In 1702, Governor Cuerbó equipped 250 men, including 150 Indian allies, for an expedition against them. Then a Navaho chief hurriedly offered compensation in Taos, and the campaign was canceled. But in 1705 the Navahos again began marauding. Cuerbó sent a large force under Roque de Madrid against them. Madrid crossed the Río Grande near Taos, swung toward the northwest and marched along the Piedra de Carmeno, the Sierra del Cobre, and Río Chama

[8] Vargas diary in Ralph E. Twitchell, *The Spanish Archives of New Mexico* (Cleveland, 1914), II, 111.

and caught up with the Navahos at Belduque Creek. The Indians sought refuge on a high rock plateau but were defeated and surrendered.[9]

This campaign reached the northernmost part of New Mexico, almost to the Colorado border. If this were the locale of Segesser I, the mountain chain behind the pass would be the San Juan Mountains, which extend north and eastward and have a number of towering basalt peaks. But the Navahos appear never to have used conical tents. One could expect buffaloes in this region, up the dry bed of the Río Grande, but not pot-shaped drums or tipis.

In a report written in 1692, Governor Vargas mentioned for the first time an Apache group called the Faraons, who had maize fields east and southeast of Taos beyond the Río Pecos but to the Canadian River and approximately as far east as 100 degrees longitude and who repeatedly attacked Pueblo villages to steal maize, horses, women, and children. The Pueblos often begged their Spanish protectors to punish the marauders. From time to time the governor called councils of war, but the expeditions usually returned without having accomplished anything.

After New Mexico had been reconquered in 1692 and the second rebellion of 1696 had been put down (although it flared up again in some areas in 1698), the occupation troops, which were probably from the south, were withdrawn again. No Spanish reports from this period have been discovered, which indicates that the punitive expedition depicted in Segesser I must have been carried out before their departure.

Nor are there in existence any reports about earlier expeditions against the Faraon Apaches, except the one in 1702, in which Governor Cuerbó attacked their rancherias. Unfortunately there are no details about this engagement.

The Faraon Apaches were not caught again. The reconqueror of New Mexico, Diego de Vargas, died in 1704 while, as governor of the province for the second time, he pursued them along the eastern slope of the Sandia Mountains,[10] which are spurs of the Sier-

[9] *Relaciones de Nuevo Mexico* (3d Series, Mexico, 1856), 180, 187.

[10] Twitchell, *The Spanish Archives of New Mexico*, 127–33.

ra Blancas, the mountain chain in south-central New Mexico. The Plains Apaches had to cross this range to raid the northern Pueblo villages.

In 1712, Mogollon marched against the same tribe. Valverde claimed to have chased them eastward in 1714, but there is no evidence of any engagements. In a 1715 expedition Ulibarri had little more success in finding them. If Segesser I is based on actual events, then this painting shows either Cuerbó's 1702 expedition or one that took place even earlier.

VIII
The Plains Apaches and Their Destruction

That the Faraon Apaches were daring raiders can be substantiated in modern times. The present-day Mescalero Apaches, who are probably descended from the Faraons, still have a bold, self-confident attitude, and they are still proud horsemen, in great contrast to the Pueblos, who impress the modern observer as members of a different race. The difference in looks and behavior of the latter may be partly due to the century-long admixture of Spanish blood, but probably even more to their having been settled for so long and to their agricultural and handicraft activities.

In October, 1541, Coronado wrote to the Spanish king about Plains hunters he had found living off enormous herds of buffaloes:

> After a seventeen days march [from the Tiguey Pueblo] I came (most of the time riding through buffalo herds) to a camp of Indians who are called Querechos [Apaches]. They follow these cows, eating the meat, occasionally raw, and drinking the blood when they are thirsty. They dress the hides of the cows, and all the people of this region use them for clothes. They have small tents made of hides, in which they live while following the cows. They have dogs to carry their tents, poles and other burdens. These people have the best shapes of all that I have seen in India.

This is the first Spanish report of tent-dwelling Apaches of the Plains.

Some aspects of the story of the High Plains, especially the fate of the groups of Apaches who lived there, were the subject of many years' correspondence between George E. Hyde and me. Because of the important role played by the Apaches in Segesser I, some of the fruits of this correspondence are summarized below.[1]

From the documents of Coronado it is evident that the Apaches visited Quivira at the eastern border of the Plains and even spent entire winters there, on the Arkansas River in the southern part of present Kansas. In addition, they visited villages of Pueblo Indians in New Mexico, carried on trade with them, and occasionally wintered among them. Thus, during the 1540's the Apaches controlled the Southern Plains from the eastern to the western extremities and from northern Texas to the Arkansas River. Since the Apache tribes, Athapascan in origin, migrated southward through the Plains from the valley of the MacKenzie River, it can be concluded that Apache groups occupied the plains of Colorado, western Kansas, western Nebraska, western North and South Dakota, eastern Wyoming, and perhaps even farther north, of Saskatchewan. In Ash Hollow Cave near the forks of the Platte, in Nebraska, tree-ring datings have placed the Apaches' occupation of the region as early as 1684.[2] Because several layers contain fragments of Apache pottery, one can assume that the tribe had at that time been living in Nebraska for a considerable period.

Because of these and many other archaeological findings, the Apaches can be considered to be one of the earliest divisions of Plains Indians of late prehistoric and historic times. Other nations, those at the eastern edge of the Plains, ventured onto the prairies only after they had become horsemen. The Apaches were divided into two language groups, the Lipans of the Plains and the Arizona or Western Apaches, and a study of dialects indicates that the Navahos were the first group to break off from the Western Apaches, while the Gattakas, or Plains Apaches, were the first to leave the eastern group.[3]

In 1598, Oñate sent sixty-nine men under the command of Záldivar from Pecos eastward into the Plains, where he found a number of Apache settlements, among them a party on the North Canadian River who had just returned from a trading expedition

[1] See also George E. Hyde, *Indians of the High Plains: From the Prehistoric Period to the Coming of Europeans* (Norman, 1959).

[2] J. L. Champe, *Ash Hollow Cave* (Lincoln, 1946), 55, 86.

[3] Harry Hoijer, "Southern Athapaskan Languages," *American Anthropologist* (New Series), Vol. XL (1938).

to Picuris and Taos. Here Záldivar saw a camp of fifty red and white tents "with smoke flaps and doors, all very clean."[4] After Oñate learned that the Apaches lived mainly on buffaloes, he stopped calling them Querechos and referred to them as Vaqueros.

At one time this "people on foot" came as poor nomadic groups to the fairs at Pecos, Taos, and Picuris to trade below the walls of the terraced houses or simply to beg. But after the Pueblo revolts of 1680–92 they came in strong mounted bands, arrogant and proud, wearing rawhide armor in imitation of the Spaniards. With them they brought slaves captured in raids. In exchange for the slaves they demanded from the Pueblos and Spaniards metal weapons—long Spanish daggers, picks, and sword blades, which they used for spearheads, having learned that stone arrowheads were no match for metal weapons. Most of the slaves were taken from their eastern neighbors, the Caddo tribes (Quiviras), and from the Pawnees, who had not yet acquired horses.

This "golden age" of the Southern Plains Apaches lasted until the Utes and the Comanches came down from the mountains of Colorado, first only to hunt but later, about 1735, to establish themselves permanently as buffalo hunters in the Southwestern Plains after destroying or pushing out the Apaches. These tribes succeeded the Apaches as slave traders.

But in the Northern High Plains as far as the Black Hills, hundreds of village-like settlements, containing the remains of square huts and pottery, have been excavated by archaeologists in recent decades, evidence that the Plains Apaches were probably the first nation to establish villages and cultivate the soil in the High Plains. They lived in the High Plains from about 1640 to 1800, following a seminomadic life they had learned from the Pueblos. The same reverse processes thus occurred among the Plains Apaches as among the Cheyennes, Arapahoes, and Crows, who pushed the Teton Sioux west across the Missouri and were themselves soon forced by the Ojibwas to follow them. To all these tribes the same thing happened. Within a few decades after 1700 they changed from settled,

[4] Herbert Eugene Bolton (ed.), *Spanish Exploration in the Southwest, 1542–1706* (New York, 1916), 226.

maize-farming village dwellers with permanent houses to roving buffalo hunters with portable tents, giving up their agricultural and cultural habits and their pottery making and canoe building.

The plan of the Ute and Comanche raiders seldom varied—to attack suddenly in the spring when the Apaches were planting their crops or in the fall during the harvest. They killed as many as possible, stole some women and children for the slave market in New Mexico, plundered the villages, and destroyed the huts. With each attack the Utes and Comanches became stronger and the Apaches weaker and more frightened. The attackers had an insatiable desire for horses and on every raiding expedition drove away all the horses they could capture, leaving their victims without mounts and thus making it impossible for them to hunt buffaloes successfully in the summer or to hunt for other food in the winter. Thus they were deprived of their main livelihood, for the Apaches' crops were small. Their maize growing and therefore interest in acquiring land was their fatal weakness. While at work in their fields, they could be found easily and were particularly vulnerable to attack.

About 1726, El Cuartelejo was abandoned, and from that time little is known about the Apaches living in Kansas or on the Arkansas River. The French had betrayed them by disregarding orders from Paris and equipping their enemies with firearms. The Spaniards, with whom the Apaches were getting along well, put them off and promised help only under the condition that they become Christians and give up their nomadic life. They did both and thereby subjected themselves to the Spanish missionaries. The Spaniards could have used these able horsemen as border guards but instead denied them not only firearms but also axes and other tools that might be used for arms. Meantime, the French traders were supplying hostile Comanches with better guns than any Spanish soldier in New Mexico was permitted to carry. Thus, about 1730, was the fate of the Plains Apaches—at least those of the Southern Plains—sealed. The Spaniards watched idly as the shield of friendly Apaches (Jicarillas, Carlanas, and Palomas) at their northern frontier was smashed and replaced by hostile Comanches who soon set up a reign of terror which the Spaniards dared not oppose. After 1800 only the northern groups, the Gattacka Apaches, could maintain themselves on the Plains. The Gattackas were reported as an independent tribe for the last time by Paul Wilhelm, Duke of Wuerttemberg, who in 1823 bought from the Skidi Pawnees a Padouca scalp.[5] The Gattackas later came to be called Kiowa Apaches when they became closely associated with the Kiowas and later were absorbed into the tribe.[6]

In Texas the Lipan Apaches survived, though between 1845 and 1856 they suffered heavy losses in the Texas wars aimed at exterminating the Indians in Texas territory. In 1905 the nineteen survivors were taken to the Mescalero reservation in southeastern New Mexico. They belong to the branch of the Plains Apaches whom the early-day Spaniards called Faraons. They were never considered as warlike as the Arizona Apaches, the mountain people about whom Father Segesser so frequently complained and who survived in far larger numbers owing to their determined resistance.

[5] Paul Wilhelm, Duke of Wuerttemberg, *Erste Reise nach dem Noerdlichen Amerika in den Jahren 1822 bis 1824* (Stuttgart and Tuebingen, 1835), 373.

[6] One small group of Gattackas lived apart for a while longer and was mentioned by the English traveler Charles Murray (*Travels in North America* [London, 1839], II). This group was probably later absorbed by the northern Comanches.

IX
Skin Tanning and Colors

Close examination of the hides (either buffalo or cow) making up Segesser I indicates that they were tanned in the technique of the Plains Indians. The skins are soft and similar to chamois in quality. Since the skins were to be painted, they were so strongly pumiced that experts are unable to identify the kind of animal from which they came because the grain is no longer recognizable.

The tanning techniques employed by the Plains Indians should be summarized briefly. First, the inside of the fresh hide was carefully cleaned with the help of a flesher, usually a deer or elk tibia whose thinner end was used as a chisel. A leather strap was fastened to the upper end of the bone and wound around the upper arm of the tanner to increase the pressure. The fleshing was done as soon as possible after the hide was removed from the carcass, while it was still soft and moist. It was stretched fleshy side up on the ground on pegs or was tied with leather strips to an upright frame. The skin was then stroked with the instrument away from the body.

To remove the hair, the Indian used either an ax-shaped piece of wood or the horn of a wapiti to which was tied, at right angles to the handle, a stone or iron blade in a rawhide sack. Several women worked together on the hide, which was now stretched hairy side up and padded with old dressed skins to soften the force of the blows and thus prevent tearing. In the meantime, the brains of the animal had been removed from the skull, spread out, and then cooked slightly in water to which a little fat had been added. Finely chopped liver, powdered yucca, and sometimes salt were added to this mixture, which was then brushed on the hide with a sponge or yucca fiber. Next a bundle of dried grass was laid in the center of the hide and the hot mixture poured over it. Then the corners of the hide were folded over the grass like a bag, and the skin was twisted into a tight ball and hung up overnight to become thoroughly saturated.

There were some variations from this procedure. Poncas, Omahas, and Otos used meat broth instead of brain and liver and soaked the hide overnight in running water. The Maricopas in southern Arizona used castor-bean oil in the tanning process.

Next the hide was stretched over a frame consisting of two forked poles across the top of which was laid a cross pole. The lower end of the hide was pegged to the ground. The tool next used was a blade (first made of stone, later of metal), about six inches long, fastened into a bone handle in such a way that it resembled a small hoe. It was held horizontally with both hands, the blade pressed hard against the hide and drawn from top to bottom, causing a thin stream of water to be pressed out of the hide. As one woman neared the bottom, another followed the same path before the moisture could work back into the skin again. In this fashion the entire surface was treated, after which the skin was left suspended in the frame to dry and bleach. When dry, it was stretched again.

The graining was done with a round piece of bone, as large as could be held conveniently in the hand, cut from the spongy part of the humerus of a buffalo or other large animal. With this implement the entire surface of the skin was rubbed as with sandpaper to reduce the hide to uniform thickness and smoothness and to remove any remaining fibers. The straps holding the skin to the frame through the holes were shortened frequently to stretch the skin. Any tears and holes were then repaired with an awl and sinew thread.

Last of all came the process of working and softening. This was done by drawing the skin for some time in seesaw fashion across a rope of twisted sinew stretched between two trees. The skin was sometimes drawn first around the trunk of a rough-barked tree, two women working together, one at each end of the skin. This treatment gave the skin its final smoothness. Afterward a thick wash of white-chalk clay dissolved in water was spread on the skin with a brush made of root fiber or dried grass. When the clay had dried, the residue was brushed off.

This tanning process was used on skins that were to be made into clothing, blankets, bed curtains, quivers, pouches, and tipi covers. For heavy robes, containers, drums, bags, and shields the Plains Indians used untanned hides from which the flesh and hair had been removed.[1]

About the method of preparing skins used by the Pimas there are few reports. The Pimas were using very little leather for clothing by the close of the nineteenth century, and in describing their techniques Frank Russell's informants drew largely on their memory. According to them, the hide was soaked in water for two or three days to soften it. Then it was laid over a slanting block, and the hair scraped off with a deer rib. Two tanning mixtures were used: brains and saguaro seed. The brains were mixed with dried grass to form cakes and stored dry until they were needed, when they were softened in water. The seeds were obtainable at all times, since a supply was also kept for food.[2]

The skins used for both Segesser paintings are only slightly thicker than the painted leather robes of the Plains Indians. They are somewhat stiffer, perhaps owing to the fact that the entire surface was painted.

Like the skins themselves, the colors and the manner of their application on the Segesser paintings are typical of Plains Indians materials and techniques. The colors used in Plains skin painting were usually earth colors. Brown, red, and yellow were obtained from iron-bearing clays. A red color was also obtained from a yellow ocherous substance by heating.[3] A black earth and certain kinds of charcoal yielded black.[4] There is some doubt about whether blue was used by Plains Indians before the arrival of white traders, but

[1] For tanning methods, see James Mooney in Hodge, *Handbook of American Indians*, II, 591–94.

[2] Russell, *The Pima Indians*, 118.

[3] Frances Densmore, *Teton Sioux Music*, Bureau of American Ethnology *Bulletin No. 61* (Washington, 1918), 226; and various Indian informants.

[4] W. C. Orchard, *The Technique of Porcupine Quill Decoration Among the North American Indians* (New York, 1916), 11.

it is certain that a blue color was obtained by the Indians and used by their painters near the beginning of the nineteenth century.[5] The same doubts exist about green, though Lewis and Clark found green color being used by Indians living near the Rocky Mountains in 1804,[6] and the Blackfeet Indians made a green color from the chlorophyll of certain dried water plants.[7] The Cheyennes mixed cottonwood seeds or ashes with buffalo blood to make black and used it to paint figures on buffalo robes.[8] Before 1776 the Assiniboin Indians were making gifts of cinnabar, which is frequently mentioned as a favored trading article in the reports of fur traders who carried on trade with the Plains Indians at the beginning of the nineteenth century.[9]

No specific information is obtainable about the Opatas' use of colors, but since they are members of the Pima family, available information about the Pimas probably applies also to them. According to Russell, the Pimas usually painted only their faces, though they painted their entire bodies on festive occasions and sometimes to prevent cracking of the skin and for warmth. Men used black to emphasize their tattoos. Both men and women painted black vertical lines below their eyes. The faces of newborn babies were immediately painted with red ocher mixed with the mother's milk to keep their skin soft. Later the color was mixed with fat, or the fat was applied to the skin first and then the paint was applied.[10]

Father Philipp remarked, somewhat unsympathetically:

> When a cow is butchered they [the Pimas] paint their entire body with its blood. Others paint themselves with yellow, red, or white

[5] Densmore, *Teton Sioux Music*, 116; R. H. Lowie, "Crow Indian Art," American Museum of Natural History *Anthropological Papers*, Vol. XXI (1922), 227; C. Wissler, "Decorative Art of the Sioux Indians," American Museum of Natural History *Anthropological Papers*, Vol. XVIII (1916), 207.

[6] Meriwether Lewis and William Clark, *The Original Journals of the Lewis and Clark Expedition* (ed. by Reuben Gold Thwaites), (8 vols., New York, 1904–1905), VI, 161.

[7] Walter McClintock, *The Old North Trail* (London, 1910), 216.

[8] Grinnell, *The Cheyenne Indians*, II, 19.

[9] Alex Henry, *Travels and Adventures in Canada, and the Indian Territories, Between 1760 and 1776* (New York, 1809), 273–81.

[10] Russell, *The Pima Indians*, 160.

> color so that they look more like ghosts than human beings. They paint themselves so especially when they go to the dance, which occurs in the Pimeria Alta almost every night, with singing or shouting but without any understandable words until the padre rings with the church bell the *satis* ("enough").[11]

Russell also mentions leather pouches in which the Pimas kept a light ocher and other minerals with which they painted their faces and bodies and even their hair.[12] Cattail pollen was also used for yellow color. (It is quite possible that some such substance as pollen was used for the coloring of the surfaces representing the ground on the Segesser paintings, since the yellow is much more faded than the other colors, except where it was covered by a molding.) The Pimas obtained color from the Mohaves and later from the Yumas. The Papagos from beyond the desert furnished red and black.

Russell does not mention skin paintings as a Pima art form, but Father Velarde reported that the Pimas wore red and yellow cotton blankets,[13] and Obregon and Alegre observed that Indian women of the Pimería Baja wore colored buckskin skirts.[14] Whether figurative designs were used was not reported, but if the Segesser painting originated with Pimas, then this would have to be assumed, for, as observed earlier, the sureness of the artist of the paintings indicates a long-standing artistic tradition.

For an analysis of the chemical makeup of the colors in the paintings, P. Karrer, of the Chemical Institute of the University of Zurich, was consulted. A small piece of green-colored skin was used to make the analysis. Karrer reported his findings as follows:

> The analysis of the colored piece of skin revealed the presence of calcium, aluminium, and some iron (mostly calcium). It can be

[11] "Relación," 31.

[12] Russell, *The Pima Indians*, 160.

[13] Padre Luis Velarde, "Relación of Pimería Alta 1716," *New Mexico Historical Review*, Vol. VI, No. 2 (April, 1931).

[14] Balthasar de Obregón, *Obregón's History of 16th Century Explorations in Western America* (trans. and ed. by George P. Hammond and Agapito Rey), (Los Angeles, 1928), 174; Francisco Xavier Alegre, *Historia de la Compañia de Jesús en Nueva-España* (3 vols., Mexico City, 1841–42), II, 124.

assumed that the greenish-blue color is due to the effect of the sulphate of iron on the hide. Sulphates of iron produce with some tannins greenish-black to black precipitates or solutions; inks also belong to this group.

However, since brains and liver consist mainly of protein, they cannot produce greenish-black precipitates with sulphates of iron. The calcium, aluminum, and iron more likely came from the kinds of clay which were used as coloring materials and whose iron content could produce yellow and reddish colors, but not green. In reply to a further inquiry in this respect, I learned that to obtain green an additional organic substance, perhaps from a plant, would have had to be used.

Since the tanning method and the color application of the Segesser paintings correspond to those of the Plains tribes, it must be assumed that the preparation of the colors was also characteristic of those tribes. The colors were pulverized in stone mortars and stored in small leather pouches until needed.[15] Then they were mixed with a thin glue obtained by cooking animal-skin scrapings or beaver's tail.[16] The glue made the colors adhere to the surface of the skin and brightened them. Occasionally the color was mixed with water, and the glue was applied as a coating. During the painting the colors were kept in hollow stones, shells, turtle shells, or old pots. The first brushes were made of bones, horns, or wood.[17] A prized brush was one made from the spongy porous part of the leg bone of a large animal. One end was sharpened to a point for drawing fine lines, while the flat side was used to apply color to larger areas. Occasionally pieces of willow or cottonwood trees were chewed to make loose, fibrous brushes. In the late nineteenth century the Plains artists used tufts of antelope hair tied to a stick. For each color a special brush was used. With thin, sharp-cornered pieces of bone, sharply pointed sticks, or pieces of mountain-sheep horn, the out-

[15] Russell, *The Pima Indians*, 160, Fig. 77.

[16] Garrick Mallery, *Picture-Writing of the American Indians*, Bureau of American Ethnology *Tenth Annual Report* (Washington, 1893), 221.

[17] Clark Wissler, "Material Culture of the Blackfoot Indians," American Museum of Natural History *Anthropological Papers*, Vol. V, Part 1 (1910), 135.

lines were made in brown or black (in brown on both the Segesser paintings); the outlines of human and animal figures were thin; trees, mountains, and, in the case of the Segesser paintings, palisades were outlined with broad strokes.

In summary it can be said that the skins comprising Segesser I and Segesser II were tanned in the same way the Plains tribes tanned skins they used for clothing; the colors were applied as Plains Indians applied colors to such items as leather shirts. Where these tanning and painting techniques originated is not known; they need not necessarily have been Mexican in origin.

X

Characteristics of Plains Skin Paintings

Despite the importance of the buffaloes to Plains tribes, they were not often depicted on skins painted by artists of the Plains. They appear only on 7 per cent of the known skins.[1] Drawings of bears and deer are even rarer, and, strangely enough, dogs do not appear on a single skin. However in Segesser I all these animals, as well as other species, are represented.

Characteristically, skin paintings of the Plains show:

1. Time counts, or calendars, comprising rather long periods of time, each year being represented by a simple small picture depicting a noteworthy event;

2. Pictures of individual deeds of war, biographies, or events of tribal history; or

3. Imaginative portrayals of visions.

In such paintings the individual pictures are isolated, usually appearing side by side without reference to each other. Seldom do the individual pictures show consecutive incidents or several scenes of the same event; such paintings are quite rare and represent unusual pictographic achievements.[2] Unified presentations showing principal and subordinate figures, together with foreground and background, as well as detailed settings—such presentations appear to exist only in the Segesser paintings. Both paintings far exceed the primitive art of the Plains skin paintings; each painting gives a reliable report—in a sense, a historical account—of a time and region of which no other pictorial documents exist.

[1] John C. Ewers, *Plains Indian Painting* (Stanford, 1939), 17.

[2] Such as a Pawnee wapiti-skin painting (in the author's possession), which tells the story of a horse-stealing expedition.

The pictographic painting of the Plains consist mainly of human and animal forms, usually in profile and without background or setting. Nowhere is the sky included as background. The predominant figures are human and horses, both of which appear on 90 per cent of the extant painted skins, doubtless because of the Plains artists' preference for reproducing deeds of war. The painted skin was a Plains warrior's decoration, a record of his deeds, and a symbol of his wealth. The Segesser paintings were obviously designed and executed with larger purposes in mind, one of which was to produce works of artistic quality. There are, nevertheless, many characteristics of typical Plains paintings in the Segesser paintings. For example, the colors were applied on a plane; there was no attempt to achieve shading or modeling. Moreover, primary attention was given to outlines; the drawing element dominates the picture. The artist of the Plains painted his figures in two dimensions. The horses and men have height and width but no depth. Color nuances, highlights and shadows, and other artistic techniques giving the illusion of depth are lacking.

When faced with the problem of presenting figures at varying distances from the viewer, the artist of the Plains either placed the more distant figure behind the nearer one so that it was partly covered by the latter, or he drew the more distant figure above the one in the foreground. Rarely did he reduce the size of the distant figure. To avoid the problem of foreshortening, figures, particularly faces, were presented in profile, even when the body was turned entirely or partly to the front. Quite often the head and legs are seen in profile while the shoulders are turned to the front.[3]

These characteristic styles also apply to a certain extent to the Segesser paintings. Six of the twenty women shown in Segesser I are looking forward, watching the battle scene in the foreground. But it is clear from their faces that the artist had ventured onto unfamiliar ground and was not equal to the demands of painting the full face. On the other hand, he presented the profile positions far more realistically than the artists of the Plains, especially in

[3] Ewers, *Plains Indian Painting*, 21.

shoulder positions and the legs. He shows all twenty-five male figures in profile, partly to facilitate the presentation of offensive and defensive action.

It is not known for certain when the Plains Indians began to paint on skins, but undoubtedly the art developed long before they came in contact with white men. The first definite reports of skin paintings are found in the writings of the early explorers. Coronado heard about painted buffalo hides while traveling through the Zuñis' territory. On August 3, 1540, he wrote to his superior, Mendoza, that the Indians had some beautifully decorated skins which he was told were dressed and painted soon after the animals were killed. Coronado also sent Mendoza two skins painted with animals but complained about their poor execution and reported that he had seen much more beautiful and better proportioned pictures on the walls of the Indians' houses.[4] The skins either had been obtained by the Pueblo people on their periodic buffalo hunts or had been traded from the neighboring seminomadic Apaches.

What Coronado wrote about the Zuñis and their artistic ability probably also applied to the other Pueblo tribes of New Mexico at that time. Today among the Hopis many skilled artists may be found whose figures strikingly resemble those of the Segesser skins. Such similarities make it possible that the Segesser paintings originated in a New Mexican pueblo.

If there are similarities between Plains and Pueblo paintings and the Segesser paintings, there are also close similarities to paintings of the Uto-Aztecan relatives of the Sonora Indians. An examination of pictographic efforts of the Mexicans leads one to suspect that the Segesser paintings originated not far from Sonora, especially Segesser I, which gives the impression of being a product of a region influenced by Mexican Indian cultures. But in Lord Kingsborough's *Antiquities of Mexico* may be seen paintings showing women's clothing and hair styles represented much like those in Segesser I.[5] Even more striking is the similarity of the figures in Segesser I to

[4] Winship, *The Coronado Expedition*, 560, 562.

[5] Lord Kingsborough (Edward King, third Earl of Kingston), *Antiquities of Mexico* (9 vols., London, 1831–48), VI, 45ff., Plates 58–62.

those found in Mexican pictographs—in the Codex Telleriano Remensis, in the Mendoza Collection, in the Codex Vaticanus, and elsewhere. One is strongly tempted to place, if not the locale then at least the origin of the painting, within the boundaries of present-day Mexico. Dietschy, the noted interpreter of Mexican pictographs, was reminded of them even upon seeing Segesser II, which has a more European style than Segesser I.[6]

Other Mexican figures in the Vaticanus, Cortesianus, Persianus, and Borgia Fejervary codices,[7] though similar to those of Segesser I, are somewhat stiffer and more rigid. However, it must be realized that the purpose for which the paintings were made would help determine the schematic treatment of their components. A similar impression is received from the Codex Troano and to a lesser degree from the Dresden Codex.[8] The pictures of the economic life of the Aztecs on the Lienzo de Tlaxcala[9] show even stronger similarities, as does the cut-stone disk from the Caracol in Chichen Itzá, Yucatán.[10]

In Chichen Itzá there lived, surrounded by Maya nations, a branch of the Nahuas, relatives of the Pimas (who had invaded Yucatán about 1200 and had become mixed with the Itzás). In the Temple of the Jaguars and Shields at the large ball park in Chichen Itzá there is a mural from the Nahua culture, dating from 1200 to 1450. In this mural the tree trunks stand on a light-green ground (not yellow, as in Segesser I), and are a bright rose color (whereas in Segesser I they are a strong reddish-brown). The trunks are divided into six to eight branches, and a root system is indicated, but the green foliage on each branch has a compact shape, and the groups of leaves are much like those in Segesser I. The color of the animals

[6] Hans Dietschy, "Zur Entzifferung einer mexikanischen Bilderhandschrift," *Anthropos*, Vol. 35/36 (1940–41).

[7] Cyrus Thomas, *Notes on Certain Maya and Mexican Manuscripts*, Bureau of American Ethnology *Third Annual Report* (Washington, 1881–82).

[8] Cyrus Thomas, *Aids to the Study of the Maya Codices*, Bureau of American Ethnology *Sixth Annual Report* (Washington, 1884).

[9] Georg Buschan, *Illustrierte Voelkerkunde* (Stuttgart, 1922), 187, Illus. 164; *National Geographic* (June, 1937), 730, 731.

[10] Karl Ruppert, *The Caracol at Chichén Itzá, Yucatán, Mexico* (Washington, 1935), Fig. 169.

in the mural is pale yellow to reddish-brown, whereas they are pale to strong brown in Segesser I. The human figures, and even more so the animals, are more lifelike and natural (which is not surprising, since the temple paintings are the products of a longer tradition and intensive artistic training). The skin of the human figure is truly flesh-colored, a color probably unavailable to the painter of Segesser I, as were various shades of yellow, blue, and green.[11] However, the style of the paintings, though sharing to a certain extent characteristics of Plains and Central tribal art, fails to disprove the conclusion that a Pueblo Indian, whether an Opata or another Indian of Sonora who lived in contact with white people, or perhaps a Tarascan or Tlascala Indian stationed there, was the artist of Segesser I.

The question to which race and to which tribe the painter belonged is of greater importance to the ethnographer than to the historian. With the exception of the border, Segesser I was the work of an Indian, as was Segesser II, although the specific characteristics are not so strikingly evident in the latter painting. Because of its distinctive characteristics, Segesser I should be classified as a work of folk art rather than one of primitive art.

[11] A. P. Maudslay, *Biologia Central-Americana, Archaeology* (London, 1895–1902), III, Plate 40.

SEGESSER II

XI
Setting and Figures

From both the lower and the upper left edge of the picture two streams flow to the left, obliquely to the central axis of the painting (Plate 8). At the left of the junction of the streams the river becomes wider. Along the banks of the river are shrubs of too little definite character to be identifiable.

On the left bank of the river tower four trees (Plate 9). The trunk of the smallest tree, at the right, extends over the lower branch of the river. The trunks of the taller trees are broad and sturdy and appear to have gray bark. The leaves of the trees are too indefinite in shape to be of help in determining the species. Bushes and tree crowns are painted the same green color, which was originally a dark, rather strong sea-green but has faded to a light color. The outlines of the trunks and branches are thinner and finer than in those of Segesser I, but the treetops in the upper left corner are of the same style as those of Segesser I.

The landscape at the left side of the painting reminds one at first glance of the paintings of the early French impressionists, while the stereotyped foliage suggests the so-called French primitives of the nineteenth century.

At one time a frame or molding covered the edges of the painting, and the colors there are less faded. The present weak reddish-brown to ocher parts of the painting were originally a strong rusty brown. The ground was a bright yellow. Those sections that have faded to a pale blue were once dark blue, almost surely indigo blue. Dark brown can still be recognized as such in a few areas of the painting, but has generally faded to a dark gray, as in the animal figures. The narrow strip between border and painting is also dark gray and may have been painted that color, as in Segesser I. The outlines are dark brown, as in Segesser I, but finer in stroke.

In the foreground at the lower left are twelve small bushes whose leaves suggest small agave plants.

Three animals also appear at the lower left edge of the picture, turned to the left, two antelope and a rabbit. Above the animals three soldiers and an Indian walk between the trees toward the left, out of the picture. The last soldier, the one directly above the rabbit, is somewhat larger than the men walking ahead of him. Most of the human figures in the painting measure between seven and nine inches tall, the taller ones generally being Indians.

The coats of the soldiers' uniforms are knee-length, and are braided from the hips down to the lower seam and slightly scalloped. The sleeves are rather wide in front and have broad cuffs of a different color from the coats. Each soldier wears a sash around the right shoulder and a sword which is broad at the point and curves backward. Below the sword scabbard hangs a fringed pouch and a powder horn. The leggings extend to the thigh. On their heads they wear the typical three-pointed hats of the eighteenth century, colored brown, and trimmed with what appears to be white or silver tape. Their powdered or very light hair falls over the neck in two braids; however, only one is visible from the side view. The footgear consists of low shoes, perhaps moccasins.

On their left shoulders the three soldiers carry flintlock guns with extraordinarily long barrels. The exaggerated length of the guns was probably intentional. All the white soldiers of the party with the three-pointed hats carry such guns. Many of the Indians carry, in addition to their native arms, bows and spears, European weapons, tomahawks, or sabers like those of their white comrades.

The Indian allies of the soldiers with the three-pointed hats are naked, and their heads are shaved or close-cropped. Around their heads are narrow, brown, roll-shaped bands, one end hanging down over the right or left ear. These bands are either a sign of tribal affiliation or of recognition. The lower legs and forearms of each Indian are a different color from the rest of the body, making it appear that they wear leggings; actually it is a peculiarity of the body painting of the tribe. The genital organs of most of the Indians are oversize and clearly visible.

Because of the unusual significance of many of the human figures in the painting, the subsequent pages will be devoted to detailed descriptions of them.

PLATE 9

Figure 1. First soldier: Coat, blue; cuffs, yellow; at the hilt of the saber, two large, round, bluish disks, probably shells used as a guard. The soldier wears a belt which is brown like his scabbard. His shoulder belt is rusty brown, as are his leggings.

Figure 2. Second soldier: Coat, russet brown; leggings, darker brown; shoulder belt, ocher; leggings, blue; at the sword hilt, one disk.

Figure 3. Indian behind second soldier, unarmed, leaning on a stick: Body, dark brown; face, lower legs, and forearms, ocher, formerly perhaps russet brown; the area from the eyes to the ear apparently not colored. The profile is quite individualistic, with a receding chin and a fleshy throat.

Figure 4. Soldier between the second and third trees: Coat, russet brown; leggings, light blue; shoulder belt, blue; hilt, distinctly light blue and long, with small oval disk as guard; cuffs, pale blue. His face is unusually dark.

Figure 5. Indian, at the right of the third tree, walking from left to right: Body, beige-ocher; outline, reddish-brown; lower legs and forearms, sepia. In his right hand he carries a tomahawk, in his left, a bow. On his back he carries a quiver on a strap extending over the right shoulder. Above the elbow, at the color line of the forearm is a light stripe. There is a dark-brown stripe between the wings of the nose and from the eye to the ear.

Figure 6. Indian nearest the small tree: Body, grayish-white; forearms and lower legs, reddish-brown; the middle of the face, yellow; sash with ends hanging down behind the knees, brown ocher. He has a quiver on his back, and in his right hand is a weapon in the shape of a hoe with two long, widespread slightly bent prongs. In his left hand he carries a bow and arrow.

PLATE 10

Figure 7. Indian at the far left, crossing the river: Body and forearms, dark brown; upper arm and upper face, light-colored; chin and forehead, ocher; line above the eyes, gray. In his left hand he carries a gray bundle, but neither quiver nor bow. The right forearm is just above the water.

Figure 8. Indian in front: Body, dark brown; forearm, reddish-brown; chin, gray; nose and cheeks, light-colored; line from the upper lip to near the ear, gray; line above the eye to the back of the head, gray. The warrior's bow, arrow, and what is probably a quiver lie on a blue bundle which he holds above his head as he wades chest-deep in the water.

The width of the streams does not indicate their actual size. On the peninsula are the best-preserved figures in the left half of the picture. Beginning with the bottom row of figures above the left tributary and the figures just above them whose legs are partly hidden by the lower row:

Figure 9: Indian whose back is obscured by foliage: Body, dark brown; forearms and lower legs, ocher; right hand, reddish; headband, strong dark brown, including the end hanging over the ear; upper part of the face and skull, yellowish; face, rusty red; a brown and perhaps also a narrow white line from the nose to the back of the head. In his left hand the warrior holds a beautifully carved double-curve bow and an arrow whose stone point is the only one of the entire painting which is drawn correctly in form and size, most of the others being exaggerated in size. In his right hand he carries a two-pronged hoe. His feet are hidden by the bushes along the river as are the feet of all the figures in this row.

Figure 10. Second Indian at the right of the tree: Body, gray with reddish-brown crosses painted on it; forearms and lower legs, dark brown; lower part of the face and wings of the nose, yellow or white; upper part of the face, gray; from the base of the nose a reddish stripe extends across the eyes to the back of the head; another stripe extends from the middle of the forehead toward the back. In his left hand the warrior holds a bow and an arrow with a large head; in his right hand he holds a blue-colored saber slanting upward. From his quiver protrude dark arrow shafts or shaft feathers.

Figure 11. Soldier in front of Figure 10: Narrow-brimmed conical hat, rusty red; from the point of the hat hangs a bow with two blue ribbons; coat, blue; breeches, white; cuff, brown. Below the garter on the left leg is what appears to be a turned-down or white legging. At his right side hang a brown powder horn and a rectangular gray pouch with a three-cornered flap; underneath may be seen the long barrel of a pistol, the butt end replaced by a spheroid. The soldier holds his gun before him, pressing the butt under his right elbow. A brown scabbard protrudes from his coattails.

Figure 12. Soldier above and slightly in front of Figure 11: Hands and face, gray; cuffs and leggings, yellow; coat and breeches, blue. His powder horn and shot pouch hang from a strap over the left shoulder. The braid of his wig is clearly visible, as is the strap over his right shoulder, from which, no doubt, is suspended his saber, although it is not drawn. He has just fired his weapon at an enemy far to the right, who is falling from his horse.

Figure 13. Soldier directly in front of Figure 11: Coat, white or yellow; cuff, ocher-brown; breeches, reddish-brown; leggings, dark brown. He is firing toward an enemy who has fallen from his horse and is lying on his back before a bush or a stand of trees. Powder smoke is spreading in front of the muzzle, and from the lock flashes the priming spark, above which a small cloud of smoke has formed.

All the soldiers of this group carry long, shafted pistols under their pouches, behind their powder horns.

Figure 14. Indian in front of Figure 13: Body, from calves to chin, dark brown; forearms and lower legs, rusty red; upper part of face, light, except for a rusty red wedge from the base of the nose and mouth to the lobe of the ear. There is a light-gray stripe from the middle of the forehead to the ear. His quiver is dark. In his left hand he holds bow and arrows; in his right hand, a tomahawk. The genitals are clearly visible, indicating that the dark body color is not clothing but body paint.

Figure 15. Indian diagonally above Figure 14: Body and lower part of face, reddish-brown; upper part of face, forearms, and lower legs, light. A gray stripe runs from the base of the forehead and from the point of the nose, tapering off toward the back. Headband, dark brown. A light-gray scarf seems to be hanging over his chest and back, but as later descriptions indicate it is a form of body painting, which tapers at the lower front and back. In his left hand he carries a bow and arrow and on his arm an oval shield that reaches from the chin to the knee; in his right hand he carries a saber.

Figure 16. Indian at the bottom near the seam: Body, white; lower part of face, forearms, and lower legs, dark brown; triangular wedge around the eyes, faded reddish-brown; forehead, light. The different-color areas of the face are separated by gray stripes, which may have been unpainted. In his left hand he carries a bow and arrow; in his right hand, a tomahawk. He has no quiver.

Figure 17. Indian at the right, above Figure 16: Body and lower part of face, white or light yellow; upper part of face, gray with dark-brown stripe from the forehead and nose to the back of the head; forearms and lower legs, dark brown. In his left hand he holds a bow; in his right hand, a tomahawk with the blade upward, raised high.

This is not yet part of the front, but on the far side of the seam is a falling horse, whose rider probably did not break through the ranks of the attackers and was ferreted out of a depression with a stand of trees or brush around it. The thicket is outlined, and the ground before it is strongly colored with ocher, which seems to have been added later with oil paint. The three soldiers already described also seem to be firing their guns. Even though the priming spark is indicated for only one gun (because there was an open space to allow for it), the yellowish-brown gun flash overlies the colors of the figures standing behind it. The white-painted warrior is at the point of splitting the head of the fallen rider or decapitating him.

Let us now describe the rear group of seven figures on the rising ground:

Figure 18. First shield-bearing Indian at the right above the small tree: Body, dark brown from the mouth to the moccasins;

shoulders and knees, light, probably white; forearms, reddish-brown; forehead, yellowish with a center stripe of sienna; above the eye, and from the wing of the nose toward the back, a light-blue or light-gray stripe; area around the eye and the base of the nose, light; the area behind it, yellow; between nose and mouth is a yellow cross stripe. A quiver hangs from his right shoulder. Over his left shoulder and passing under his right elbow to his left elbow is a carrying strap, evidently for his long shield, which is rectangular with rounded corners. The bow and arrow he carries in his right hand are also held almost upright. His left leg is forward, making his long penis visible.

Figure 19. Second Indian above and at right of Figure 18: Body, reddish-brown from chin to calf; lower legs, light or gray; forearms, light; forehead, reddish-brown with a sharp dividing line of the same color above the eye and from the chin toward the back; rest of face, yellow with colorless stripe from the nose to the ear. He holds his bow and arrow beside his left knee, the string of the bow at the top, as customary when the bow is held horizontally. In his right hand he holds a tomahawk slanting upward.

Figure 20. Third Indian, above and at the right of Figure 19: Body, dark brown; lower legs and forearms, reddish-brown; light stripe on right forearm; lower part of face, pale reddish-brown; upper part of the face, yellow; stripes at the throat and under the headband, light gray. All over his body are painted large, light-gray crosses. In his left hand he carries a wreath with thornlike objects, probably a sun symbol. (This Indian may be a "Priest of the Lance," similar to the Zuñis' "Priest of the Bow.") In his right hand he holds a long lance with an iron tip covered with small dark brown feathers from the tip to the lower part of the handle.

Figure 21. White-painted Indian crossed by feathered spear: Body, white; lower legs and forearms, dark brown; upper part of the neck, light gray; chin and lower jaw, reddish brown; stripe from nose to ear, gray; wedge stripe to the ear, yellow; lower part of the forehead, light; upper part, gray. In his right hand he carries a saber with a large, disklike, handguard.

Figure 22. Soldier in front of Figure 21: Coat, blue;

breeches and stockings, light blue. He carries a long-barreled flintlock on his left shoulder. Underneath his shot pouch he wears a long, shafted pistol, barrel downward.

Figure 23. Soldier in front of Figure 22: Coat, red; leggings, light; stockings, light blue; breeches, cut off above the middle of the thigh, gray; visible shoe, dark brown; garter below the knee, light. The soldier's pistol hangs far below the bottom of the coat.

Figure 24. White-painted Indian in front of Figure 23, at seam: Body, white, originally perhaps yellow; lower legs and forearms, once reddish-brown, now weak ocher; face above the upper lip, reddish-brown, with light-colored stripes from the middle of the nose and above the eye across the eyebrow toward the ear. Behind his shoulder he carries a quiver with an ornamental cover or flap; the protruding arrowheads are brown. In his left hand he holds a bow and arrow; in his right hand, a tomahawk which like the bow extends across the seam of the skin.

Figure 25. White-painted Indian, in front of and directly above Figure 10: Body, white from hairline and mouth to lower legs; lower legs and forearms, brown; upper part of face, dark brown; shaved skull line above the headband. In his right hand he carries a tomahawk.

Figure 26. Soldier in front of and above Figure 25: Coat, faded red or yellow, open in front, with stiff pleats; cuff, blue; stockings, blue; garters, light-colored; pouch, gray; powder horn, brown with light-colored bottom. He wears a long pistol. On his shoulder he carries a very large flintlock. From behind the coat swings a sword which is evidently unsheathed, for it is blue. The sword handle and cross guard protrude in front of the powder horn. In his bearing and stride this figure appears highly aggressive.

Figure 27. Soldier wearing grenadier's hat, in front of Figure 26: Coat, red; cuffs, blue. He carries the same weapons as Figure 26, but in bearing seems hesitant in contrast to Figure 26. Around the middle of the hat is a thick roll. On top is a reddish pompom from which hang two blue ribbons. Leggings, dark brown; breeches, once reddish-brown, now ocher yellow, which go to the middle of the thigh. He is evidently not carrying a sword.

Figure 28. Indian with large red crosses on body, above Figure 27: Body, pale-colored; crosses, reddish-brown; area from mouth to chin, dark brown; stripe across nose to ear, white; wedge stripe around the eye, reddish-brown. In his right hand he carries a tomahawk; in the left, a bow and arrow.

Figure 29. Indian in front of Figure 28: Body, strong reddish-brown; lower leg, yellow; stripes across calves of legs, light-colored; forearm, gray; face, ocher yellow; neck, light gray; the wedge around the eye is lighter, and it may therefore be assumed that the ocher was once red and the reddish-brown color of the body much darker. Under his right elbow he carries a long-handled tomahawk. In his left hand he holds a bow and arrows. He seems to be wearing a frayed cape.

Figure 30. Soldier wearing three-pointed hat below the left foot of Figure 29: This soldier is so badly faded that even his three-pointed hat appears white; coat, once red or straw-colored, with stiff pleats; cuffs, blue; stockings, blue; garters, light-colored.

Figure 31. Indian, above, to the left, and ahead of Figure 30: Body and head, dark brown; chin, light-colored; forearms, neck, and lower legs, white or yellow; stripes from the neck and the shoulder across the chest and tapering off at the middle of the back, light gray; stripes across the forehead to the ear, light-colored. In his right hand he carries a tomahawk; in the left, a bow and arrows.

Figure 32. Indian above and at left of Figure 31: Body, from upper lip to lower legs, blue; forearms and lower legs, reddish-brown; light stripes separating colors; wedge stripe in the middle of the face, ocher yellow; forehead and back of the head, reddish-brown. On his shoulder is a gray quiver. In his left hand he holds a bow and arrows; in his right hand, a two-pronged fork with blue prongs and a brown handle.

PLATE II

Lower front row of three Indians just above the bushes along the stream which disappears at the lower edge of the picture:

Figure 33. Indian, appearing on both sides of the seam: Body and arms, bluish-gray with large reddish-brown dots; a painted triangle of indeterminate color extends below the nose and across the chin, throat, chest, and back; stripe above triangle, yellow; nose-eye wedge, light-colored; forehead, yellow; hands, dark brown. In his right hand he holds a saber; in his left, a bow and arrow. On his left forearm is an oval shield. His legs are hidden by shrubbery. He has a strikingly thick mouth, whose corners, as well as the tip of the nose, are pulled down.

Figure 34. Indian in front of Figure 33: Trunk of body, dark brown; stripe at hip, light-colored; forearm, bluish-gray; thighs and upper legs, strong reddish-brown; below the knee two light stripes alternating with two reddish-brown ones; lower leg, bluish gray; moccasins, brown. The painting of the upper body gives the impression of a short jacket. The colors of the stripes extending like rays from the ear to the forehead, nose, and chin cannot be determined.

The profile of this figure has a sharply receding forehead and a chin like those of the other Indian profiles, in contrast to the generally vertical profiles of the white soldiers. This figure also has a quiver behind the left shoulder; the light strap stands out clearly against the dark color of the warrior's body. In his right hand he carries a tomahawk; in the left hand, a bow and arrow, held low, standing out against an upright, oval shadow, which is probably a shield.

Figure 35. Indian with sash, in front of Figure 34: Body, reddish-brown; lower legs and forearms, light-colored, probably originally white; upper part of the face, light-colored; forehead, possibly yellow; skull, like all the parts above the dark-brown headband, relatively dark. In the left hand he carries a bow; in the right hand, a sword. Around the middle of the light-colored calf is a narrow reddish stripe, and there is a broad light stripe around the middle of the thigh. Across the chest and shoulder and along the back of the outline of the upper arm runs a sharply drawn, light stripe with a reddish-brown outline; two similar stripes encircle the body. The warrior wears an ocher-yellow sash tied at the small of the back with two bows, the long, free ends hanging down almost to the heels. The part of the sash around the body is placed very low. The manner of wear and the way it is fastened remind one of the dance bustle worn by the Plains tribes and Hopis on the small of the back.

Above the three Indians described above are the two foremost enemies, in a separate battle scene which takes place behind the actual battle line. Unfortunately, these very interesting figures are obscured by powder smoke. On the seam can barely be discerned the head of a horse that is falling forward; the belly, crupper, and hindquarters of the horse appear on the right side of the seam. A man appears to be riding on the animal, dressed in leather coat, blue breeches or stockings, and red jacket. The rider is sinking down on the left side of the horse's neck, evidently wounded by a shot from one of the soldiers shown on the skin at the right. The yellow- or white-painted Indian (Figure 17) on the first skin brandishes his tomahawk in his right hand, preparing to bring it down on the head of the man or the horse. Behind the horse stands a red-painted warrior, face front, grasping the right foot of the rider to push him off the horse. The horseman has lost his lance, which extends across the seam to the first skin. Behind the falling horse, on the right, lies another enemy on his back, evidently dead or dying, struck in the throat with a tomahawk. At his right, a warrior facing toward the left bends slightly toward him holding his bow in front of him. He is paying no attention to the fallen enemy whose skull he has just split with his tomahawk.

The six figures of this scene are described below:

Figure 36. The falling rider: Coat, probably unpainted leather, which is now much darker than the horse. The rider's head hangs down between the brownish-yellow sleeves of his jacket. The stirrups are faintly indicated by outlines and blue stripes (see Figure 65). On the rider's visible foot is a shoe with a wide, oddly curved boot top.

The head of the brown Indian whose skin is covered with painted dots (Figure 33, in the seam of the skin) stands out against a dark spot at the left wrist of the rider. The shield has slipped out of his hand. All the white participants in the war party have such shields. Its unusual outline can be clearly determined in spite of the seam. Obliquely above it lies a spear which has also fallen from its bearer's hand. The iron tip is visible across the seam in the direction of the shot of Figure 13. At the right of the shield and below the horse which has sunk to its knees is a dark spot between the heads of the first two lower Indians of the second skin, which extends to the left across the seam, and may represent the horse of the second enemy lying on his back, but is more likely the powder smoke from the muzzle of the flintlock of Figure 13, as in the case of the dark spot at the left of the head of Figure 37, which is smoke from the weapon of Figure 12.

Figure 37. Warrior standing face forward behind the horse, seizing the rider by the right foot and pushing his lower leg upward: Body, reddish-brown; forearms, brown; chin, gray; face from the mouth to the middle of the nose, yellow, then light-colored; forehead, yellow.

Figure 38. Soldier with round hat, lying on his back: breeches, blue; coattails, light blue; leggings, reddish-brown; shoes, dark brown; soles, light.

Figure 39. Squatting or kneeling Indian, front view, with broad face: Body, weak brownish-gray; the light spots on his right shoulder, on his left knee, and in the middle of his chest indicate a variation of the body painting of Figure 18; left forearm, dark brown; right forearm, somewhat faded. In his left hand he holds a bow vertically; his right hand, held low, is thrusting a tomahawk into the throat of the prostrate figure. Behind his right shoulder he carries a quiver with flap.

Figure 40. Indian bending over at the right of Figure 39: Body, faded dark brown; oval, strong reddish-brown dots from the elbow to the calf; wrist and hand, light-colored; chin and neck, yellow; calves, yellowish-gray but without dots. There is a brown stripe from the mouth and another from the eyebrow to the neck; the forehead is lighter. In his right hand he holds a tomahawk whose blade is buried in the forehead of the prostrate man. He also carries a quiver with long flap behind his right shoulder.

Figure 41. Indian with feathered spear above the fallen rider: Body, pale gray with dark, reddish-brown, oval spots, similar to those of Figure 40; lower legs and forearms, dark brown; lower part of the face up to the eyes light-colored, almost colorless; wedge from above the eye tapering toward the ear, reddish-brown; forehead, gray. In his right hand he carries a large lance with a lancet-like point; the shaft seems to be adorned with small feathers, or perhaps wrapped with strips of fur. In his left hand he carries a bow horizontally.

Figure 42. Warrior whose feathered spear cuts across the foliage of the grove near the center of the scene: Body and throat, dark brown; lower legs and forearms, gray; edge of the chin and lower jaw, light gray; stripes from the mouth horizontally toward the edge of the ear, ocher yellow; middle part of the face, gray; eyebrows, pale gray; forehead, ocher yellow. His quiver, which has no flap, is carried by a light strap across the right shoulder. In his right hand his spear is slanting upward to the right like those of the other spearmen. He holds bow and arrows in his left hand. The profile of this man is strong and controlled. The large dark spot in front of his chest and face appears to be oil paint added by a bungler attempting restoration work on the painting.

Figure 43. Indian above the spearman in the rear (Figure 41), with left lower leg on the left side of the seam: Body, dark brown; the lower part of the face is indistinct owing to damage to the skin by insects. From the base of the nose across the eye to the upper edge of the ear is a reddish stripe; the upper part of the face is light-colored, as is the crown of the head above the headband. The head is very small, and the forehead does not recede as sharply as do those of the other warriors; he has a receding chin. A light-colored stripe resembling a strap extends across the back, the left shoulder, under the right arm, and across the chest; there is a similar stripe at waist level around the body and one around each thigh. The stripes resemble those of Figure 35, as well as those of the figure above him. Lower legs and forearms, light yellow or white; right moccasin, brown; left moccasin, light-colored. In his right hand he holds a tomahawk; in the left, a bow. His stride is vigorous.

Figure 44. Lanceman ahead of Figure 43: Body, gray, covered with light disks and stripes; lower jaw, brown. A gray stripe extends from the upper lip and eyebrow to the ear; otherwise, the face is light-colored, formerly perhaps gray or the color of the ground since today it appears uncolored like the latter. Lower legs and forearms, dark brown; below the knee there are two lighter-gray stripes. He has a long, slender penis. In the left hand he holds a bow; in the right, a lance, which is decorated with a bunch of small brown feathers near the tip.

Figure 45. Warrior above the grove, partly hidden by foliage, at the right of the spear of Figure 42: Body and upper arm, blue; forearm, light-colored; upper part of neck, light-colored; lower part of the face to the nose, reddish-brown; to the eye, gray; a blue stripe extends from the base of the nose to the brow and back to the ear; forehead, faded reddish-brown or yellow. On his left side is a quiver on a light-colored strap. In his right hand he carries a tomahawk; in his left hand, a bow and arrow whose point is distinctly triangular.

Figure 46. Uppermost lance bearer, at the right of the seam: Body from the nose to the waist, dark brown. At the waist is a light-colored stripe around the body. A similar stripe extends from the left shoulder under the right elbow across the neck, similar to the stripes on Figures 35 and 43. Area from the hip to the ankle, white or yellow. Left moccasin (visible behind the blade of a tomahawk), dark brown; a light-colored stripe extends from the upper lip to the lobe of the ear; from the nose to the ear is a reddish-brown stripe; area around the eye, light-colored; lower part of forehead, reddish-brown; upper part, light-colored. Behind his left shoulder he carries a quiver with an ornamental flap. In his left hand he carries a bow and arrow; in the right hand, a lance with a shaft decorated with a thick bundle of what appear to be feathers; below the bundle are two tail feathers of an eagle. Since such feathers usually have black tips, it may be that the dark-brown color on the painting is also meant to represent black. The blue (and therefore iron) lancehead ends in two pointed, barbed hooks, as do all the lanceheads in this section of the painting.

Above and behind the lancehead is a pronghorn without horns, running to the left. The buck ahead of it, also running to the left, has small horns. The animals of the painting are not distinguished by sex. The two animals' faces are pale brown.

Figure 47. Saber-carrying Indian in front of Figure 46: Upper part of body up to the mouth, reddish-brown; stripe around the waist, light-colored; area below stripe, pale brown to the calf; from the calf to the ankle, light reddish-brown; forearms, dark brown; from the upper lip to the ear, a light-colored stripe; to the middle of the nose stripe from below the eye, light-colored; the area from the base of the nose to the lower line of the forehead across the eye, dark reddish-brown; the area above to the headband, white. The penis is distinct. He carries a quiver with an ornamental flap; in the left hand he carries a bow; in the right hand, a saber.

The battle scene at the upper edge (damaged and soiled) shows mounted Indian spearman being pursued by warriors on foot. In this scene there are four warriors, the first of whom, the one in front of the rider (at the right edge of Plate 11), draws the eye of the viewer into the action, for he, too, is advancing and appears to be looking back incredulously to find that he, an attacker, is followed so closely by a mounted enemy. But the rider is concerned only with escape, for he is cut off from his own group and is hard-pressed by two warriors.

Figure 48. Indian bowman shooting arrows, in front of Figure 47: Body, dark brown; lower legs and forearms, ocher yellow; left foot, gray; his right foot is hidden by the head of Figure 45. Shoulder, chest, and back, light-colored, perhaps indicating that the bowman is wearing a light skin wrapped around his shoulders. Between the mouth and the middle of the nose, there is a darker (perhaps brown) stripe. The area from nose and eye to the back of the head, yellow; forehead, blue. His quiver is behind his left shoulder. He is running and aiming his arrow at the same time, bending forward with the effort. One of his arrows has reached its target: an arrow protrudes from the rider's right hip.

Figure 49. White-painted Indian in front of and slightly above Figure 48: Body, ivory white from the nose to the ankles;

shoe, pale gray. Broad cross stripes are superimposed on the light color of the upper arm and body. Forearms, light gray below the elbow. Below the eye is a gray cross stripe; between eye and eyebrow, a blue one; the forehead to just below the headband, yellow; above the headband, light-colored. This warrior has almost reached the rider from the left side and is raising his tomahawk high over his head for the blow.

Figure 50. Fleeing mounted lance bearer: The first Indian of the attacked party, seen from the left, has so far escaped the fate of the two riders at the left, but he is about to meet a like fate; his pursuers are close behind him. As mentioned earlier, he has already been struck by an arrow in the right hip. He is trying to reach the horse guards farther to the rear, riding left past the camp of his codefenders. The rider, like the other members of his tribe, wears a knee-length coat with wide flaps. These Indians also seem to wear trousers or leggings and a special riding boot with a curved brim in addition to moccasins. Attached to the right stirrup appears to be a spear rest and perhaps also one for the gunstock. Such a support seems to be sewed onto the coat at the right, below the hip. (The white defender, Figure 109, has the same design on the right side of his coat, and it seems to be a common design in all the leather coats.) The two blue stripes hanging from the stirrup are the same Mexican cross stirrups as those used by the white members of the party.

In the back of the horse is a blanket which is of the same light-gray color as the coat and leggings of the rider; all three items are probably tanned leather. A bridle with snaffle and crupper completes the horse's equipment. The knobs in front of and behind the rider probably represent pommel and cantle. The Indians of the Plains copied such high saddles from the Spanish saddles.

The horse itself has a forelock, but only a few brown lines of the mane are still visible. The gray outline of the sketch of the horse shows longer forelegs, bigger hooves, a broader neck, a longer mouth, and more distinct nostrils than the painted final form. The animal is probably a stallion. Behind the rider's head seems to have been sketched the stretched-out head of a horse which was not completed. There are many faint black lines around this figure which make it difficult to discern the details. In the right thigh of the horse is an arrow. The rider's face is not painted. His hair is brown, probably faded from black. It is divided in the middle, tied together at the neck, and ends in a small knot. On his left shoulder is a quiver with the flap hanging down. In his left hand the rider holds a bow; in his right hand, gripped below the middle of the shaft, a lance with slightly convex edges. The stronger blue color at the middle of the blade probably indicates a socket in which the point of the shaft is placed. The spear is the same as that used by the white soldiers and is therefore probably of European design.

Figure 51. Warrior in front of Figure 50: Body, dark brown; lower legs, forearms, chest, throat, and lower part of face, light gray. A dark-brown stripe extends across the lower part of the face from ear to ear, while the area around the eyes and up to the upper part of the ear is light gray. The forehead is white. The end of the headband hangs beside the right cheek. In his left hand he holds a bow and arrow; in the right, a sword, as do most of the warriors near the front.

Below Figures 50 and 51 is the actual battle scene, consisting of two firing lines. The soldiers in front are firing, while those behind (one warrior and two white soldiers) are loading or standing ready to take their turn. A complete encirclement has already taken place around the defenders' camp. The scene illustrates clearly the custom of white soldiers of that time to fight in a closed group, a method which proved impractical in the colonial wars and was later abandoned.

Figure 52. Uppermost Indian of the second rank of the front line, in front of the warrior (Figure 45) with the tomahawk above (actually behind) the bushes: Body, reddish-brown; below the knee and elbow are light-colored stripes; lower legs, forearms, and hands, blue; moccasins, light gray; face from chin to the headband and the back of the head, light gray or white, except for a blue stripe from the lower lip to the upper edge of the ear and a reddish-brown wedge from the nose and eyebrow to the middle of the ear; tip of nose, light-colored; top of the head, yellow; he has a distinctive, large round ear, like that of the uppermost white-painted Indian at the right of the seam at the left. His penis is painted across, alternately light- and dark-colored. In his left hand he carries a bow and arrows; in the right hand, a tomahawk, part of which is hidden by the hat of the grenadier, the uppermost soldier of the front rank. Of special interest is this warrior's long, rectangular shield with rounded upper corners which hangs at his left side and is carried on a strap over his right shoulder. It is similar to the shield carried by Figure 18. He does not have a quiver. He is walking with his body bent forward slightly, following the man in front; he seems about to push forward past the left end of the first line of skirmishers.

The shape of the shields and the manner in which they are shown being carried makes it likely that they were not used frequently. The material from which they were made cannot be determined. Wooden shields of this size would be rather heavy, but might explain why so few of them were taken into the battle, which evidently followed a rather long advance. Other possible materials are rawhide or wickerwork.

Figure 53. Soldier in conical hat below Figure 52: Hat and coat, ocher yellow; cuffs and leggings, blue. Under his bright-colored shot pouch is a large-bore pistol; powder-horn, brown; shoes, yellowish; conical hat without tassle at the tip. He is holding his flintlock upward as if he were about to lower it to take aim.

Figure 54. Soldier with three-pointed hat loading his weapon, below Figure 53: Coat, blue; cuffs, reddish-brown; leggings, yellow; collar and shot pouch, light gray. There seems to be some ornamentation on the left sleeve. From behind the seam of the blue coat protrudes a brown scabbard which becomes broader toward the front end. He is holding his flintlock with his left hand at about the middle of the barrel and pushing the ramrod home with his right hand; the muzzle and a part of the ramrod are visible just below the cuff of the right arm.

Figure 55. Lowest rifleman of the second rank, directly below Figure 54: Coat blue; cuffs and conical hat, ocher brown; shot pouch and leggings, whitish; powder horn and shoes, dark brown. The outlines are faded. A small soldier, he holds his gun slanting upward, preparing to aim and discharge it.

Figure 56. Indian behind and below Figure 55: Body from waist to mouth, dark brown; waist to ankles, whitish; shoes, dark brown; forearm, dark ocher; face from mouth to eyebrow, dark ocher; forehead, gray. On his chest is painted a yellow disk. He holds bow, arrow, tomahawk, and quiver.

Figure 57. White-painted Indian above and to the left of Figure 56, behind Figure 55: Body, white up to the mouth; from there a faded dark gray; nose-eye area, brown; lower part of forehead, gray-brown; upper part, yellow. There is a whitish stripe from the eyebrow to the upper edge of the ear, and a similar one across the wings of the nose to the lobe of the ear. Right forearm, dark brown. No quiver is visible, though a shoulder strap and the outline of a shadow may be discerned in front of the body. In his right hand he holds a tomahawk; in the left, a bow and two arrows. In his left arm is a shield held tightly before the body. It is a long, narrow shield with rounded corners, making it oblong in shape.

Now to the figures in the front line:

Figure 58. Indian with saber and sash striding forward, directly below the fleeing rider, Figure 50 and in front of Figure 52: Body from calf to leg to mouth, dark brown; cheeks, whitish; area from the eyes to the headband, yellow, with blue cross stripe through the middle of the forehead and temple; lower leg and forearm, white; right shoe, gray. A bright-colored penis is shown in exaggerated size. In his left hand are bow and arrows. On his back, slanting backward, is a quiver with the customary ornamental flap. One sees behind the left wrist, in the continuation of the upper line of the strap, a line which is probably the strap of a shield, and the curved line in front of the chin must be the upper rim of the shield. Its upper rim is considerably more rounded than that of the shield carried by Figure 52 and appears to resemble the shield borne by Figure 57. In his right hand he carries an oversize sword of the usual form with a large handguard. Just below his waist he wears a broad blue sash looped across his lower back and tied in bows with dark fringes reaching almost to the ankles.

Figure 59. White-painted Indian below and ahead of Figure 58: This warrior has almost reached the entrenchment. Body from calf to chin, white; chin and upper lip to the neck, dark ocher. Stripe from upper lip to the neck, dark-brown. Nose-eye area, yellow; forearm and lower leg, dark brown. In his right hand he carries a blue-colored sword; in his left, a bow and arrow. He carries a quiver on his back.

Figure 60. Kneeling soldier with conical hat, behind Figure 59: Coat and cuffs, blue; the coattail has wide, stiff pleats; leggings, light gray; he wears a brown, conical hat, bent backward, with a narrow brim, and a pompom on the top from which hang two bows of the same color. The soldier's hair is worn in a braid that begins near the ear and lies stiffly on the back. From behind the lower seam of his coat protrudes the end of the brown scabbard. Although the rifleman is kneeling, he does not prop his left elbow on his knee but holds his arm under the barrel, which is either propped on his fist or leaned on the thumb, which is hidden behind the shaft, and laid on the rear knuckle of the index finger. He is pressing the long barrel under the elbow of his right arm as a standing rifleman would do. His right index finger is at the trigger. Evidently he has just fired the weapon; a small cloud of smoke is spreading above it. The white-painted Indian seems to be standing somewhat too low (too far to the right) for the soldier to be able to shoot straight ahead. But he is really having to turn a little to the right so as not to hit one of his comrades, who have climbed over the barricade and are continuing to fire from there at the enemy.

Figure 61. Second rifleman in the first line from the left, below Figure 60: This soldier is shooting from a standing position, aiming at one of the two foremost Indians in the entrenchment. The butt of his rifle extends behind his right arm. The outline of his back and the brown scabbard behind the seam of his stiff-pleated coat are still recognizable. Coat, light reddish-brown; leggings,

PLATE 8. Segesser II. Photo by Yves Debraine, from *The Old West: The Spanish West*, © 1976 Time-Life Books Inc.

PLATE 9. Junction of two rivers (the Loup and the Platte) (Segesser II). Photo: Blair Clark.

PLATE 10. Pawnee and Oto attackers and (fictitious) French soldiers (Segesser II). Photo: Blair Clark.

PLATE 11. The French firing line (Segesser II). Photo: Blair Clark.

PLATE 12. The breakthrough into the Spanish camp (Segesser II). Photo: Blair Clark.

PLATE 13. The battle scene at the right of the Spanish camp (Segesser II).
Photo: Blair Clark.

PLATE 14. The Spanish horse guards (Segesser II). Photo: Yves Debraine.

PLATE 15. Detail of battle scene at the Spanish camp (Segesser II). Photo: Blair Clark.

yellow; shoes, brown. He is wearing a shot pouch, a powder horn, and a pistol.

Figure 62. Third rifleman of the first line, wearing a three-pointed hat: Coat, ocher brown, probably originally reddish-brown; cuffs and leggings, blue; garter, light-colored; shoes, blue. He is holding his weapon at the ready, having just fired a shot. The spark from the lock is shown, as well as the muzzle fire.

Next are shown two riflemen kneeling above a fallen soldier who is being dragged to safety by an Indian ally. The presentation of these two soldiers in kneeling position is a masterpiece of primitive composition.

Figure 63. Left-hand kneeling rifleman, wearing three-cornered hat: Coat, blue; cuffs, ocher; breeches, light-colored, perhaps white, barely visible; shot pouch and powder horn are visible.

Figure 64. Right-hand kneeling rifleman: Conical hat, blue with ocher-colored ribbons; coat, light ocher, perhaps originally straw-colored like that of Figure 61; cuffs and leggings, pale blue.

Figure 65. Fallen soldier, below Figures 63 and 64: There are no weapons visible; he could, therefore, be an officer. In the battle he has lost his ocher-colored, conical hat with bluish lining. An Indian at his left in the picture is dragging him from the front line. The outlines of the soldier's face and head are almost obliterated; one can discern only eyes, nose, and mouth by brown spots. Coat, ocher brown; cuffs and bandolier that runs from the right shoulder to the left hip, blue. Around his coat is a light-colored belt, which is not part of the uniform of the other soldiers. The lower front corners of his coat are turned back to show the blue lining; there is a light cross trim of cords above the belt. The light stripes below the belt are the front seams of the coat whose ends are turned back.

The figures on the first skin of Segesser II wear two-colored leggings and breeches. The uniform of Figure 65 has leggings apparently made of one piece, for they are of one color, ocher brown, except for a wedge-shaped piece of leather from the knees up the inside of the thighs, which is often seen in riding trousers even today. The injured soldier is shown as though from above. His right foot is pointed upward so that not only the brown upper but also the light sole of the low shoe can be seen. Of the left shoe only the light outline of the sole is visible. At the left of the bandolier an arrow protrudes from his chest.

Figure 66. Indian pulling the wounded soldier from the battle line: Body, dark brown, separated from the reddish-brown lower legs and forearms by light-colored stripes; lower part of face, light ocher. Across the lower part of the nose a horizontal reddish-brown stripe extends from ear to ear. The area around the eyes is white or yellow; the area above and below, gray; the portion of head above the headband, brown; his eyes, nose, and mouth are barely discernible. He holds a bow in his right hand, and is pulling the fallen soldier with his left hand. His left shoe is faded dark brown. His quiver strap extends across the left shoulder; so his quiver hangs behind his back. The tapering, rounded-off lower end of the quiver, which is evidently circular in cross section, touches the right knee. This warrior is rather small and thickset.

It is interesting to note that the figures become increasingly smaller as one moves from the upper to the lower areas of the picture, perhaps because the artist painted from the top downward and did not have enough space for everything he wanted to include. Conversely, he may have begun at the bottom and enlarged the figures toward the top to fill the remaining space.

Figure 67. Soldier wearing three-cornered hat, at the right of the wounded soldier: Coat, blue; cuffs, reddish-brown; leggings, light ocher; shoes, brown; bandolier, reddish-brown; crossing it is a narrower, light-colored bandolier, visible on the back. The butt of the flintlock seen below the right elbow is unusually light, as are the shot pouch next to it and the powder horn below. The scabbard is faded and colorless. He is aiming his weapon to the right, diagonally upward at the white defenders in the entrenchment.

Figure 68. Soldier at the right of Figure 67, seen from the side: Coat, reddish-brown; cuffs and leggings, blue; shoes and scabbard, dark brown; bandolier, blue; garter on left leg, light-colored.

The soldier is firing his weapon; the front part of the gun barrel is obscured by a cloud of powder-smoke. The priming spark is quite clear.

PLATE 12

Figure 69. Third soldier in the lower row, viewed from the rear (Plate 12, far left, bottom): Coat, blue; leggings, light-colored; bandolier, reddish-brown; three-cornered hat seen half from the rear; small braids over left and right shoulders. He wears a long scabbard. His gun is aimed upward and is being discharged; the priming spark and smoke are visible.

Next the participants in the attack at the lower edge of the picture will be described, then the corresponding action at the upper edge of the picture, and finally the happenings within the defensive position.

Figure 70. Fourth soldier of the lower rank, at the right of Figure 69, above the head of the collapsing white-painted Indian: Three-cornered hat, dark brown with light-edged brim; coat and leggings, yellowish-white; bandolier, blue; cuffs, pale reddish-brown. His hair is divided at the neck into two small braids. From the position of his legs and weapon he appears to be "shooting from the hip." The muzzle of his weapon seems to be pointing toward the fallen soldier who lies behind the left upper corner of the tent, or the shot may be intended for one of the nearby soldiers.

At the right of Figure 70 lie two mortally wounded Indians.

Figure 71. White-painted Indian on hands and knees (bottom of Plate 12): Body, white (white was considered by various tribes, among them the Apaches, as the best color for war paint[1]); stripes on arms and legs, gray; forearms and lower legs, reddish-brown; chin, brown; the rest of the face is covered by the left upper arm; neck and middle part of the face, gray; forehead, yellowish; moccasins, brown. An arrow juts from the left hip of the warrior, and another from the left side of his chest. He seems to be trying to

[1] Wellman, *Death in the Desert.*

crawl away, dragging his left leg. His weapon, a tomahawk, has fallen from his hand and lies beside his left knee.

Figure 72. Indian lying on his back, at the right of Figure 71: Body, dark brown; stripe above the white forearm and lower leg, gray; chin, faded reddish-brown. Across the mouth is a gray stripe, above which is a white stripe; around the eyes is a reddish-brown stripe, and around the forehead is a gray stripe. The end of the headband lies at the right of his head. The light-colored sole of his left shoe (brown) is turned toward the front; its sharp outline indicates a moccasin of the Plains Indians, with the sole sewed on. The dead or dying warrior appears to be lying on a rise of ground. Arrows have pierced his stomach and collarbone; his body is rigid in the agony of death. His double-curved bow has fallen from his opened right hand and lies under his last arrow and underneath his arm. There is no other weapon.

Figure 73. Indian at the right of Figure 72, above the two bushes in front of the tent: Body, strong reddish-brown; light-colored stripe above the blue forearm and lower leg; sharply outlined light-colored quiver; face, light-colored or white to the middle of the nose, then a strong reddish-brown to the eyebrows; forehead, light with reddish-brown cross stripes. In his left hand he carries a bow; in the right hand, a tomahawk. The figure, especially the head, stands out boldly against the pale-gray tent.

Figure 74. Indian in front of Figure 73: Upper part of body, blue; lower part, white; stripe around calf of leg, gray; forearm and face, white; upper forehead, blue; moccasins, gray. In his left hand he carries a bow and two arrows but no quiver. In his right hand he carries a two-pronged weapon.

Figure 75. Indian at the left and in front of Figure 74: This is the first figure shown from the rear; it is unusual in that the body painting is in two colors vertically from head to feet. This manner of body painting may have been characteristic of the clan to which the figure belonged. The moccasins are faded brown. The end of his headband hangs down at the left side. With his left arm he is drawing a very short bow, and the nocked arrow is plainly visible. In his left fist he holds some reserve arrows. No quiver is shown. He seems to be standing in a gap in the wall of the camp.

The tent toward which Figure 75 is aiming is a conical military tent. The central post of the tent has been broken in the battle. The tip hangs to the right, and the tent wall is puffed up to the left, partly obscuring a defender lying with head downward. Where the canvas of the tent is fastened to the protruding end of the post, two rolls or rings are clearly visible.

Figure 76. Dark-painted Indian at the right of the bush, in front of Figure 75, seen from the side: Body, dark brown; a light stripe on the reddish-brown forearm and the lower leg. From the nose and across the eye a lighter stripe extends to the ear; the area between the stripes is a dark reddish-brown; forehead, light-colored, with a broad, dark-brown stripe from the eyebrow, and a narrower one, a little higher, extending to the back of the head. He carries a tomahawk, bow, and two arrows and has a quiver on his back.

Figure 77. Indian seen from the rear at the right of Figure 76: Body, reddish-brown; back of his head, gray with two broad reddish-brown stripes. His drawn bow is foreshortened; he holds reserve arrows at the left of the bow.

Figure 78. Indian carrying a sword, at the right and diagonally below Figure 77, marching to the right: Body up to the chin, blue; there is a light-colored stripe across each reddish-brown forearm and lower leg. Across the chin is a narrow light stripe, then a broader one, reddish-brown, from the middle of the chin and upper lip to the ear. From the upper lip and across the eyebrow are light-gray stripes, between which is a blue wedge. Across the middle of the forehead is a reddish-brown stripe; the area above it is light gray. The back of the head is blue. In his right hand he carries a sword; in the left hand, a bow and arrows, held vertically. He has no quiver.

Figure 79. Indian with white upper body, in front of Figure 78, marching to the right: Body from the hip upward, white, including the head; extending from the lower part of the nose to the ear is a broad reddish-brown stripe, tapering toward the rear, and above it, a white stripe; area around the eyes, dark brown; a white line accentuates the eyebrow. There is a reddish-brown stripe across the middle of the forehead and around the back of the head. The upper part of the forehead, yellow. On the right arm, above the edge of the reddish-brown color, is a light-colored stripe; a similar stripe extends around the calves of the legs. Forearm, reddish-brown; lower leg, dark brown; moccasins, white. He holds bow and tomahawk. His quiver is brown. He also carries a shield clearly outlined, shaped somewhat like an hourglass, cut off straight at the bottom.

Figure 80. Soldier, above and between Figures 78 and 79, aiming between the two conical tents: Coat collar, light-colored; coat, brown ocher, slit in front of the left thigh; garters, light-colored; shoes, dark brown. From beneath his three-cornered hat are two short braids, one on each shoulder. On the left, in front of the brown scabbard, is a narrow, light-colored bandolier for the light-colored shot pouch above the broad blue bandolier, to which is attached a long broad pouch with light-colored fringes. Underneath the pouch on the right protrudes a small pistol with a blue barrel. The light-colored butt of the musket rests on a brown powder horn.

Figure 81. Soldier in front of the light-colored conical tent, at the right and below the defensive position, at the right of Figure 80, and crossing both sides of the seam of the painting: Coat, bright blue; cuffs, reddish-brown; leggings, dark brown; garters, light-colored. The ocher-colored broad bandolier, joined above the sword, ends in a light-colored, fringed sash that extends to the seam of the coat. The originally dark brown scabbard is now a light gray. The hilt and guard of the sword are clearly visible. Between hilt and blade is a light-blue disk outlined in brown, probably the outline of the guard bent toward the pommel. The face of this soldier is exceptionally well formed, and his hair, which appears to be braided, is neat and well cared for. He is the only rifleman of the attacking party who is shooting from right to left. He is shooting at the second soldier of the defenders wearing round hats, at the left of the left corner in the front rank of the square. The muzzle fire and priming spark are ocher brown. The butt end of his weapon is visible behind his back.

The enveloping action of the right wing of the battle ends here. At the left the artist appears to be showing action at the rear. The left and right wings are trying to advance, but in the center the movement of the attackers becomes in part an attack on the rear of the camp, and in part a flight before the counterattack of the horse guards.

Next the events pictured at the upper edge of the painting, at the left wing of the advance, should be examined. To do so, it is necessary to consider the last two figures in the upper part of the center of the picture, below the Indian looking back (Plate 11, upper right corner):

Figure 82. Indian between bush and front legs of the galloping horse (Figure 50): Body, blue; lower legs and probably also the hidden forearms, dark brown; face, yellow, with a blue stripe from ear to ear across the eyes. Only the upper parts of his bow and arrows are visible.

Figure 83. Indian below and to the right of Figure 51 and in front of Figure 82: Body, light reddish-brown (or orange) up to the chin, including the arms. Down his right side, arm, and leg is a light-colored, perhaps white, stripe. His face is gray, with a reddish-brown wedge around the eye; the mouth area is yellowish. He carries a bow and a tomahawk and a quiver behind his left shoulder.

Figure 84. White-painted Indian directly in front of Figure 51 (Plate 12, upper left corner): Body, from knee to mouth, white; face, gray, with a faded yellowish wedge around eye; forearm and lower leg, blue. In his left hand he carries bow and arrows; in his right hand, a sword. His feet are hidden by the barricade.

Figure 85. Soldier at the right of and a little below Figure 84: Three-cornered hat, dark-colored; coat, grayish-yellow; cuffs and bandolier, brighter yellow, perhaps originally reddish-brown.

His face is round and marked by a bottle-shaped nose. He wears a pistol, pouch, and powder horn. He and the rifleman at his left are aiming into the entrenchment.

Figure 86. Soldier at the left of Figure 85: Coat, blue; cuff, yellowish; on the right front seam of his coat light-colored lacing is clearly visible; breeches, light gray; leggings, yellow. He wears a brown powder horn and a white pouch. The face appears very youthful and intense. A wig extends over the right ear. (None of the soldiers are shown with their ears exposed.) A short braid hangs down the right side. Neither Figure 85 nor Figure 86 appears to have a sword.

Figure 87. Indian at upper edge between and above Figures 85 and 86: Right side of body from chin to foot, blue; left side of body, apparently white (white and blue were used widely among the Plains tribes as symbols of war and peace); face, light-colored, perhaps originally white. There is a yellow cross stripe below the eyes and a reddish-brown stripe above the headband extending to the back of the head. In his left hand he holds a bow; in his right hand, a large tomahawk. He carries a quiver on his back.

Figure 88. Indian in front of Figure 87: Body from waist to mouth, dark brown; area from mouth and nose to neck, reddish-brown; across the middle of the nose is a narrow light-colored line; above the line the face is dark brown; forehead, gray. This figure is unusual in that the spear he carries is without decoration and his shield is more clearly outlined than that of any other warrior shown in the painting. From its position it appears that the Indian is holding it on his forearm, ready to pull it across the front of his body. The shield, which appears to be about three feet long, has an elongated oval shape, curved back at the top and bottom. The outline of the rim is thicker at some points than others, indicating a wooden frame, perhaps covered with hide or bast. It is too long to represent a plain leather shield such as was common among the Plains tribes. In his left hand he carries a bow and two arrows; in his right hand, a spear. The spearhead has two barbs parallel to the line of the shaft. The blade of the spear is unusually broad.

Figure 89. White-painted Indian in front of and below

Figure 88: He is crouching behind some object and his body is thus hidden below the waist. Above the waist he is painted white, except for a dark-brown cross stripe across the lower lip and a gray stripe above his eyes. The lower half of his forehead is yellow; the upper, gray. He carries a short lance with a much smaller head and thinner shaft than that carried by Figure 88.

Other attackers have already climbed over the wall at this place and either routed the defenders or forced them to lay down their arms.

Figure 90. Indian with sword, bent forward, climbing over the barricade, in front of Figure 89: Body from shoulders to calves of legs and upper arms, dark brown; light-colored stripes extend around the calves and forearms; below the stripes the forearms and lower legs are reddish-brown. From the shoulders across the back and in front to the chest are light-painted sections, evidently what is called shoulder-wrap painting. Face below the nose and along the chin to the ear, reddish-brown with a gray stripe above it; from the stripe to the brow, faded dark brown; forehead, yellow; back of the head, light gray (part of the shoulder-wrap design). In his hands he holds a bow and a sword. He is following two companions who are already engaged in battle with the main force of the enemy. (It is difficult to identify the objects forming the barricade; they may be saddles and saddlebags.)

Figure 91. Warrior walking behind and at the left of Figure 90: Body, reddish-brown to the mouth; chin, somewhat darker; lower trunk from light-colored stripe around the waist to calf, dark brown; forearm and lower leg, light brown; area from the mouth and middle of the nose to the neck, yellow; area around the eyes to the back of the head, dark reddish-brown; a light-colored stripe extends from eyebrows to the back of the head; forehead, yellow; footgear, faded dark brown. In his left hand he carries a bow and arrows; in the right hand, a tomahawk.

Figure 92. White-painted Indian in front of Figures 90 and 91: Body from calves of legs to the chin, white; forearms and lower legs, dark yellowish-brown; lower part of the face to the nose, yellow; from nose to eyebrow and tapering toward the back, strong reddish-brown; forehead, light-colored with yellow stripes. He carries a bow and two arrows and a sword.

Figure 93. Indian in front of Figure 92: Body, blue; forearm and lower part of the lower left leg, white; footgear, brown; face, white (or yellow) with a blue stripe across the eyes, a narrower one across the nose, and one across the lower part of the forehead to the back of the head; across the middle of the forehead is a reddish-brown stripe. In his right hand he carries a wreath or hoop; in his left hand, a bow. He is evidently a medicine man; there is no record of a weapon shaped like a hoop. It may be a deer-hoof rattle.

Figure 94. Indian in front of Figure 93: Body from chin to calf, dark brown; forearm and lower leg, white or gray; lower half of face, light yellow, white, or gray; forehead, ocher yellow; a broad reddish-brown stripe extends across the forehead and around the back of the head; two parallel light-colored lines extend from the eye to the middle of the nose; across the lower part of the nose is a narrow gray stripe; lower part of the face, light yellow; chin, light gray. He carries a quiver on his back; in his left hand he carries a large double-curved bow; in his right hand, a tomahawk.

Figure 95. Soldier below and a little behind Figure 94, facing front: Coat, blue; cuffs and bandolier, pale reddish-brown; collar, white. The hilt of his sword can be discerned; his scabbard is hidden. He is firing a long-barreled flintlock; no powder smoke is shown, but the muzzle fire is visible. The legs of the soldier are hidden by the barricade.

Figure 96. Soldier behind the tent, beside Figure 95, facing front: Coat, faded reddish-brown; underneath the coat can be seen a waistcoat with points at the lower edge; breeches, gray. The straps of his pouch, powder horn, and bandolier extend cross his chest. This soldier is also firing into the defenders. His flintlock is painted as though seen from above.

Figure 97. Indian directly above Figure 96: Body to chin, reddish-brown; forearm and probably also lower part of leg, gray; the area from chin to mouth, yellow; area from mouth to nose and the back of the head, white; area around the eyes and the upper half of the ear, gray; forehead, upper part of the ear, and back of the head, reddish-brown; crown of the head above the headband, dark gray. His quiver is ocher yellow; the quiver straps are clearly outlined but evidently not colored. In his left hand he carries a bow and two arrows; in his right hand, a long-handled tomahawk. Several outlines have been faintly sketched in this section of the painting, indicating that the artist had some difficulty deciding upon the details he wanted to include.

PLATE 13

Figure 98. Indian with pickax in front of Figure 97, crossing the seam of the skin (Plate 13, upper left corner): Body from calves of legs to mouth, dark brown; lower legs and forearms, reddish-brown below narrow light-colored stripes; a light-colored wedge extends from the middle of the eyes to the middle of the forehead and the ears; area across nose to back of the head, reddish-brown; upper half of forehead, yellow; quiver, pale yellow. In his right hand he carries an ax with long prongs.

The advance and envelopment movement on the right flank at the bottom of the painting have thus far been traced only as far as the seam in the skin (Plate 13, left side). Next to be considered are the defenders (Plate 12).

A breakthrough has been made from the left wing of the front, and another at the left flank. The defenders are still vigorously resisting the frontal attackers, their right flank (lower part of the painting) being subjected to the strongest fire. Two Indians and two soldiers have pushed through to the center of the defense (Plate 12, left center), supported by three warriors at their left, who have climbed over the barricade.

Figure 99. Indian defender, below small tree (Plate 11, center, right edge), lying with his face on his outstretched arms, which are turned toward the camp. The figure is small and faint.

Figure 100. Kneeling Indian, just below Figure 99, facing

left: The figure is unpainted except for his hair, which is dark brown and tied at the neck. The same is true of the other Indians in the party of defenders, indicating that their clothes were natural-colored leather and that their faces were not painted.

The defenders' quivers, bows, and arrows do not differ in detail from those of the attackers, but their physical appearance is strikingly different. They have higher foreheads and softer facial features than those of the attackers. They have rather round heads, and their long hair is tied at the neck or braided. They seem more thickset and shorter, perhaps because their clothes cover the entire body. They wear tightly fitting leggings reaching to their shoes and knee-length leather coats cut like those worn by their white allies. Some of the coats appear to have raglan sleeves, others appear to have set-in sleeves, and still others appear to be sleeveless and worn over a long-sleeved shirt. The sleeves of the white defenders are red and blue and contrast with the leather of the coat. The coats of the long-haired Indians pictured here are cut like uniform coats but without their ornamental borders and cuffs. Either they are an Indian imitation of a European uniform, or, more likely, both white and Indian warriors were equipped with such coats for this campaign as protection from arrows.

Figure 101. Indian defender drawing his bow (Plate 12, left edge, facing left): His leather armor has the same cut as the coats of the soldiers except that it is sleeveless. The warrior's left arm is stretched out, the bow bent so that the arrowhead and the feathering of the reserve arrow stand out from it. The size of the arrowhead is probably exaggerated. His quiver, which hangs across his back from the right shoulder, is of the same design as those of the attackers, with the ornamental flap at the rear of the upper edge. The curve of the upper edge suggests that these quivers were made of soft leather.

Next appear the attackers who are forcing their way into the defenders' fortification.

Figure 102. Firing soldier, above Figure 101: Coat, blue; cuffs and leggings, yellow; breeches, visible above the knee between the coattails, light-colored. He wears a three-cornered hat. Since he is presented in profile and is advancing, his pistol, light-colored pouch on a light-colored strap, and brown powder horn are visible; of his sword only the handle is visible; the scabbard extends behind the coattail. His brown shoes reach to the ankles. A small cloud of powder smoke above the lock and a flash from the muzzle indicate that he has just fired his gun, which he is aiming past the soldier on the left and the two Indian allies at the right. He appears to be grinning with enjoyment. The Indian in front is probably standing lower than the firing soldier, which would indicate a depression in the ground.

In order to take full advantage of the height of his picture and to give a clear composition with as few overlappings as possible, the artist placed action and figures progressively higher toward the rear, as did medieval artists in painting pictures of cities and battle scenes. It is the varying expressions on the faces of the figures in Segesser II that reveal the artist's talent for creative characterization and mark him as far more than primitive. The main force of the defenders is so placed that it creates the impression that they are standing lower than the assault detachment at the place where the attackers have broken through.

Figure 103. Second soldier at the point of the breakthrough, at the right of Figure 102: Coat, yellow; cuffs and leggings, blue; breeches, light-colored; hat, brown. He too has just fired into the crowd of round-hatted defenders. He appears to be a less well seasoned soldier than Figure 102. He stares openmouthed at the defenders before him, as though just now realizing that he is killing other human beings.

Figure 104. Indian at the left of and above Figure 103: Body from calves of legs to throat, dark brown; forearm and lower leg, white; lower part of the face up to the eyebrows, including neck and ear, white; a gray stripe runs from ear to ear across the lower part of the nose; forehead, ocher yellow. His quiver hangs at the left in front of his chest; in his left hand is a bow; in the right hand, a short-handled tomahawk whose blade appears to be semicircular.

Figure 105. Indian wearing a sash, at the right, below and in front of Figure 104: Body from calves to the nose and upper arms, reddish-brown; forearms, gray; lower legs, ocher yellow below a gray stripe separating the colors; face from nose and cheeks upward, white; forehead, pale gray with white stripes. He is drawing his bow and aiming at the hostile Indian just stepping out from behind the left rear corner of the square. His mouth is open wide. This figure is one of the two most strongly colored figures in the painting and gives the viewer some idea of how strikingly the figures stood out in contrast to one another before the colors faded.

The rather detailed outline of the Indian's hand and of the feathering at the end of the arrow shows that he and his fellow tribesmen held the arrow against the cord with thumb and bent index finger, bending the other three fingers at the same time. This detail seems to indicate that the artist was aware that different tribes held their bows and arrows in various ways. As with all the other Indians who are attacking with bows and arrows, no second weapon is indicated. His quiver hangs at the left side of the body. Around his abdomen is a wide, yellow-brown sash tied in a loop in the small of the back; its ends reach almost to his heels.

Figure 106. Indian at the left of Figure 105 (in the painting, at the right): Right half of body, blue; left half, white; face, white; on the forehead is a large blue disk which is partly hidden by the headband; temples and middle of the face, white; lower jaw, faded brown. This man is shown in three-quarter front view. He has climbed over the barricade from the left flank of the attack and is advancing with his sword held ready toward the Indian defender before him. In his left hand he carries a bow.

Figure 107. Indian at the left of Figure 106: Body, light bluish-gray with scattered small reddish-brown crosses with white disks around them; forearms and lower legs, reddish-brown. On his chest is a large reddish-brown disk, probably symbolizing the sun.[2] The figure, which has a white appearance, is emerging from

[2] Cf. The disks of bristles and beads embroidered on the leather shirts of the Plains Indians. The disk painted on the forehead of Figure 106 is also found

the bluish haze of powder smoke, like one from the nether regions. The body painting was obviously designed to elongate his appearance and strike terror into his enemies.

Figure 108. Indian looking back over his shoulders, in the picture at the right of Figure 107, next to the crease in the skin: Body, white from nose to lower back; buttocks and legs, blue; forehead, yellowish; stripe from tip of nose to lower eyelids, vivid blue, making it impossible to determine his facial expression; lower part of the face, pale gray. In his left hand he holds his bow and an arrow. The figure is badly faded and very small, almost dwarf-size. This warrior seems to be regretting his zeal, for he is retreating from the spears of the defenders, after having shot an arrow into their midst. The two soldiers facing him and firing from above seem to be covering his retreat.

The Camp of the Defenders

The defensive position is near the actual center of the painting, indicating the central importance of the action taking place there. The pale color, owing to the uncolored uniforms, emphasizes the blue tipi above and at the right of the scene, and the light-colored triangles of the tents in and below the foreground emphasize the squeezed-in position of the men in the square. The dark-colored tent with its forked poles is a genuine tipi, but the smoke flaps are missing; the rolls around the poles on top are the turned-over edges of the tipi cover.

The center of the front row of defenders is closest to the viewer (the deep crease in the leather passes through this section); the third man from the left forms one corner of the square. The soldiers standing to the left of that point have turned toward the attacking enemies and their right wing; the defenders at the right of the corner, as seen by the viewer, are battling the extreme right wing

among their designs. In Francis La Flesche, *The Osage Tribe: The Rite of Vigil*, Bureau of American Ethnology *Thirty-ninth Annual Report* (Washington, 1917–18), is the photograph of a participant in a ceremony with a round spot on the forehead, in addition to the dark painting of the chin which occurs so frequently on Segesser II.

of the attackers (at the lower edge of the picture) and the enveloping troops attacking them from the rear.

There are seventeen visible soldiers standing in the square. Three of them are seen from the rear (of two only their hats are visible); three are turned toward the front; three are turned in the opposite direction; three are turned half to the right; and five are turned half to the left, partly toward the center of the front and partly toward its right wing.

The face of each soldier has individual features and an expression of its own, which suggests that the painter knew each one individually.

All the soldiers are wearing short breeches that barely cover the knee; their stockings reach the bend of the knee. The breeches are light or dark blue; the stockings, ocher yellow; or vice versa. Their knee-length leather coats, both sleeved and sleeveless, are stiff and have short, straight collars. They are seamed at the sides and have deep slits for pockets or three-pointed ornaments. Underneath this leather armor they wear long-sleeved jackets of the same color as their breeches or their stockings. They wear wide-brimmed dark-brown hats; the brims are occasionally turned up at the sides. Their brown shoes are rather higher than those worn by their white enemies. Their hair or wigs are braided.

Their weapons are swords, spears, or flintlocks, and nearly every man carries a shield.

Figure 109. The defender turned to the right, as seen by the viewer, at the right of Plate 12: He is watching an Indian attacker who, bleeding from the mouth, is falling through an opening at the rear of the camp, having been struck by a spear by an Indian ally of the defenders who has rushed up behind him (Plate 13). Figure 109 seems to be hypnotized by the spectacle of the wounded enemy falling toward him. He has distinctive features: a prominent nose and lower lip and a receding chin. The large brim of his hat is turned up at the sides. His leather coat is shown in detail. The long seam down the side can be plainly seen. Between this seam and the one in front are two yellowish-brown stripes extending upward above the pocket and meeting at the elbow. There appears to be ornamentation or an insignia on the pocket. The long sleeve of the jacket is ocher yellow, as are the stockings. The coat is open, revealing blue breeches. The brown shoes cover the ankles. His shield appears to be a long oval, but other shields painted broadside have single notches at top and bottom. At the upper end, near the forward rim, is a flexible handgrip, probably of leather. There is also probably a loop for the forearm. The shield reaches from shoulder almost to knee. His sword is very long and narrow; the metal hand guard is disk-shaped, a regular sword guard.

Figure 110. Soldier turned to the rear, a rifleman, at the left of Figure 109: He is firing his flintlock, as indicated by the muzzle fire and the priming spark; the long trigger guard runs parallel to the stock. The barrel is considerably shorter than the barrels of the attackers' guns, making it possible to hold the weapon at the hip with one hand when firing it. This practice did not permit careful aiming.

The round face of Figure 110 beneath the large hat brim does not look at all martial. His fleshy mouth is open. His gun barrel is pointed in the direction of two Indians hurrying up.

The forward grip of his shield, which is placed vertically near the rim, and the hand grasping it are clear and sharply outlined. His leather coat has a short, upright collar, ornamentation on the pocket, and, on the front side, brownish stripes. His jacket and stockings are blue; his breeches (as in all the following figures, visible only at the knee, below the seam of the coat) are not colored. The inner surface of the shield has a brownish-yellow tint.

Figure 111. Soldier behind Figure 110, seen in profile: His face, with its flat eyes, short nose, and mouth drawn down at the corners, indicates that he may be a mestizo. The sides of his hat are turned up. He has placed his pike, which has a long, straight blade, before him, but his weapon is a spear; because of its short blade, it is probably a spontoon, a half-pike carried by lower-rank officers and noncommissioned officers.

Figure 112. Third soldier from the right in front (rifleman), above the top of the tent: This soldier appears to be firing at the back of the Indian walking between the tents who has killed a white defender with his spear. The gaze of this energetic, strong, big-boned man is directed with concern at the oncoming enemies, not at his victim. Damage done to the painting by insects and dirt has obscured parts of this figure. The grip of his shield, held sideways, is visible. His jacket and breeches are yellow-brown; his stockings, blue.

Figure 113. Hatless soldier with spear, at the right of and behind Figure 112: The man has a troubled look on his sharp-featured face, as though repelled by the horrors surrounding him. He is supporting himself with the shaft of his spear. He is not wearing a leather coat or a hat. A lock of blond hair falls over his forehead.

Figure 114. Hat of a man carrying sword, behind Figure 113: The figure is facing toward the blue tent, and only the rear side of his uncolored hat, with turned-down brim and narrow hatband, and the point of his sword can be seen.

Figure 115. Soldier in the front row, fourth from the right: His face, which is ghostly white, seems to express terror or benumbed horror. He has just fired his weapon, which now simply points into space. His shield is pulled in front of the left side of his chest. His straight-brimmed hat is not colored; his jacket and breeches are blue; the stockings, yellow-brown. His right arm stands out unusually dark against the light-colored front row of soldiers.

Figure 116. Soldier with uncolored light hat and curls reaching to his shoulders, at the right of Figure 115: His broad face with somewhat drooping cheeks and thick mouth bear an expression which shows that the man is in no doubt about the outcome of the battle. The lower part of his face is lighter than the upper part. In his right hand he holds upright a lance. His jacket is yellow-brown with a straight, uncolored collar. He is not wearing a leather coat.

Figure 117. First rifleman in the front line, turned toward the left (as seen by the viewer) of the man with the dark sleeve, in the crease of the leather: The upper part of the figure is badly damaged, but one can discern the energetic eyes, small nose, and broad, angular chin under the straight line of his hat. His unusually short-barreled gun is being fired across the defensive position toward the central front. It is the only weapon that shows the complete and unshortened stock with the strong bend of the lower edge away from the small of the stock. His shield is in front of the left side of his chest. The sleeve of his leather coat covers half of his upper arm. From his coat protrudes an arrow. His jacket and breeches are ocher brown; stockings, blue; shoes, brown.

Figure 118. Wounded soldier sitting at the feet of Figure 117: This figure is very dramatic and shows strong expression. He is pressing his right hand to his breast above the reddish-brown bandolier. Blood is oozing from underneath his hand. His left hand lies on his coat, on his right thigh. A reddish-brown scabbard with a light-colored tip is at his left side. His sword lies at his right side. His gun is pressed into his right side. His head is bent backward in a death agony; his mouth is open wide in pain. His face is pale and bloodless, showing the lines of death. His head is bare, revealing light-colored hair. His jacket is blue; his breeches, ocher yellow; his stockings, which are not colored, may be leather leggings; his shoes are brown.

Figure 119. Soldier falling forward, to the right behind the second conical tent from the right, at the right of Figure 118: Protruding from the back of his leather coat is an arrow shot by the Indian standing in front of the tent (Figure 77), who is now sending a second arrow over the head of the wounded man toward the end soldier on the front line (Figure 117). Figure 119 is sinking forward, his left knee already on the ground. He is stretching out his arms to break his fall. Blood is flowing from his right side and downward. His weapon cannot be seen.

Figure 120. Wounded soldier sinking forward toward the left, at the left of Figure 118: This soldier has placed his hands on the ground in front of his feet to hold himself up, but his head has already sunk so far forward that one can see the underside of the brim of his hat. His mouth is open, and his ocher-yellow sleeves are red with blood. He is writhing in pain. He wears an ocher-yellow jacket and breeches. His shoulder belt and scabbard are sharply drawn. The stockings are not colored and thus are probably made of leather; his shoes are brown.

The three dying men just described form a composition of genuine artistic merit.

Figure 121. Soldier behind the first fighter in the front row (Figure 117): He has a full face, with a narrow chin and piercing eyes. The brim of his hat is turned down. He wears a leather coat and carries a shield and lance.

Figure 122. This soldier, at the right of and behind Figure 121, is shown with his profile turned to the right. He is young, with soft features and round cheeks, slightly opened lips and bowed head, as though deep in thought. He wears an ocher-yellow jacket. His lance crosses with that of Figure 116.

Figure 123. Hatless soldier, shown with his profile turned to the left: All but his face is hidden by the hat of the soldier in front of him. He seems spellbound and has set his lance upright beside him. He has a rather lean face with a receding chin. The yellow color of his hair is probably a faded brown.

Figure 124. Soldier wearing a hat, above the blond head of Figure 123: Only the back part of the brown hat and the upright spear of this soldier are visible.

Figure 125. Second soldier from the left corner of the square, firing his gun toward the left: His face shows an almost unconcerned expression, and he is looking, not in the direction of his shot, but rather toward the front, out of the picture, as though posing. His mouth shows no emotion; he has a short nose; his eyes are half-closed. The broad brim of his hat appears to shade half his face. The barrel of his gun is a little longer than that of the man beside him. The stock has a pronounced curve. His shield covers the left side of his chest and leaves only his right shoulder exposed. His jacket is blue.

Figure 126. Soldier behind Figure 125, in the middle of the three riflemen: Of this soldier only his hat can be seen, evidently from the rear. The yellowish area beneath the brim of the hat must be the hair above the nape of the neck. It is uncertain which weapon is his. It may be the lance cutting across the left knee of the blue-legged hostile Indian at the rear of the square.

Figure 127. Rifleman on the outside, at the far left of the three men firing toward the left: In contrast to the other figures of the group, who are rather heavy, this figure is a slender young man with a sharply etched profile and a rather lean face, with prominent cheekbones and narrow cheeks. Especially pronounced are the mouth and chin and the middle part of the face. He wears a brown hat with the brim turned up toward the back. He is firing his flintlock, whose barrel appears to be almost twice as long as that of his second fellow rifleman at the left. The vertical line of the end of the barrel and the muzzle fire are clearly outlined. In the upper part of his shield, which covers the left side of his body, is an arrow. He is evidently wearing yellow breeches but no leather coat.

These soldiers just described give the impression of belonging to a different nation, as do the ones below.

Figure 128. Rifleman behind Figure 127, wearing a light-colored hat: His face resembles that of Figure 127, but his features are even more prominent. Traces of yellow paint in front of the mouth suggest that the man has a mustache and a small beard. The features of this man, as well as of the rifleman standing at the left in front of him, appear to be French. (There were Frenchmen who enlisted with the Spaniards and made common cause in quarrels with the English.)

Figure 129. Indian drawing his bow, at the left and a little above the square: This warrior is the most exposed defender: the entire wedge of attackers is approaching him head on. He is threatened with tomahawk, sword, arrow, and bullet. Unperturbed, he draws his bow, although he will shortly join the ranks of the dead. He seems to typify legendary Indian stoicism. Behind his head is a small knot, above which the hair is held together with a light-colored string, probably of leather. His cheeks are broad and full; chin, long and rounded; nose, rather short; forehead, prominent. It is not a distinctively Indian profile. He has been wounded; there is an arrow below the ribs on the left side. The whole figure is enveloped in a cloud of powder smoke. In his left hand he holds the bow and a reserve arrow; with his right hand he is drawing the bow. His quiver hangs on his right shoulder.

Figure 130. Dead soldier lying on his back, below the first of the three guns aimed toward the left, and in front of Figure 120: His face is almost in profile, and his mouth appears to be open. The relaxed angle of his outstretched arm makes it apparent that he is dead. Blood is flowing from a wound in the chest and also from the nose and mouth and across the forehead. His uniform is like that of the other soldiers. The shoulder belt across his chest is extremely dark.

Figure 131. Soldier in front of the lower half of of Figure 130: The brim of his hat is turned up at the sides. He carries a large shield notched in the center of the upper rim.

Figure 132. Wounded soldier whose head is hanging down between the walls of the tent with the ridged roof at the left and the conical tent at the right: The figure is somewhat difficult to discern; the lower part of his body is hidden by the collapsed tent cover. His hat is still on his head. Toward the middle of the body is a light yellow line tapering off toward the top, which may be blood flowing from a wound.

Figure 133. Soldier in front of the man with the large shield (Figure 131): Only his face and small hat with upturned brim on the side are clearly visible. His face seems to have delicate features. Other details are difficult to discern. He seems to be carrying a gun and a shield. The ramparts at this point seem to be made of short wood stakes.

Figure 134. Soldier at the nearer, lower left edge of the rampart, diagonally to the left in front of and above the head of Figure 133 and to the left of Figure 131: His head is turned to the right, away from the front line. His forehead is prominent; his hair is light. His position and expression make it evident that he is no longer fighting and has taken refuge behind the barricade. He carries no arms, and he is hatless.

Figure 135. Bareheaded soldier with barrel of weapon pointed upward, at the upper right side of the rampart: Almost all of his back is visible. He seems to be sitting on the edge of a pit. His back is slightly bent, perhaps indicating that he is ducking the bullets and arrows of the attackers. He is not firing at the attackers or reloading.

Figure 136. Large, light-colored profile seen against the jacket of Figure 135: His face is turned to the right away from the attack. He has an unusually large head. His hat is white or uncolored.

Figure 137. Soldier with large shield, at the right of and above the three soldiers behind the barricade. He seems to be standing in a depression, perhaps a trench, behind upended packsaddle frames with reinforced sides. His brown-brimmed hat is turned up at the sides. His face is turned toward the front line. His face is bony, with long chin and a thick upper lip.

Figure 138. Dead soldier lying on his back behind the upper left corner of the ridge tent: His head has been placed on a low stool or support of some kind. His head has fallen backward in death, his pale, broad face turned upward. From the corner of his mouth blood trickles down over his cheeks and jaw. His round hat is lying behind his head, upside down. The shape of his hat makes it clear that he is one of the defenders. His coat is reddish-brown; at his throat he wears a band resembling a modern-day clerical collar. The decoration on his coat and the fact that an effort was made to make him comfortable in his dying moments indicate that he is the officer commanding the front line. A shield-bearer is standing in front of the body to protect it from attackers. As will be seen later, this figure is of particular significance in the painting.

Figure 139. Shield-bearer behind the left corner of the saddle-roofed tent: This man is defending the gap between the two tents (Plate 12, lower left). His gun is aimed past the rear of the conical tent toward the center of the front line. From his coat it is likely that he is also an officer.

Figure 140. Wounded or dead defender, turned to the right and lying on his knees and forearms with his head directly before the face and throat of Figure 139: This figure is indistinct in the plate, discernible only through color patterns.

Figure 141. Head of an Indian at the left, in front of the

conical tent, at the left front corner of the camp, beside the two tears in the skin: He, too, is one of the defenders; his brown hair is tied together at the neck. He is drawing his bow, preparing to defend himself against the guns of the two soldiers facing him. His face shows determination. Nothing else can be seen of him, because he is kneeling behind a saddle with a yellowish blanket. One can see the girth and the end of the stirrup strap, which extends below the blanket and ends in a round eye set on the quadrangular stirrup. Eye and stirrup are blue and therefore iron. In the almost square stirrup a hole is cut which is straight at the bottom and curves up in a semicircle. More will be said later about the significance of the stirrup.

The arrangement of the defenders' camp can be compared to that of an ancient Roman military camp. At the forward half of the camp, the one nearer the enemy, the auxiliary troops have been stationed; at the rear part, the regular soldiers. On the side of the camp facing the enemy, the most dangerous position, the defenders are almost exclusively Indian. At the point of the square under attack stands a single Indian, perhaps symbolizing a larger force. Armed only with bow and arrow, he is trying to withstand the fiercest point of attack. Thus throughout history have the so-called master races defended themselves, by using the bodies and lives of those whom they have subjugated.

The figures in the camp are distributed as follows: seventeen figures in the square; five Indians, four of whom are fighting on the barricade at the front, and one covering one flank of the main position; three figures who have fallen directly in front of the square; two dead figures closer to the front line; three shield-bearers at both sides of the rampart, behind which are one figure and two heads; the dead figure directly in front of the horse; the dead figure at the left behind the ridged tent, and the shield-bearer guarding his body. In addition, there is the dead soldier with the Indian spear in his throat behind the tent at the right below and the wounded or dead soldier in the blue jacket at the right, in front of the blue tent at the top right.

At the right of the painting are sixteen additional figures of the attacking party, and at the left of the front of the attack two mounted red-coated soldiers and a mounted Indian in flight. These figures total 57 defenders as compared with 134 attackers. The overwhelming superiority of the attacking force leads the viewer to conclude that the Indian artist may have been of the same tribe as the defenders. This fact would explain the more individual treatment of the figures of the defenders, the details of their deeds and sufferings, especially on the third skin, the one at the right (Plates 13 and 14). Moreover, the enemies are pictured as large men as well as superior in numbers, to account for the defenders' defeat and to emphasize their heroism and steadfastness.

If, on the other hand, the painter belonged to the tribe of the attackers and had perhaps taken part in the battle himself, he would have wanted to show as many of his comrades as possible on the painting and to depict them as heroic. An argument can thus be made for either conclusion. It is a testimony to the artist's objectivity that the question cannot be resolved with certainty from the evidence of the painting alone. However, it is my belief that the artist either was of the tribe of the Indian defenders or was sympathetic to their cause.

Now to the scenes at the rear of the encampment.

PLATE 13

This section of the painting shows individual and small-group engagements in which the attacking force has overwhelming superiority. Among these groups are the fourteen figures who are engaged in hand-to-hand combat between the upper blue tipi and the far-right lower tent.

One of the scenes shows five combatants at the right of the blue tent (Plate 12). One defender, with blond hair, has been knocked down, and an attacker is holding him by his legs while two others are pulling him by his wrists, the warrior in front brandishing a tomahawk over the fallen man's head, a superfluous gesture, for another attacker has hurried up from the left and has plunged a spear into his heart.

Figure 142. Defender described above, lying on his back, at the rear of the dark tent (Plate 12), held by his wrists and ankles by attackers. The Indian standing directly before the entrance to the tent has grasped his ankles; another, a faintly discernible white-painted Indian, is holding him by the right wrist; and the Indian with dark circles painted on his body, by the left wrist. The third Indian is raising his tomahawk to strike; meanwhile, another warrior has run his spear between the defender's ribs. His blood, now faded to a pale ocher, is staining the ground. His jacket is blue. He wears yellow breeches fastened with garters below the knees, light-colored stockings, and brown shoes. His face is obliterated; he appears to have blond hair. He has no weapon, shield, or leather coat, indicating that the suprise attack gave him no time to seize his weapons.

Figure 143. Indian covered with painted circles in the seam of the skin (Plate 13, upper left side), holding Figure 142 by the left wrist: Body, grayish, covered from the elbows to knees with deep reddish-brown circles; lower legs, light-colored; forearms, reddish-brown; lower part of the face from neck to middle of the nose, reddish-brown; upper half of the face, light-colored. The blade of the tomahawk he holds over the defender's head is not colored. The posture of the figure is more lifelike than that of other Indians in the painting.

Figure 144. White-painted Indian at the left of and behind Figure 143: Little detail can be discerned of this figure except that he is holding the right wrist of Figure 142 with his right hand and seems to be holding a bow in his left.

Figure 145. Indian, seen from the front, holding the legs of Figure 142 (Plate 12): Body, light blue from the moccasins to throat; across his light-colored face is a reddish-brown stripe from the middle of the nose to the mouth; forehead, light blue; top of the head, ocher yellow. The end of his headband hangs down behind his right ear. His outline is faint, and the features of his face are unrecognizable. His light-colored quiver strap extends across his chest.

This part of the painting shows a great many overlappings and is lacking in several details.

Figure 146. Tall Indian in front of the blue tipi, thrusting his lance into Figure 142 (Plate 12): Body, blue from thighs to mouth (the color partly obscures the figure since the tent is the same color); forearms, yellowish-brown; lower body, including legs and shoes, white; the middle part of the face, light-colored; forehead, light gray. A yellow-brown stripe extends from the nose to the ear. The end of his headband hangs behind his right ear. In his left hand he holds a bow and two arrows; in his right hand, a narrow light spear without ornamentation.

The following group, at the right of Figure 143, is more clearly distinguishable:

Figure 147. Indian defender on his hands and knees, at the right of the seam and of Figure 146: He is sinking to the ground; his body is riddled with arrows. His attacker stands over him with raised tomahawk. The figure is clothed in a long-sleeved leather shirt. A narrow rope serves as a belt around his waist. The lower seam of his coat and the end of the sleeve at the wrist are visible. The weak-gray color of his leggings stands out against the faded yellow of the ground. Only the left shoe shows traces of paint. The hair is dark brown. Blood is spurting from a wound in the back of his head. This clearly outlined and lifelike figure gives the effect of a sketch drawn from observation.

Figure 148. Indian brandishing his tomahawk over Figure 147: Body, reddish-brown from calves of legs to upper lip; light-colored stripes around the calves and forearms; forearms and lower legs, faded dark brown; shoes, light-colored. There is a light-colored stripe across the middle of the nose, above it, a reddish-brown stripe; across the eye, a light-colored stripe; and under the eyebrow, another reddish-brown stripe, this one extending to the back of the head. Forehead and top of head, yellow. The end of his headband hangs down in front of the ear.

Figure 149. Indian defender with spear and bow, facing left, at the right below Figure 147: This figure was drawn with great care and detail. His moderately long hair is tied at the neck. His knee-length leather coat has a thick seam at the sleeve, suggesting that it is a sleeveless leather jerkin like that worn by his white allies. The coat is belted and slit in the back and therefore has coattails. An arrow protrudes from the lower left side of the coat but evidently has not reached the warrior's body, for he does not appear to be wounded. A second arrow protrudes from the right rear near the belt, and a third from the shoulder blade down over the quiver. His clothing is grayish-white; his shoes and quivers, yellowish. He carries two full quivers and two bows, one in his left hand, the other in the quiver hanging over his left hip. In his right hand is a spear. He may have picked up the extra bow and quiver from a fallen comrade, or he may be trying to bring fresh ammunition to the camp. He has evidently just wounded the white-painted Indian at the right of the lower tent (Figure 153), who has an arrow in his hip.

Figure 150. White-painted Indian at the right of and above Figure 149: He is about to shoot an arrow at Figure 149 and is holding a second one ready in his left hand, parallel to the bow. His white paint is contrasted with a deep-blue masklike stripe across his eyes and nose. Above the blue stripe is a narrow white stripe, and the upper part of the forehead is yellow.

Figure 151. Indian with dark circles on his body, below and behind Figure 149, seen from the rear: Body, painted white or yellowish-gray, covered from shoulders to shoes, including arms and hands, with dark, reddish-brown disks. From the ears and headband downward is a dark-brown triangle that tapers off to a point between the shoulder blades. The top of his head is light. His bow, which is visible above and in front of his head, has a double curve. He is pursuing Figure 149, having circled around the camp from the right and come upon the defender. One of his arrows has penetrated the defender's coat.

Figure 152. White-painted Indian, at the left of Figure 151: Shoulders, upper arms, and lower trunk, dark brown; moccasins, faded brown. In his left hand he holds a bow and two arrows; in his right hand, a tomahawk with a light handle.

The three above-described warriors attacking Figure 149 are smaller than the surrounding figures and appear to be quite young.

Figure 153. Indian attacker, bent over, in front of Figure 149: Body, strong reddish-brown; forearm, below a narrow, light-colored stripe, dark brown, now faded to yellow. Below the nose is a narrow light-colored stripe; above it a pale, ocher-brown band; then another narrow, reddish-brown band to the middle of the forehead, and a light-colored line; the upper half of the forehead is ocher yellow. The end of his headband hangs down at an angle; it is not colored. He has been wounded by Figure 149 who has run his lance into his back. The light-blue lancehead has evidently pierced his lungs; blood is flowing from his mouth as well as from the wound. The dying warrior seems not to be carrying a weapon.

Figure 154. White-painted Indian below Figure 153, looking back, close to the lower conical tent crossing the seam: Body, white from feet to headband, broken by a reddish-brown stripe that extends from the eyebrows across the nose and around the back of the head; chin, dark brown to nose and tapering off toward the lobe of the ear; a narrow, light-colored stripe extends from the tip of the nose to the cheeks; lower part of the left arm and the hand, weak reddish-brown. In his left hand he holds a double-curved bow and an arrow. His right arm is white; his right hand is hidden by the tipi.

Below the tent that extends across the seam is another engagement involving two or perhaps three persons. Behind and at the right of the tent is a soldier, one of the defenders, lying on his face. At the left of the tent (Plate 12) stands his slayer, holding the end of the spear which he has run through the defender's throat. At the right of the fallen man stands another warrior with raised sword. Either he has struck the fallen man or he is raising his weapon to force his way into the camp.

Figure 155. Dying soldier lying below the lower tent at

the right: He is lying on his face, with his head turned to the right. Blood is trickling from his mouth. A lancehead is buried in the right carotid artery. A stiff, light-colored braid lies on the neck; his hair is light. His right arm, in the reddish-brown sleeve of his jacket, lies between his face and the right foot of the warrior carrying the sword. Of his thick leather armor only the upper part of the back can be seen. The rest of his body is hidden by the tent. No weapon is shown.

Figure 156. Indian with the lance, at the left of and behind the lower tipi, turned to the right toward his victim, Figure 155 (Plate 12): Body, dark brown; above the mouth is a narrow white stripe; forehead, white. The end of his headband hangs behind his right ear. In his left hand he holds a bow and arrows; in his right hand, which is not colored, he holds the shaft of the lance, which is probably covered with short feathers. Here the painter shows in one single picture aggression and its result.

Figure 157. Indian carrying a sword at the right of Figure 155 (Plate 13): Body, light blue from calf to throat; throat and lower part of the face to the nose, reddish-brown; a yellow stripe runs across the cheekbones to the back of the head; the area around his eyes above the lower part of the ear and the back of the head, blue; lower part of forehead to the ear, yellow; upper part of the forehead and around the head, yellow; area above the thick headband, light yellow. He has a rather long nose, light-colored full lips, and an imposing skull structure. Forearm and lower leg, reddish-brown below light-colored stripes; his moccasins are also light-colored. In his left hand he holds a bow and arrows; in his right hand, a sword. The handguard on the sword, which is buckled up toward the blade and flattened into a disk toward the outside, is distinctive; the cross guard extends from front to back. Behind his right shoulder is an ocher-yellow quiver.

Next to be considered are the figures at the lower edge of this section, moving to the right.

Figure 158. Indian attacker with vertical stripes, at the right and below the lower tipi and at the right of the seam (Plate 13):

Body, red-and-white-striped from throat to feet; forearms and hands, reddish-brown, below a light-colored stripe. Lower part of the face, neck, and throat, reddish-brown; the wedge in the middle of the face to the ear, light-colored; upper half of forehead, ocher yellow. The end of the headband hangs behind the right ear. Skull, above the headband, grayish-yellow. Over his right shoulder and chest is a light-colored quiver strap. In his left hand he holds a bow and arrows; in his right hand, a sword.

Figure 159. Indian attacker with horizontal stripes, below Figure 158: Body, alternating light-colored and dark-brown stripes from throat to light-brown moccasins; throat, lower part of the face up to the nose, lower part of the forearms and hands, light brown. Light-colored stripe across lower part of nose; reddish-brown stripe across upper part of nose; area to eyebrow, light-colored; forehead, ocher yellow; skull, grayish-brown. The end of the headband hangs over the right ear. In the left hand he carries a bow and two arrows; in the right hand, a two-pronged ax.

The stripes shown on Figures 158 and 159 are distinctive and unusual. There is a prototype of the design shown on Figure 159, the body painting of the clown who accompanies the Hopi Katcina Humis at the Powamu festival in the annual return of katcinas to the village of Walpi, in northeast Arizona.[3]

At the right of the striped figures is a group of five figures engaged in battle with two soldiers and an Indian ally of the attacking party, who are shooting at two Indian defenders whose leather coats are spiked with arrows. The two defenders are partly enveloped in a pale-gray cloud of powder smoke. One of the men is withdrawing in the direction of the men guarding the horses (Plate 14).

Figure 160. Soldier in front of Figure 159: Coat, reddish-brown; cuffs and leggings, deep blue; breeches, white or yellow. Above his long pistol is a light-colored pouch on the forward half of which lies a brown powder horn. The blue-colored hilt of his

[3] Jesse Walter Fewkes, *Hopi Katcinas, Drawn by Native Artists*, Bureau of American Ethnology *Twenty-first Annual Report* (Washington, 1899–1900), Plate XXI.

sword extends in front of the left hip, and a brown scabbard protrudes from behind his coattail. The brim of his brown three-cornered hat is edged in white. The soldier, holding his flintlock pressed under his right elbow, is shooting at the two defenders at the right. The spark from the pan of the flintlock and the powder smoke ballooning up above it are clearly visible.

Figure 161. Soldier in front and slightly above Figure 160: Coat, straw-colored, with distinct shading at the arms and pleats; cuffs and leggings, ocher brown; breeches and garters, white; shoes, faded yellow. The butt of the pistol extends above the pouch; the barrel is not shown. The brown powder horn has a broad, light-colored base. There is no sword.

Both Figures 160 and 161 are firing without taking precise aim. The unusual length of the stocks would have made it impossible to fire the weapons from the shoulder.

Figure 162. Indian in front of Figure 161 and nearest the two defenders: Body, pale gray with white or yellow splotches covering the legs, arms, hands, and feet. The markings are similar to those of Figure 44, though less distinct. Lower part of face from upper lip to neck, white; an ocher-brown stripe extends from the upper lip to the middle of the nose, above which is a dark-brown stripe; between the eye and the eyebrow is a narrow, slightly curved white stripe. The lower half of the forehead is dark brown; the colored band above it, ocher brown. The skull above the brown headband is pale gray; the end of the headband hangs down over the right ear. The penis is painted white. He is drawing his bow, to which an arrow is fitted; a second arrow, held in the left hand, is pressed against the bow. His face looks impassive, but resolute.

Figure 163. Indian wearing sleeveless leather coat, facing Figure 162: Coat, unpainted, belted in front; jacket and leggings or stockings, reddish-brown; he is wearing light-colored garters at the knees. His moccasins, which are turned back at the upper edge, are not colored. His face and that of the other Indian defender are not painted and are therefore light like those of the white men. His reddish-brown hair is tied together at the neck in a knot. His coat is full of arrows, one in the chest, another a little above the left coattail, another below the belt, one below the left shoulder blade, one in the neck, one in the back, one in the left thigh, and one at the back between the coattails. The feathers of an arrow which seems to be buried in the right shoulder protrudes diagonally from behind the forehead. Altogether there are ten arrows in his armor. However, none of them seems to have injured him, for he is drawing his bow, aiming at Figure 162.

Figure 164. Indian defender behind Figure 163, moving right: Coat, uncolored, like that of Figure 163; hair, reddish-brown, knotted at the neck. In his coat are nine arrows, and a tenth is lodged in the quiver he is carrying in front of his body. In his left hand he holds a bow. He has two full quivers, one in front of the left side of his chest, the other, which also holds another bow, behind his left shoulder. In contrast to the concentration on the face of Figure 163, the face of this man mirrors only resentment and resignation. His right hand is covered with red splotches of blood from the arrow wound in his elbow or from one in his hand, which hangs limp and weaponless in front of his coat.

Between Figure 164 and the line of horse guards lies a strip of no man's land containing a few scattered bushes. The attackers have shot a number of arrows across this area toward the guards, before turning away, evidently because the guards are not participating in the fighting.

As in Segesser I, the offensive operation develops from the left against a fortified central position with a reserve force at the right. At the lower edge of the scene the defense is beginning to crumble; the superior strength of the attackers is prevailing.

The situation is different at the upper edge of the scene (Plate 13, right edge). There, at the right wing of the guards, two mounted men, a white soldier and an Indian, have succeeded in driving back a considerable number of attackers. Five of them are in retreat, one has fallen, and one has turned to counterattack. The mounted Indian with the bow is aiming at one of the enemies and forcing him to retreat with an arrow in his back. The horse ridden by the white defender is trampling the fallen attacker. The rider is about to run his spear through the back of a retreating soldier. An ally is coming to his rescue and firing his gun at the rider.

These six figures are the main actors of the scene, but other figures are also less directly involved:

In front of the retreating warrior with the upright spear is a man hurrying to the left, armed with tomahawk and bow; his open mouth indicates that he is uttering a cry of terror. In front of him is another warrior, also rushing away, sword high; toward him hurries a warrior with a tomahawk to rescue him. At the right of him (in the picture, at the right, below) a warrior with a pickax hurries into the battle behind the soldier firing his flintlock. The Indian painted gray and white is in full retreat.

Figure 165. White defender on horseback, armed with lance and shield (second figure from the upper right edge of Plate 13): He has a round, plump face and wears a large reddish-brown hat with the brim turned up on the sides; his light-colored hair is tied in a braid. His bandolier and scabbard are ocher yellow. The bandolier does not have an ornamental flap like the bandoliers of the attackers but is plain at the end. In front of the scabbard is the oval-shaped guard, painted blue and therefore metal. The cross guard can be discerned, as well as the half of the bandolier beginning at the scabbard and crossing the back. His coat is pleated or seamed at the side. His lance is leveled at the back of the soldier in front of him. It is a spontoon, which broadens toward the back like a sword, with two short metal blades curving outward and forward. From the base of the lance the shaft extends behind the rider's back. The rider's broad back is hunched forward to thrust his spear into the fleeing soldier. Around the upper part of the figure powder smoke billows from the weapon of the soldier at the left. The front of his body is hidden by his oval shield, which is notched at the top and bottom.

His light-colored, sleeveless coat reaches to the calf of his leg and is slit for ease in riding. The armhole shows that it has armor-like thickness; the visible left jacket sleeve is ocher yellow, as is the left stocking. On his foot is a light-colored (probably leather) shoe with a collar at the upper edge. The stirrup seems to reach in front only to the instep, but its sole is regular length and is covered up to the tip by the rider's shoe. At the front of the sole of the stirrup is a reddish-brown spot in the shape of a foreshoe. Across the overshoe is a strap, to which is tied a black spur. It is not clear what the bright-blue object in front of or around the brown toepiece represents. It is probably a lightweight metal or cloth decoration on the stirrup, perhaps bearing the insignia of the rider's troop.

The broad saddle blanket, uncolored like the coat and the shield, hangs slightly below the horse's belly; on the rump of the animal is a special, light-brown cover. On the bridle at the side of the mouth is a short blue, therefore metal, bow. The rein, which disappears behind the front rim of the shield, is held in the rider's left hand. The horse is sturdy and fiery-eyed and carries its head high—a real warhorse. Its mane and tail are light-colored. Its front legs are trampling the fallen warrior.

Figure 166. Mounted Indian with drawn bow following close behind Figure 165: In his left hand he is carrying a reserve arrow. At the right, in front of the saddle, almost completely hidden by the horse, hangs his full quiver. He is standing up in the stirrups, leaning against the pommel, to fire over his horse's head. He wears the same sleeveless leather armor as that worn by his white allies and underneath it a long-sleeved jacket. He also appears to be wearing breeches and leggings.

Unlike most Indians, who rode without saddle or bridle, this rider has both, as well as stirrups. The stirrup strap is visible in front of the rider's knee. The blue stirrup is almost entirely hidden by the tail of the horse in front of him but appears to be of the broad Spanish-Moorish design. The bridle leads from the snaffle to the pommel. The saddle blanket is narrower and shorter than that of Figure 165. At the rear of the saddle is a fastening for the crupper.

The horse itself looks shorter and heavier than that ridden by Figure 165. Both are represented realistically.

The riders' features are strongly Indian, almost Mongolian in the slant of the eye and the high cheekbone.

Figure 167. Fallen soldier underneath the horse ridden by

Figure 165: Face, light-colored; clothing, ocher yellow; cuffs, coat lining, and stripe at collar, blue; hat, reddish-brown; braided hair or wig, light-colored. Since the soldier is lying on his back, it is obvious that he was resisting when struck down. His gun lies beside his right hand whose fingers are still spread wide as if the weapon had just fallen from it. This gun is a good deal shorter than most of the others carried by his allies. The man has obviously been run down by the horse. His left hand is groping for the weapon he has dropped. His hat has also been knocked off. He has drawn up his left knee in an effort to protect himself from the horse's hooves. Evidently he has no sword. He is lying on top of his shield. The reddish stripe on his upper lip and at the side is blood flowing from his nose or mouth. The fact that the genitals of the fallen soldier are exposed to mutilation (surely meant to be an insult) is one of the strongest arguments supporting the view that the artist was an Indian belonging to the tribe of defenders.

Next to be considered are the four figures at the left of the fallen soldier.

Figure 168. Grenadier in front of Figure 167, with his flintlock on his shoulder and a drawn sword in his right hand, moving left: Coat, blue; leggings, light-colored; shoes, brown. His face is rather thin, with a high-bridged nose, a protruding thick underlip, mouth drooping at the corners, and an angular chin. His helmet-like hat has a broad visor and a rounded top with a ring from which hang two blue ribbons. Part of his light-colored braid is visible. The guard on the sword is clearly outlined. His light-blue sword is raised as though to strike. On his left side is a brown scabbard, hanging from a long sword belt with a long ornamental flap and a light-colored fringe at the bottom.

Figure 169. Indian at the left in front of Figure 168, walking toward Figure 170. Body, gray, with white disks evenly distributed over it—the third figure in Segesser II so painted. His forearms are entirely white, as are his neck and face up to his nose; a horizontal stripe crosses the lobe of the ear and encircles the neck. Above and parallel to it is an ocher-yellow stripe up to the eye; above it is a pale blue stripe which extends around the back of the head. The upper half of the forehead is ocher yellow; above the eyebrow is an apparently triangle-shaped spot. In his right hand he carries a tomahawk; in his left hand, a bow and two arrows. Evidently he, too, is fleeing from the rider with the spear.

Figure 170. Soldier in three-cornered hat in front of Figure 169, facing and firing to the right: Coat, reddish-brown, with long stiff pleats; cuff, blue; breeches, bright blue; stockings, light blue; shoes, light brown. The fire from the muzzle of his flintlock can be seen behind Figure 168, and the smoke spreads out at the right beside the head and upper part of the body of Figure 165. His left arm is stretched forward, the left hand apparently grasping a supporting bolt on the gun extending downward from the stock in front of the lock. In front of the butt can be seen the outline of a ball of a pistol. Such wheel-lock pistols with rear balls, called "hand guns," were invented in the first half of the seventeenth century. About the beginning of the eighteenth century the rear ball evolved into a butt, which broadened from the barrel toward the rear and ended in a plate. Segesser II shows the old-fashioned ball. Modern sidearms had evidently not yet arrived in the region.

In front of the soldier's left hip may be seen the handguard, and cross guard of his sword; behind the seam of his coat is the curved end of the scabbard. His profile is characterized by a prominent nose and a receding chin. His face is gray, much darker than the light-colored or uncolored faces of the Indians.

Figure 171. Indian behind and at the left of Figure 170, moving right, partly hidden by the head of Figure 147: Body, dark brown from ankles to upper lip; forearms, light-colored; middle part of the face up to the eyebrows and back of the head, light-colored. Across the lower part of the forehead is an ocher-yellow stripe that tapers off toward the sides; the upper part of the forehead, up to the headband, is light gray or pale blue. Headband, dark reddish-brown; top of the head, ocher yellow. The end of the headband lies in front of the ear. Shoes, light-colored; quiver, yellow; quiver strap, light-colored. In his left hand he holds perpendicularly a bow and two arrows; in the right hand, a pickax whose prongs spread across each other behind the handle like scissors.

Now to the uppermost row of retreating Indians:

Figure 172. Indian in front of Figure 166, moving left: Body, reddish-brown from mouth to shoe; on the right lower leg light-colored, yellow, and reddish-brown stripes up to the knee; from the light band in the middle of the right forearm to the fingers the color is lighter. There is no such distinction on the left forearm. There is a white stripe from the upper lip and the nose extending around the neck. The area around the eyes is a strong reddish-brown; behind the pale-colored flap of the headband and around the back of the head is an ocher-brown stripe, above which is a narrower light stripe. The forehead and the top of the head are yellow; the headband is a faded dark brown.

The warrior has an arrow protruding frim his back, evidently buried deep. He has put his right arm around his quiver, whose upper half is painted white and which hangs in front of the right side of his chest. In his right hand he holds a smooth-shafted lance with a triangular lancehead, underneath which is a bundle of bleached feathers wound around the shaft. At the rear of the spearhead are two barbed hooks. In his left hand he carries a bow.

Figure 173. Indian in front of Figure 172, also moving left: Body, blue up to the mouth; right lower leg and right forearm, light-colored or faded. From the corner of his open mouth to the base of the nose is a light stripe; across the nose and up to the eye is a blue stripe that extends across the lower half of the ear to the back of the ear. Across the area from below the nose to above the eyebrow and across the upper half of the ear is a broad light-colored band; the upper part of the forehead is ocher yellow; the skull, grayish-yellow. The end of the headband hangs behind the ear down the neck. The quiver, which is faded yellow, has slipped in front of the right side of the body. The dark-brown feathered ends of the arrows are visible. In his right hand is a tomahawk, which is large in keeping with the unusually large size of its owner; in his left hand he clutches bow and arrows.

Figure 174. Indian leading the retreating warriors, in front of Figure 175, moving left: Body, from thighs to nose, white, including arms and hands; legs, dark blue; shoes, light-colored. From the bridge of the nose to the eyebrow is an ocher-brown stripe which tapers off around the back of the head; above it is a white-gray stripe reaching to the headband; the top of the head above the headband is yellow. His clearly drawn profile is emphasized by a narrow, prominent lower lip. Close inspection reveals a light-gray neck and shoulder collar painted over the white, tapering off to a point in the center of the chest. In his left hand he carries a bow and arrow; in his right hand, his sword, held before his face almost like a banner. The sword guard is basket-shaped, and the cross guard below it has two unequally long ends; the one toward the sharp edge of the sword is considerably the longer.

Figure 175. Indian in front of and facing Figure 174, moving from left to right: Body, blue from hip to nose; legs and forearms, white; face, white from nose to eyebrows; receding forehead, yellow-brown; the top of the head, yellow-gray. The end of the headband hangs down behind the right ear. The light strap of his yellow quiver curves over the right shoulder. In his left hand he carries a very large bow and arrow; in his right hand, a tomahawk.

One figure in this section of the painting was deliberately placed by himself and given more space than any other figure. That is the Roman Catholic priest, near the central point of Plate 13, pursued by six warriors. The three nearest pursuers have raised their swords in an almost ceremonial attitude. An arrow is embedded in the priest's right hip and another in his back, and the archer hurrying up behind him is threatening him with a third. He has pulled the lower half of his robe over his head for protection. He appears to be hastening to administer last rites to the dying men in the camp. In view of his own perilous situation he has little chance to reach his goal. The single Indian in front of him with the arrows in his coat is pushing through toward the encampment. His task is to lead the priest to the dying defenders. He will not succeed, for he is threatened on all sides by attackers.

The heroic action in which the priest is engaged and the sympathy and detail with which he is treated seem to confirm the assumption that the painter of Segesser II belonged to the Indian tribe allied with the defenders.

Figure 176. Catholic priest carrying a crucifix: Robe, bluish-green; stockings and garters, grayish-white; shoes, dark brown with light-colored soles. The rather lean face of the priest, seen in profile, is that of a young man with a well-formed head; he looks rather pale in the frame of the dark robe. The expression is attentive and anxious. His left eye is drawn realistically and is his dominant feature. His head is tonsured. In his left hand he carries a large crucifix; with his right hand he holds up his robe to protect his head from arrows.

The priest is obviously the chaplain of the defenders. According to Friederici, every expedition into the interior was accompanied by a medical officer, an apothecary, and two clergymen, to care for the troops' physical and spiritual needs. Final absolution was, of course, an overwhelmingly important aspect of the faith of the Spanish conquistadors.[4] The significance of this figure will be discussed in subsequent pages.

Figure 177. Indian with saber, half hidden by the priest, walking at his right beside him and turned toward the viewer: Body, including trunk, arms and hands, reddish-brown; face, blue from the mouth to chest, in a triangular design, coming to a point near the navel, set off by a narrow white stripe. Across the mouth and nose is a light-colored stripe, above which is a broader reddish-brown stripe, and above this a very narrow white line below the eyebrows and across the upper eyelids. The lower part of the forehead and eyebrows are yellow. The area of the forehead below the headband is light gray. The yellowish ends of the brown headband extend from behind the right cheek.

In his right hand he carries a blue-colored sword. The guard is clearly visible above the cross guard, which is somewhat shorter toward the blade than on the opposite side. The cross guard is only

[4] Georg Friederici, *Der Charakter der Entdeckung und Eroberung Amerikas durch die Europäer* (3 vols., Stuttgart, 1925), 419–22.

weakly outlined and colored; the pommel is not as thick as that of other swords of this type.

Figure. 178. Indian behind Figure 177, looking back: Body, pale brown up to the throat, with lighter patches on the arms and left hand; shoes, light yellow; chin, pale gray; cheeks and mouth, white; across the nose and eyes is a brown stripe; the forehead is somewhat lighter. The darker coloring of the upper part of the face has the effect of a mask. The end of the headband hangs down in front of the right ear. The warrior is evidently looking back toward the line of horse guards. In his right hand is a sword; in his left hand, a bow and arrow.

Figure 179. Warrior opposite Figure 178, at the left of the priest (in Plate 13, at the right and behind the right foot of the priest): Body, dark brown; below the knees are a narrow white stripe and a brown one; lower legs, white; low-cut shoes, yellowish, with a cuff at the upper edge. Around the small of the back, just above the hip bone, is a blurred, narrow, light-colored stripe slanting downward in front. The left forearm and hand, holding bow and arrow, are white; right arm, brown. In his right hand he carries a blue-colored sword. A light-colored triangular shoulder decoration begins underneath the chin and runs across the chest and the back of the head and across the back, tapering to a point. The face from the throat to the pupil of the eye is brown, a stronger brown than the body. Forehead, temples, and the back of the head up to the headband are white, tapering off toward the rear. The end of the headband hangs in front of the ear.

Figure 180. Indian between the two warriors guarding the priest from the rear: Body and limbs, blue; the triangular shoulder decoration is clearly visible on the back, curved inward and tapering off to a point at the small of the back. His moccasins are not colored and are only faintly outlined. Neck and jaw are white. Above the white area is a broad blue horizontal band which reaches to the nose and the lower end of the ear. A narrow white stripe crosses the nose; a reddish-brown stripe extends to the lower eyelid. The forehead is white. The headband is dark reddish-brown; its tip hangs down on the turned-away side of the face. The man carries no quiver, but the two arrows already buried in the priest's robe seem to have come from his bow. Because the arrowheads are not colored blue, they must be of flint, although their large size would seem to contradict this conclusion. Flint-headed arrows of such large dimension would not carry far and would also lose much of their penetrating force because of their thickness. By contrast, the arrowheads shown in Segesser I are extremely small.

Figure 181. Indian below Figure 180: Body, white from above the middle of the thigh to the nose, including the arms; legs from the thighs down, reddish-brown; shoes, light or uncolored. Across the upper part of the face is a very strong reddish-brown stripe extending around the back of the head. The forehead is yellow, and the area around the eyes is light-colored. Three light-colored stripes encircle the lower right leg.

Figure 182. Indian behind and slightly above Figure 181: Body, strong reddish-brown from below the knee to the upper lip. Below the knees and elbows is a white stripe, below which the body color is lighter; the lower legs and forearms appear yellowish. His shoes are light-colored. There is a light stripe across the lower part of the nose, and a broader, ocher or brownish-yellow one to above the eyebrows. The lower part of the forehead is uncolored or white; the upper part, gray. The headband is stronger ocher. In his left hand he holds bow and arrows; in the right hand, a tomahawk.

Figure 183. Indian painted with leopard-like spots, in the painting at the right of and behind Figure 182: Body, including limbs, neck, and jaw, gray, upon which are painted reddish-brown spots, like those of Figure 151. Across the upper lip is a brownish-yellow stripe that tapers off toward the ear; the forehead above the eyebrow is the same color; the top of the head is yellowish. The headband is brownish. The area around the eyes and lower lip and part of the cheek is white.

The body painting of the Figures 151 and 183 may be in imitation of the jaguar, which was common in Sonora and in parts of Chihuahua; on rare occasions it was also seen within the present boundaries of the United States, in central Texas, central New Mexico, or northern Arizona.[5] The spots may also represent feathers, like the painting seen on the Hopi Keca katcina, representing the kite.[6]

In his left hand the warrior holds a bow and two arrows; in his right hand, a pale-blue sword.

PLATE 14

Behind the group of fighters described above, at the far right side of the painting, is a group of horses guarded by mounted defenders. The two riders leaving the line of guards connect the scene with the battle action, as do the Indians and soldiers at the lower edge of the picture who are advancing against the horse guards.

In the no man's land in front of the guards are arrows both in flight and buried in the ground. Such arrows appear in pictographic paintings of Plains tribes to indicate that attacks are being made on the figures behind them. The scene is one of the more carefully composed scenes in the painting. The horse guards are shown in close formation. They are composed of four mounted Indians and four white horsemen. Behind them, closely bunched together, are the unsaddled horses, facing left. Farther back are five horses and two mules, turned toward the right, posed as though they are in flight. The Indian below and behind them is putting his horse to a gallop to head them off.

Figure 184. Indian horseman at the bottom of the group, turned to the left and positioned somewhat behind the other guards: Little color can be discerned on this figure; this section of the painting has suffered from wear and damage. His hair is dark; his coat, leggings, and moccasins are pale gray. His coat is short and belted at the waist. In his left hand he appears to be holding the reins, which begin at the snaffle, above the neck of the horse. There is no saddle. In his right hand he appears to be holding a weapon, which is unidentifiable. The horse's mane, forelock, and tail are dark brown.

The bridle on this horse, as on the other animals whose mouths are visible, has no bit. Since the rings of curb bits are shown on the horses of some of the attackers, the omission of bits here must be

[5] E. W. Nelson, *Wild Animals of North America* (Washington, 1930), 96, 99.
[6] Fewkes, *Hopi Katcinas*, 78.

deliberate, and the bridles are intended to be Indian-style. Similarly there is no throatlatch or cheek strap, but behind the cheek and parallel to the headstall is a strap that extends around the neck and through the looped right end and leads behind the chin to the rein.

Figure 185. Indian horseman next to and a little in front of Figure 184: Coat, pale gray, evidently similar in cut to that of Figure 184, through details are unrecognizable; hair, tied in a knot at the neck, dark brown; details of leggings and moccasins are also unrecognizable. His face has a low forehead, plump cheeks, and thick lips. In his left hand he holds rein and bow; his right hand is placed on the neck of the horse and supports his left elbow. His quiver hangs behind his right shoulder. He is riding bareback; the brown mane of his light-colored horse is somewhat paler than those of the animals near him.

Figure 186. Indian horseman above Figure 185: This figure is characterized by a sharply drawn face and a long braid down his back, held in place with a light-colored leather band which circles the top of the head and extends the entire length of the braid, to the back of the saddle. He appears to be wearing sleeveless leather armor like that worn by the white soldiers. In his left hand he holds the rein, a bow, and an arrow; his right hand is not visible.

The horse, now gray, was probably originally reddish-brown; the mane and tail are dark brown. On its back is a blanket that extends far down the side and a saddle with a high back that curves backward and a pommel that curves forward. While this horse and the one of the Indian rider above him (Figure 187) have cruppers, the horses of the white soldiers have rounded-off blankets reaching from the saddles to the horses' tails. A chin strap can be seen at the left corner of the horse's mouth. The back of the saddle is visible in the slit in the rider's coat. A strap is wound around the pommel.

The prominence and size of this figure, together with his saddle and leather armor, indicate that he represents a chief or outstanding warrior; his distinctive hair style may indicate that he belongs to a different tribe from that of the other Indian defenders.

Figure 187. Indian horseman above Figure 186: He appears to be wearing a short, belted coat; the absence of the double line at the armhole indicates that it is not sleeveless armor worn by other horsemen. The corner of his mouth above the thin lower lip is drawn upward; he has a sharply angled forehead and a prominent nose. His dark-brown hair is uncolored below the headband, probably through oversight. His short braid lies on his back in front of his pale reddish-brown quiver and quiver strap. The quiver flap hangs behind the quiver. In his left hand he holds a bow, colored brown; his right hand is not visible.

His horse is pale yellow, like the ground at the horses' feet and in the no man's land in front of the guards. Its mane and tail are light gray. It is equipped with blanket and saddle. The connecting piece between chin strap and neck rein is braided.

Figure 188. Mounted soldier above Figure 187: His body is hidden by his shield, which has the same shape as those of his two comrades at the right behind him and the other shield-bearers in this party, oval-shaped with notches at top and bottom. His leather jacket reaches below the knee; his leg is hidden by the Indian below him. The rider's mouth is thin; he has high cheekbones. His wig is light-colored and tightly braided. His hat brim is turned up at the sides.

The horse is light gray, including mane and tail. The horse's visible left eye is particularly well drawn and gives the animal an intent, alert look. The saddle blanket is ocher yellow; the crupper cover was probably the same color originally but has now faded. The rein ends at the lower edge of the lower lip, lower than those on the Indians' horses. It disappears under the edge of the shield, as does the brown scabbard. The large barrel of his gun extends from behind the front (left) rim of the shield. The back of the saddle is seen through the slit of the coat.

Figure 189. Mounted soldier at the right, behind and above Figure 188: Coat and shield, grayish-brown; bandolier, yellow; breeches, blue, below a bit of the ocher-brown stocking; scabbard, ocher yellow with a blue tip. The rump of the horse is light-colored tinged with reddish-brown; the saddle blanket with a tinge of gray. The reins lead directly to the pommel. The soldier's gun is held more erectly than the one carried by Figure 188.

Figure 190. Mounted soldier behind Figure 189: Coat, light-colored; breeches, yellow; stockings, blue. This rider is larger and heavier than the two men in front of him and larger than the Indian with the long braid. He has a big head with a prominent nose and fleshy chin and cheeks. From beneath his shield extends a narrow, ocher-yellow scabbard with a blue-colored iron tip. Only a small part of the guard of the sword is visible. The barrel of his flintlock extends in front of his shield. The wide upper edge of his short-legged boot has a strap around ankle and heel that leads one to assume that the rider is wearing spurs, which, however, are not visible. His saddle and blanket are of the same design as those of the two riders in front of him. The horse's mane and forelock are light-colored.

Figure 191. Mounted soldier at the right behind Figure 190: He has been wounded and is falling backward. His left arm hangs limp. A portion of the yellow sleeve of his jacket is visible between the shield, which he is still holding or which is tied to his forearm, and his leather jacket. His right arm is bent at the elbow and stretched upward; his mouth is open wide from pain. Above and behind his head is the front half of a lance; it must be his own weapon, for there is no horse's head behind him, as there would be before the tear if there were a rider in front. Across his body lies a short-barreled gun; one can see its barrel, shaft, and curved butt, as well as the flintlock and the large trigger guard. His sword is not visible. A tear in the painting has obliterated part of his horse. Below the belly of the horse only its forehoofs can be seen, and the front part of its head can be seen in front of the rider. The horse's body, originally reddish-brown, is now faded to gray. Its thick forelock was dark brown or black.

As is evident in Plate 14, there is a rent in the canvas cutting through the herd of horses. Evidently a narrow strip of the canvas has been lost, for some of the animals are incomplete, and other sections do not exactly align, although at some time the tear was carefully repaired.

Below Figure 191 is a herd of seven unsaddled horses. The first horse, turned to the left, is yellowish with a brown mane. The faces of this animal and the others in the herd are quite expressive. Behind this animal is seen part of a reddish-brown horse. The second horse, facing right, is reddish-brown with a dark-brown tail and a lighter mane. The tear in the painting crosses the animal's face. Of the third horse, turned to the left, only the neck and head, in front of the shoulder of the second horse, are visible. The eye is dark brown; coat and mane are light gray. The fourth horse, turned to the right and partly hidden, is yellowish with a brown mane. The fifth horse, turned to the left, is a lighter color with brown mane and forelock. The sixth horse, turned to the right, is light brown or gray with brownish mane and tail. The seventh horse, turned to the left, is only partly distinguishable. At some time this area of the painting has been smeared with red and yellow oil paint.

Figure 192. Indian horseman, riding toward the right: Coat, gray or uncolored, probably leather. He is wearing short breeches like those worn by the soldiers and calf-length stockings. He has a distinctive hair style: his long brown hair is braided and wrapped in leather or uncolored cloth almost to the ends. In his left hand he carries a bow; in his right, a long switch, curved and forked at the upper end. He is probably the herdsman and is pursuing the horses that have begun to stampede from the herd. It is also possible that he is trying to escape.

The pony is yellowish with a dark-brown mane and tail. It has a broad body, and its front legs are pulled up to indicate that it is in full gallop. The bridle appears to have no fittings. The saddle blanket, like the rider's coat, is gray. The broad stirrup, which is not painted blue, is probably wooden, like those of the Plains tribes as far north as Canada, who copied the broad Mexican stirrup. The stirrup strap disappears just above the foot beneath the saddle blanket.

At the right of the tear in the painting (not visible in Plate 14) are six horses and two mules. The eighth horse or pony (also not visible in Plate 14) is under the curled-up torn edge. Only the reddish-brown back of the ninth horse is visible. The tenth horse, a little higher in the scene, has a light-colored coat and brown mane and forelock. The pale-gray neck and head of the eleventh horse are visible at the edge of the painting. The twelfth horse is partly hidden by the head of the tenth horse, and is behind Figure 192. The horse was probably reddish-brown, with a dark-brown mane. The thirteenth horse, the uppermost horse moving to the right, was also probably reddish-brown.

The first mule, below the thirteenth horse, has long ears and a short, light mane. Its coat is light; its eye, dark brown. The second mule is also in the front row, turned to the right. The tips of its long ears are tinted brown. Its brushlike mane is characteristic of mules, as is the broad, straight neck. The body is brownish; the mane and tail, darker brown.

The fourteenth horse, below the second mule, looks stockier and more compact than the other horses. Its coat is faded brown; mane and tail are dark brown.

At the extreme right edge of the painting is a narrow strip which was under the molding that once framed the painting. The colors are more intense in this strip, indicating that the ground color was probably yellow.

The horse herd is the best-composed part of the painting. The lack of depth perspective permits the viewer to see directly into the square, framed by mounted guards, in which the bodies and necks of the horses roll like waves against one another, their manes forming the crests of the waves.

In the camp there are thirty-eight defenders but only one horse. In addition there are five defenders between the camp and the horse guards, and another unmounted defender lies at the left of the front of attackers behind his mounted comrade. The defenders would thus require a total of forty-four mounts. In the herd there are only sixteen animals. Since the artist was careful to show the weapons and equipment of both attackers and defenders—most of them in faithful detail—it is somewhat surprising that he did not provide mounts and pack animals for all the actors in the scene.

The composition of Segesser II is lens-shaped, narrow at the left and right edges and widening at the center (see Plate 8). The figures almost completely fill the painting. Each element of the composition points toward the main battle, at the center of the scene. The unity of the composition is readily apparent. Whether the artist worked consciously toward this unity or achieved it instinctively cannot, of course, be conclusively determined, though the relative sophistication of the composition seems to indicate that the artist planned the work carefully.

Including the missing portion of the right side of the painting, the distance from the right edge to the rear entrance of the camp is about the same as that from the rear of the advancing attackers at the river crossing to the front entrance of the camp. The camp thus lies in the center of the painting. The neck of land on which the battle takes place serves as a geographical introduction to the painting and gives some idea of the landscape and the mood of the scene—that is, it serves as the backdrop for the drama. The huge trees at the left seem to brood over the scene, setting a forbidding tone. Nature seems to sustain the attackers as they sally forth into battle. Quite different is the mood at the right, where only stunted bushes animate a desolate prairie and give the impression of a drying up of the sources of life.

Also worth mentioning are the different sections along the front that create suspense: at the left, the line of riflemen in front of the barricade, then the section between the attackers and the left edge of the defensive position, then the defenders at the right and below, and, finally, the bowmen to the left in front of the line of guards.

Three corners of the painting, and the edges outside the ellipse that comprises the main scene, are filled with wild animals, a common means of filling space in primitive art. The animals have no relationship to the action shown in the painting and were lightly colored by the artist. Their presence is largely decorative.

At the right of the seam in the second skin are two pronghorns running toward the left, toward the bank of the upper fork of the river. Ahead of them, at the left of the top tree, is a smaller unidentifiable animal with a bushy tail and a pointed nose. In the upper right corner is a similar animal with heavy paws. These animals may be coyotes, which Father Philipp thought were a species of fox.

In the lower left corner are three animals, two pronghorns and a rabbit, also moving left.

There is more space available in the lower right corner of the painting, below the mounted Indian horse guard turned to the right. There one may discern two does among the shrubbery, running to the right. The head and forequarters of the leading doe are cut off at the right edge of the painting, also indicating that a portion of the right side was cut from the painting. These deer have longer tails and larger ears than the pronghorns at the left, and are evidently meant to represent red deer.

The upper right corner of the painting is filled with the usual bushes resembling agave plants. At their left, at the edge of the leather, is a spot of yellow oil paint under which appears to be an unidentifiable animal. At the left is a buffalo galloping toward the right, following another buffalo whose tail is visible at the right edge of the tear. The buffalo was originally reddish-brown and today is faded to a tan color. It is quite accurately drawn.

At the left of the buffalo are two pronghorns, turned to the left. The pronghorns' bodies and legs are a dull light brown or reddish-brown; the hoofs are of the same color but lighter, and were originally dark brown. The foreheads, eyes, and noses are distinctly yellow and clearly outlined, indicating the mask which is characteristic of these animals. The length of the horns indicates that they are young animals.

At the left of the leading pronghorn is a small animal with short legs, perhaps a coyote.

XII

The Significance of the Stirrups

In the effort to determine the subject matter and the persons portrayed in Segesser II, it was necessary to rely on the uniforms and equipment shown in the painting. One intriguing piece of equipment is the distinctive stirrup shoe of Figure 165, which has a blue band extending around the front and hanging down in two wide tips.

In his work *Archaeologisches zur Geschichte des Schuhs aller Zeiten*, Robert Forrer fails to describe or picture such a shoe, nor have I found such a description in other publications. What seems to be a blue flap wound around the foreshoe and hanging down from it on the foot of Figure 165 must be in reality an unusually large stirrup, evidently made of iron, since the iron parts of weapons and the bits worn by the horses are also painted blue.

The red spot must be either a strip of leather added to reinforce the soft overshoe of the rider or a shoe cap of very hard leather to absorb the pressure of the heavy stirrup on the instep. The shoe worn by Figure 36 has no such reinforcement of the cap but otherwise is the same kind of shoe in a similar stirrup. There is a minor difference in the two stirrups; that of Figure 36 seems to have a slightly curved upper edge on which the eye for the strap is mounted.

Still another distinctive stirrup is visible, this time seen from the front, but without the large lateral projections. It may be seen in front of the head of the Indian defender drawing his bow, Figure 141, and above the three-cornered hat of Figure 69, the soldier shown from the rear in three-quarters view, at the lower right wing of the line of attackers. This stirrup is clearly of Spanish-Mexican design. The development of Mexican stirrups has been traced by Zschille:

Especially rich in variety of forms are the stirrups of Mexico, a land in which the art of riding has always been especially cultivated and where at all times unusual luxury was applied to riding equipment. To be sure, the Mexican stirrups could not compete with the magnificent products of the Renaissance; they lacked the finished style and workmanship which we admire so greatly in the Renaissance stirrups. But many Mexican stirrups and spurs were beautiful and artistic creations of cut and open iron work. Where his artistic ability fell short in purity of style, the Mexican resorted to other means to enrich his stirrup. It was greatly enlarged to allow for as much ornamentation as possible, and its value was enhanced by the work of the silversmith. Certain parts of the stirrup were inlaid with silver, or the whole stirrup was silver-plated. Those who wanted to make a special show not only had spurs and bridoon made entirely of silver but also had the stirrups and the bridle silver-mounted or richly embroidered. Just as the Swiss mercenary had special affection for his "Swiss dagger" as his constant companion and trusted help in distress and gave it an elaborate vestment in its artistic scabbard, so did the Mexican equip his faithful companion, his spurs and stirrup, with special luxury, since he spent half his life on his horse. By the opulence of his spurs and stirrup one determined the quality of the horseman; exactly as in the Middle Ages harness and shining armor let one recognize from afar that a man of high rank was approaching.

The oldest stirrups of Mexico are extremely large and very heavy; they are in the form of a cross and therefore are called *estriberas de Crux*—"cross stirrups." . . . No doubt, the note of Francisco López de Gómara in his *Historia de la Conquistas de Hernando Cortes*, published in 1826 by Carlos de Bastamente, refers to the enormous stirrups: ". . . that the Spanish leaders cut down the Aztecs who had not yet fallen under the blows and thrusts of their swords and lances in the battle of Otumba, with their huge iron stirrups, called *mitras*, whose form resembled more that of a cross than a bishop's miter and were very heavy." This note dates from the time of the wars of Hernando Cortes against the Aztecs between 1519 and 1521 and thus gives us some clues about the approximate age of these stirrups. In any case, this form originates in the Gothic style and we have here merely exaggerated enlargements of some stirrup parts which were already to be found in the Gothic stirrup: The unusually long lower part is nothing but a very exaggerated enlargement of the flap of the sole which extends vertically downward in the Gothic stirrup, as we find it especially in the German stirrup of the Gothic. It is also found occasionally in French and Spanish stirrups. . . . The motivation here, too, was to create as much room for ornamentation as possible. The same purpose was achieved by the broadening of the side rods, as already observed in the Renaissance stirrup. We see here, too, this principle developed to the extreme by the use of broad oriental forms of stirrups on the occasion of the creation of Spain of the showy stirrup for Charles V by Alonso Miergillo of Seville. . . . In the early Mexican stirrups . . . the same principle was applied but was executed differently. Instead of broadening the side rods toward the front, they developed them into broad flaps on the sides and thus created the cross shape together with long flap of the sole and a correspondingly enlarged ear for the strap. It is possible that the stirrups of the Spanish leaders were not yet as large as Mexican stirrups, but, once established, the design was further developed in Mexico. There are many examples of similar developments. . . .

But it remains strange that up to now stirrups in the shape of the cross have been very rare in Spain. It is absolutely clear from the above-mentioned note that similar spurs, althought perhaps of a less eccentric form, were developed and worn in Spain in the first quarter of the sixteenth century. Cortes and his fellow leaders no doubt brought this form fully developed from Spain. In Mexico the Spanish conquerors then developed the Mexican stirrup from the original Spanish form. . . . Many of these rather rare stirrups are cut extremely fine in iron, in delicate filigree work, and are engraved with designs of leaves and occasionally animal figures. The ornamentation reminds one of the Renaissance but also shows the work of exotic artists. They are evidently products of a later period than the Conquest but probably originated not much later than about sixteen hundred. With the more active settlement of Mexico in the seventeenth century, other forms were also introduced from Europe and seem to have found acceptance.[1]

At any event, Segesser II proves that the *estriberas de Crux*

[1] R. Zschille and R. Forrer, Die Steigbuegel in ihrer Formentwicklung (Berlin, 1896), 17.

were still in use in the eighteenth century, for it seems definite that it is such stirrups that are shown in the painting. Thus the horsemen of the party were Spaniards who probably operated from Mexico or were attacked in a forward province of this country, which at that time was still called New Spain.

Little other evidence of typically Spanish or Mexican equipment could be found in Segesser II. The riding boot, which was worn over the ordinary shoe and to which the spur was fastened, was a wooden shoe similar to the Dutch *klompjes*. The gauchos of Argentina still use these boots to protect the foot from the hard rim of the stirrup and at the same time protect the regular shoe from briars, which was probably its purpose in earlier times in Spanish and other European pasture lands. Because this wooden sole was exclusively a riding and stirrup shoe, in Segesser II it is worn only by the soldiers of the Spanish-Mexican mounted party.

XIII
The Spanish Defenders

After intensive study of the painting it finally became evident that not only the stirrups but also the weapons and clothes of the unmounted defenders are Spanish in origin. The headgear was identified as a typically Spanish hat, which is still worn today in rural areas on festive occasions. In Spanish plays staged in earlier times, male actors usually appeared in short breeches which did not fit so tightly above the knees. Called *bombachos*, these breeches were worn by certain classes of Spaniards until near the end of the nineteenth century. The uncolored heavy sleeveless coats are very likely similar to the coat that Father Philipp described as being worn by the soldiers in place of a cuirass: ". . . made of deerskin, five to six folds sewed together, thick and heavy, so that arrows do not pierce it." Father Philipp also mentions "carbine and sword and pike and lances, of which the Indians were very much afraid."

Both at the rear of the hard-pressed defenders in the square and at the side of this formation, which is turned toward the viewer, can be seen the carbine, which, in comparison with the extremely long rifles of the enemy foot soldier, look almost like toys. No doubt, they too are exaggerated in size; otherwise, they could not have been fired from the hip.

Father Philipp speaks of shields "made of thick paper with which they catch the flying arrows," but he does not mention anything about their shape, nor does he explain what he means by "paper," which was doubtless smooth rawhide that resembled parchment and was formerly used also in place of paper. It was also established that the shields notched at the top and bottom not only were used in the New World but were shields of Hispano-Moresque design dating from the fifteenth century. Such a shield with two loops on either half can be seen in a mural painting from the fourteenth century in the courtroom of the Alhambra.[1] The Artillery Museum in Paris possesses a similar small, round shield (*adarga*) made entirely of soft leather, dating from the end of the sixteenth century. It is larger than the shields of the riders but has the same distinctive shape. There is a slight difference in the shields of the Segesser II riders in that the half covering the right side of the body has a somewhat lower cheekpiece on top, which makes the buckler asymmetrical but allows the soldier to see over the rim of the shield without exposing the left side of his head.

The defender at the right corner of the square is turned in profile to the right, revealing the inside of his buckler, as well as the entire length of his sword. The guard behind the long, thin, straight blade is either a bell or two shells, of which only one is visible, curved upward toward the knob. It looks more like a bell. An illustration of an early nineteenth-century Spanish ceremonial or court sword with similar bells or shells indicates that the sword shown here is of typically Spanish design. The guard is present, but the straight bars are missing.[2] Such swords may also be found in the Landesmuseum in Zurich and in most other public and private collections in Europe.

Because the painter of Segesser II obviously lived in the Spanish-Mexican culture, he also provided the enemies' swords with bells and cross guards.

[1] August Demmin, *Die Kriegswaffen in ihrer historischen Entwicklung* (Leipzig, 1886).

[2] August Demmin, *Ergaenzungsband* (supp. vol.), (Wiesbaden, 1893), 164, Fig. 79.

XIV
The Indian Attackers

It is not possible to identify the Indian attackers from their appearance. Warriors of many North American tribes went to war naked, armed with bows and arrows. The warpaint and headbands could also be characteristic of a number of tribes.

After it was established that the defenders shown in the painting were Spaniards, the possibility that the attackers belonged to one of the northern tribes was dismissed. Where the French established their mighty arc from Canada to the Mississippi Delta, an acquisition which they squandered disgracefully, in the southern regions they often enlisted the aid of tribes living there, and it was never difficult to win them over whenever they were needed. But clashes between Frenchmen and Spaniards were of minor importance. For example, Pensacola, which was settled by a colony of Spaniards from Vera Cruz in 1696, was conquered by the French in 1719 but returned to the Spaniards the same year. In an effort to identify the tribal membership of the attackers, every likely southern group was studied from cultural, ethnological, and historical aspects, and efforts were made to determine the conflicts they had engaged in. Pictures of Indians wearing their hair cut short and headbands were also examined in detail. One particularly helpful work was the three-volume *Indian Tribes of North Amercia*, by McKenny and Hall. Despite close study of the portraits, however, it proved impossible to reach any positive conclusions. The hair styles and the use of a turban-like headband strongly suggested the Creeks, but there were no other comparable characteristics. It was therefore necessary to turn to other evidence provided in the painting.

The animals shown in Segesser II offered possible clues to the location of the battle. One, the buffalo, seemed to eliminate the eastern part of the continent, for it had virtually disappeared from there by the eighteenth century; moreover, the pronghorn probably never lived east of the Mississippi.

The animal species thus strongly suggest a western setting. At the time of the painting, the English generally confined themselves to the Atlantic Coast regions, and since only a few traders and hunters crossed the watershed to the eastern tributaries of the Mississippi Basin, it seems conclusive that the white attackers of the Spaniards were Frenchmen. Yet historical and ethnographical works available to me made no mention of any engagement that would fit the scene shown in Segesser II. Nor did the soldiers' uniforms provide much help. The style and colors of the uniforms led experts at the Artillery Museum in Paris and the Victoria and Albert Museum in London to believe that the soldiers might be Frenchmen. But the style was insufficiently detailed to be certain; soldiers of many other European countries wore similar uniforms. Even the distinctive conical hats worn by the soldiers could not be identified, despite thorough investigation.

After a long period of intensive investigation I submitted the case to authorities in the United States. John C. Ewers, curator of the Department of Anthropology of the Smithsonian Institution, directed my attention to the 1720 massacre of a Spanish expedition led by Villasur in what is now the state of Nebraska. In this engagement the attackers were said to have been Pawnee and Oto Indians and Frenchmen. The various accounts of this event were contradictory in details of the battle, the participants, and the locale of the battle. But several important details were common to all the accounts and so closely correspond to the details shown in Segesser II that there could be little doubt that the Villasur expedition was indeed the subject of the painting.

Further investigation revealed that the naked Indian attackers were Skidi Pawnees and Otos. The hair styles of these tribes corresponded closely to those shown in the painting. True, there is no evidence that they wore headbands, but they were common headdress of the period and region.

It is unfortunate that early-day explorers and observers had so little interest in the culture of the Indians. Information about body painting of the period is scanty and inconclusive. From the evidence provided in Segesser II, it appears that the entire body was painted, including the close-cropped head. The colors were not always solid. Stripes, circles, and other shapes were either painted separately or painted over a basic color. The faces were frequently divided into sections tapering off toward the back or ringing the head.[1] It proved impossible to determine whether body painting indicated the rank or tribal affiliation of the individual warriors. The painter was probably unfamiliar with the tribes making up the attackers and the significance of the war paint.

Special attention was given to the most striking and often repeated design, which is shown on at least sixty of the ninety-eight Indian figures: the glovelike paintings of forearms and hands, in a different color from that of the other main parts of the body, and the stocking-like painting of the lower legs. This pattern is repeated so often that it is clear the painter was basing his work on careful observation. Such patterns were found among various Indian tribes, among them the Choctaws and the Natchez and other tribes of the Mississippi Basin.[2]

As mentioned earlier, the spotted design painted on ten of the Indian attackers may be an imitation of the markings of the jaguar or the bobcat. Three of the warriors have such markings on their arms and legs as well. These Indians may belong to a special warrior class or group, like those common among many Plains tribes. Other stripes may be imitative of such animals as badgers, squirrels, raccoons, and skunks.

Another body-painting design shown in Segesser II proved to be of interest: the triangular back or chest design found on ten of the figures, usually a lighter color than that of the rest of the body. No similar designs could be found anywhere in the literature on Indian

1 Cf. the portrait of Little Elk in McKenney and Hall, *The Indian Tribes of North America*, II, 306. Little Elk was a chief of the Winnebagos, the parent tribe of the Otos. (See also the portrait of Nowayke-sugga of the Otos, *ibid.*, II, 16.)

2 *National Geographic Magazine* (January, 1946), Plate VII.

body painting, except for a coincidental resemblance to a later Creek costume. Here again, the design was repeated too frequently to have been a product of the artist's imagination. On four of the figures are painted large dark crosses, and one man, carrying the wreath and spear, is decorated with light-colored crosses.

Among the Forest and Plains Indians the cross was the symbol of the four directions of the world, or the four winds, which were ruled by deities. The symbol was used on war shields, battleaxes, moccasins, tomahawks, war shirts, whip handles, and elsewhere. It was believed to serve as protective magic. Among the Pawnees it was a symbol used in star worship. A photograph of Chief Pahu-Kah-Tah-Wah of the Skidi Pawnees, taken about 1870, shows him wearing a buffalo robe completely covered with crosses. These stars have five points, but the leggings of the much-photographed Pitalescharo,[3] of the same period, show four-pointed stars like those shown on the figures in Segesser II.

Other distinctive designs may be found on the warriors: white bands around their shoulders and knees or distinctive colors on particular sections of the body, such as the shoulders and trunks. Such designs may have been symbolic protection for those parts of the body or may have been added merely for decorative purposes or as marks of social distinction.

The large white shoulder patches and leg stripes worn by some of the warriors may be explained by the comment of James R. Murie, himself a Skidi Pawnee, who wrote that the members of a war party painted their faces and blankets with thick white clay, which was the war paint of the Pawnees and symbolized the wolf.[4]

The fact that in the early eighteenth century Pawnee warriors painted themselves from head to foot is confirmed by a statement of Captain Felix Martínez, governor of New Mexico, in which he described Pawnees[5] as "white Indians" with pierced ears who lived

[3] Both pictures were taken by the government photographer William H. Jackson and have appeared in numerous works.

[4] James R. Murie, "Pawnee Indian Societies," American Museum of Natural History *Anthropological Papers*, Vol. XI (1914), 596.

[5] The Pawnees, an alliance of several Caddo tribes, were called "Panis" in earlier times. As late as 1755 they were so called on John Mitchell's map, which

in four or five settlements along the Río Jesús María (the South Platte).[6] Since Martínez' informants saw only war or horse-stealing parties, they only saw Pawnees in war paint; but Martínez very likely knew that the whiteness of their skin was body paint, since he occasionally saw Pawnee prisoners (one of whom, François Sistaca, later became a Pawnee interpreter).

We know too little about the body painting of the Otos to be able to distinguish them from the Pawnees in Segesser II. Again, the painter's lack of familiarity with the tribes probably made it impossible for him to distinguish them.

The red disk painted on the chest of Figure 107 and the yellow disk on Figure 56 should be mentioned. Such disks were used by nearly all the Indian tribes as symbols of the sun. The Pawnees' supreme deity, Tirawa Atius, was a sun-god; the sacred name for the sun was Sakuru.[7]

Four of the warriors, Figures 6, 35, 58, and 105, wear sashes as part of their body decoration. The sashes, with their long ends falling free, were probably symbols of rank, for the four figures wearing them are prominently placed and carefully executed. They may also have been talismans worn to ensure victory in battle. The sashes appear to be made of cloth but more likely were woven of plant fibers or made of leather. Murie reported that at the beginning of the twentieth century the leader of the Brave Raven Society of the Skidi Pawnees painted his whole body with soot on the fourth

refers to the Platte River as the River of the Panis. The tribe of Skidi Pawnees is called Pani Maha. Felipe Tamariz, who kept the diary of the Villasur expedition, calls them Pananes. Some authors are of the opinion that the name came from the word *pariki*, meaning "horn," after their custom of stiffening their scalp locks with paint and curving them like a horn. The Pawnees themselves believe that the name comes from *parisu*, meaning "hunter." In the seventeenth and eighteenth century Indian and Negro slaves were called "Panis" by the French and English as far north as Canada, evidently because most of the slaves who were sold in the East were from tribes known as Panis. The Spaniards feared the Pawnees and considered them a warlike people.

[6] "Declaration of Martínez, México, November 13, 1720," Thomas, *After Coronado*, 171.

[7] Thomas B. Marquis, *Wooden Leg: A Warrior Who Fought Custer* (Lincoln, 1962), 127.

day of the Feast of the Replacement of the Spears and then donned a belt of buffalo hide with two wolves' tails and two strings trimmed with crow feathers hanging down the back. From this description it would appear that the belts in Segesser II did indeed have some religious significance.

Aside from the body designs and sashes there is another indication of religious custom. The two warriors crossing the stream are carrying bundles on their heads to keep them dry. They are probably "keepers of relics," bringing magic talismans to the battlefield to ensure victory.

In contrast to the Indian defenders, the attacking warriors are naked. James reported that in the winter of 1819–20 the Pawnee Mahas (the Wolf and Skidi Pawnees) fought Comanches and other southern Indians during a raid south of the Arkansas. Before going into battle they discarded their blankets, loincloths, and leggings and fought completely naked.[8] Such behavior, in midwinter, must have been in conformity with a very old custom. James also reported that the young Pawnee men removed their clothes when participating in hoop games in their villages.

The attackers are shown with a variety of weapons. The predominant weapons are, of course, the bows. In length they correspond exactly to the length of the bows used by the mounted buffalo hunters of the Plains. They are longer than the bows carried by the tent people in Segesser I, which were probably more familiar to the painter. Bows are carried by all the attackers except those engaged in hand-to-hand combat. Quivers are carried even by Indians with swords.

The only available picture of an Oto warrior with a bow (in a Smithsonian Institution photograph taken about 1870) shows a plain curved weapon a little less than four feet long. According to Weygold, Pawnees generally used double-curved bows. Eighty-six of the Indian attackers in Segesser II carry double-curved bows in their left hands, either vertically in front of their chests or horizon-

[8] Edwin James, *An Account of an Expedition from Pittsburgh to the Rocky Mountains, Performed in the Years 1819 and 1820*, in Reuben Gold Thwaites (ed.), *Early Western Travels* (Cleveland, 1905), II, 159.

tally in their hands hanging down; a few are shown aiming or shooting arrows.

The effectiveness of the bow is underestimated today. All reports from the fifteenth, sixteenth, and seventeenth centuries agree that the American Indians were extraordinary bowmen. The Sioux tribes of the Plains could shoot an arrow from not too great a distance through a large buffalo and with the same arrow mortally wound a second animal running close beside the first.

Fidalgo de Elvas, a participant in De Soto's 1539–40 expedition, gives a vivid description of the style of fighting and the skill in handling the bow exhibited by the southern Indians:

> The Indians are extremely adept in handling their weapons and are such quick and capable warriors that they are not afraid of foot soldiers, for when they attack them, they flee, and when the soldiers turn back, the Indians take them by surprise. They easily evade a flying arrow. They never stand still, are always running, cross from one place over to another, so that neither crossbow nor blunderbuss can be aimed at them. Before a European can get off one shot, an Indian will have dispatched three or four arrows, and he rarely misses his mark. Where the arrow hits a part of the body that is not protected by the armor, it penetrates as deeply as a crossbow bolt.[9]

The Spaniards placed a coat of mail over a basket and asked a Florida Indian to shoot at it. The savage balled his fists, shook and stretched himself to gather his strength, and let fly the arrow with such power that it pierced both armor and basket and emerged with enough force to kill a man. The Spaniards then placed a second coat of mail over the first one, and the Indian shot through both sets of armor, the spearhead protruding on one side, the shaft on the other. After that exhibition the Spaniards no longer trusted their coats of mail, nicknaming them "linen from Brabant." Thereafter they used horse blankets made of several layers of felt, "four fingers thick," to protect their horses.[10] (This accounts for the seemingly

[9] *Narratives of the Career of Hernando de Soto* (ed. by Edward Gaylord Bourne), (2 vols., New York, 1904), I, 25–26.

[10] R. Cronau, *Amerika, die Geschichte seiner Entdeckung* (1892), XI, 31.

exaggerated armor shown on the two leading horses in Segesser I.)

The question arises why none of the Indians, either attackers or defenders, pictured in Segesser II had firearms. Traders' lists of goods indicate that trade in firearms to Indian tribes began quite early. By the beginning of the eighteenth century tribes in Maryland, Viriginia, and the Carolinas, even those living some distance from trading centers, had firearms and were skilled in using them (using alligator teeth as substitutes for lead bullets). As early as 1700, English firearms were found among the Arkansas and Quapaws west of the Mississippi. The English, French, and Dutch carried on a flourishing trade in firearms with the Indians. Spain, on the other hand, had from the very beginning forbidden her merchants and colonists to trade in arms with the natives under the threat of severe punishment and saw to it that the law was obeyed. When Spanish colonies in Louisiana and Florida were threatened, they relaxed the rule to arm friendly tribes, but to a much lesser extent than their opponents did.[11]

Since the painter of Segesser II belonged to the Spanish party, he pictured the Indian defenders using their native weapons. In Segesser I, even the militia composed of Indians and mestizos had no firearms, though it seems highly unlikely that such a police unit would not have been provided firearms for a punitive expedition.

The shapes and sizes of the bows were often presented inaccurately in drawings and paintings; even the artist of Segesser II was not always exact in this respect. Since he probably came from Sonora or New Mexico, the double-curved bows of the Apaches were most likely well known to him, and he used the same shape for the bows of the attackers. West of the Mississippi, osage orange wood was preferred to any other wood for bow making. So popular was it among all the tribes of the region that it was an important trading article of the Caddo Indians, in whose territory it grew abundantly.

Many materials were available from which to make arrows. The most effective material, at least against Spanish armor, was cane, which pierced the best armor, while stone and bone arrowheads often broke.

[11] Friederici, *Skalpieren*, 31, 32.

About the arrows of the Pawnees we are fortunate in having a special report. According to John B. Dunbar, the first missionary to the Pawnees, the Indians devoted much effort to fashioning their arrows. The shafts were made from dogwood shoots. The bark was removed, and the switches were scraped between two grooved stones firmly pressed together in one hand until the desired thickness and smoothness were attained. The arrowhead, made from iron hoops, was then set into the end of the shaft, straightened, and tied with sinew. To the back end of the shaft a triple row of feathers was glued and tied, and the end was notched for the bowstring. With a small, chisel-like instrument three shallow grooves were cut along the shaft between tip and feathers, and the arrow was finished. Dunbar cited various reasons for the grooves. They were said to hold the arrow more firmly in the wound and also to allow blood to flow from the wound more readily.[12]

The making of arrows was a slow and tedious process. Only three or four could be made in a day. The Indians were so careful in their work that not only were the arrows easily distinguishable by tribes but also individuals could readily distinguish arrows they had made. After a buffalo hunt sometimes a quarrel arose over who had the right to a slain animal. If the arrow was still in the animal, the question was quickly decided by pulling it out and examining it. Sometimes an identification mark of its owner made the decision even easier.

Some Indian tribes made two types of arrows, one for hunting and another for war. Arrows used in war usually had barbed heads, loosely tied to the shaft so that they would remain in the body of the victim when an attempt was made to pull the arrow out of the wound. However, Dunbar asserts that the Pawnees never used this type of arrow.

The Pawnee bowman took excellent care of his weapons. After use, the bow was replaced in its casing and the arrows were put back into the quiver. The weapons were protected from moisture, and the bow was kept elastic and the arrows straight. Dunbar reported

[12] John B. Dunbar, "The Pawnee Indians," *Magazine of American History*, Vol. IV (1880).

that the approximate length of the bows was four feet and that the arrows were twenty-six inches long. The bows shown in Segesser II are the same length, but the arrows are somewhat longer.

Pawnee bow casings and quivers were usually made of waterproofed hide. They were decorated with porcupine quills, beadwork, or pieces of colored cloth. Occasionally the casings and quivers were made of otter or panther skins. When skinning such an animal, the hunter was careful to leave the head, the tail, and even the claws on the skin to decorate the finished quiver or casing. Such equipment, which was made waterproof by the heavy fur covering, was highly treasured.

In Segesser II, flaps are clearly shown at the upper ends of all the quivers, both of the attackers and those of the defenders. The flaps distinguish these quivers from those of the Apaches in Segesser I, which lack this detail. In the Plains quiver flaps were occasionally used as decoration, but were much more common among the mountain tribes, particularly the Shoshonis and the Navahos. The painter was no doubt familiar with the design of the western quiver; probably he had one himself.

Eight figures in Segesser II are shown carrying shields: Figures 15, 34, 58, and 88 have long, oval ones; Figure 57 has an unusually long, narrow one shaped like an hourglass; Figure 33 has a shorter oval shield; and Figures 18 and 52 have rectangular shields with rounded corners. All are carried on the left side of the body by means of a strap over the right shoulder, except for the narrow shield of Figure 57, which hangs between the arms on a strap around the neck. It is possible that this is not a shield but a bundle of some sort; it is a good deal longer than the other shields, which are about half the height of the men carrying them. It is possible that the shield-bearers belong to a special group, though they are carrying different kinds of weapons (five carry swords; two, tomahawks; and one, a spear. Plains shields, almost without exception, were round. Thus if the shields shown in Segesser II were drawn realistically and from personal observation, then they could not belong to Pawnee warriors. It is possible that they belong to Oto or Missouri Indians in the party. Because reports from early days are so scarce, it cannot be determined definitely how accurately the shields of the attackers were reproduced—though those of the Spaniards are accurate.

Ten of the attacking warriors have spears. The spearheads resemble the iron tips of sword-clubs, the broad part held forward. In Segesser II both plain and barbed spearheads are shown. Most spearheads were made of knife blades or sword tips. The beautifully shaped spearhead with the unusually wide base did not exist. The painter either used his imagination or exaggerated its size to demonstrate to the Spaniards the weapons the enemy provided their allies, while the Spaniards' Indian allies were seldom permitted to possess even knives or hatchets.

The spears in the painting are probably ceremonial spears of the type the Pawnees took into battle more as standards than as actual weapons. Their owners were members of spear societies, and they were expected to take special care of the spears, since they brought the buffaloes and protected the people.

When the village left for the hunting grounds, the chosen guards of the spears took them along and placed them near the war tent. Here they remained for anyone to borrow when he went after buffaloes. The spear bearers led the hunt and kept the advancing men in line with their spears, for no one could move out alone or too early. When the buffaloes were surrounded, the spear bearers served as a court of law, saw to the just distribution of the meat, settled quarrels, and so on. During the slaughtering they climbed a hill and watched for enemies; they were the last ones to return to camp. The spears were never taken along on raids or minor sorties but were used only to launch or repel large-scale attacks. The spears had an almost sacred position among the warriors' weapons, giving special protection to the tribe in battle. Each spear society was divided into a northern half and a southern half; the former conducted the winter ceremonies, and the latter the summer ceremonies. The spear of the northern half of the Skidi Pawnee Red Spear Society was wrapped in a dark otter pelt; the one of the southern half, in a reddish pelt. Once his spear was planted in the ground in front of an enemy, its bearer had to stay with it. He was permitted to pull it out only to pursue the enemy. If the spear was in danger, however, another member of the society could seize it and carry it to safety, and then the original bearer was also permitted to retreat.

The spears carried by Figures 20, 41, 42, and 156 are wrapped with what appear to be feathers, perhaps indicating that they were the spears of the Crow Spear Society, which in the Pawnee tribes formed the rear guard on marches and was the last contingent to leave the battlefield. The shafts of the Crow Spear Society spears were trimmed with blackbird and, later, crow feathers, as were the spears of the Brave Raven Society, a minor organization among the Skidis.

The spears of Figures 88 and 89 are not decorated and do not resemble known ceremonial spears. They are probably the warriors' personal weapons.

The presence of spears among the attackers of the Villasur expedition is documented in Spanish records. Though the eyewitness Aguilar, who escaped the massacre with nine severe wounds, speaks only of guns and arrows,[13] the chronicler of the expedition, Tamariz, mentions spears as well.[14]

The remaining weapons shown in Segesser II, including the tomahawks, are of European origin. In the painting thirty-four warriors are carrying tomahawks. In the testimony of the survivors of the Villasur massacre whose written depositions have come down to us, no tomahawks are mentioned as weapons used by the attackers, but this does not disprove their use, for Tamariz, the main witness, writes in his diary that the Spaniards' scout had earlier been threatened by warriors armed with tomahawks.

The two-bladed axes with which seven of the warriors are armed present a problem. No such weapons are mentioned in the literature on North American Indians. Since the blades are of iron, as indicated by their blue color, they must have been made in Europe or in one of the colonial settlements. It is also possible that to make the weapon the Indians filed down the blade of a French hoe or a

[13] "Testimony of Aguilar, Santa Fé, July 1, 1726," Thomas, *After Coronado*, 227.

[14] "Testimony of Tamariz, Santa Fé, July 2, 1726," *ibid.*, 229.

tomahawk so that only the two prongs remained. The bearers of these axes may have formed a special warriors' society.

In excavating the Pawnee village on the southern bank of the Republican River, not far from the little town of Red Cloud, Nebraska, A. T. Hill recovered, among other items, hoes with rather narrow iron blades which, if filed out, might have resulted in axes like those shown in the painting. It is known that the hoes were often cut up and the material used for arrowheads, scrapers, and similar objects.[15] Correspondence with historical museums in Nebraska and Oklahoma failed to produce any two-pronged tools of this design, though the Nebraska Historical Museum and the Chilocco Indian School Museum, in Chilocco, Oklahoma, had single-pronged tools. Interestingly, too, the Nebraska Historical Museum has a Pawnee spearhead that is as broad as the one shown in Segesser II.

Thus it appears that there were no two-pronged axes in Nebraska at the time of the Villasur expedition. The question then arises, Why did the painter include them in Segesser II? There are two possible explanations. The weapons may have been filed down from French farming tools. The second possibility is that the Indians carrying the weapons are Otos, who lived closer to the white trading posts and had more opportunities to obtain such implements. At the time of the massacre many Otos were already armed with guns—indeed, that is why the Skidi Pawnees called on them for help in attacking the Spaniards.

It should be remembered that the painter, or at least the Indian companions of the Spaniards, were probably farmers from the Southwest. Therefore, something which even faintly resembled an agricultural implement must have greatly excited their imagination. An ordinary ax could become a hoe, even a two-pronged hoe, for the Spaniards treated their hosts with very little consideration in providing them with iron implements, which they would have gladly exchanged for digging sticks and hoes made of bone. The painter may have been demonstrating to the stingy Hidalgos how the French showered such gifts on their proteges.

[15] *Nebraska History Magazine*, Vol. X, No. 3 (1927), 238, 251.

It is somewhat surprising to note that twenty-three of the Indians are carrying European swords, which they seem to handle with assurance. It is well known that the tomahawk, which could be used for many purposes, quite early replaced other cutting weapons, while the sword never became very popular. The typical sword shown in Segesser II is rather short, straight at the middle, then curving backward near the tip, while the back edge is straight to the tip, becoming rather broad at the curve. Many persons who have studied the painting, even weapons experts, have considered this weapon to be some kind of machete. However, it was probably the same weapon carried by their white allies in their scabbards.

None of the soldiers have drawn their swords. Why then did so many of the Indians choose the sword for their main weapon? It should be remembered that, after the bow, the main weapon of these tribes was the sword-club, which gradually broadens and curves behind the hilt. Only in the upper third does the wood curve backward at a sharper angle. It is widest at the tip, which is cut off straight across or notched at the back, creating a point like that of a sword.

> Like a pointed triangular or rhombic cross cut, the club either has a thin cutting edge and a broad, two-edged back or slants from the middle toward both sides and has a thin edge on both back and front. This wooden cutting weapon, which on the average is 24½ to 27½ inches and sometimes even longer, is strikingly similar to the short, broad European cutlass and curved swords like Turkish scimitar. . . . These comparisons play an important role in the literature of of the early colonial period; the wooden "sword" of the Virginia Indians is also a scimitar-like sword. . . . The designation "sword-club" therefore has an old meaning and indicates at the same time the essential elements of form and function.[16]

This description of the native club of the southeastern Indians and those of the Middle West explains why they were attracted to the swords of their white comrades-in-arms and why they had gained enough familiarity with them to go to war with them. It is probably

[16] Hans Dietschy, "Die Amerikanischen Keulen und Holzschwerter," *Internationales Archiv fuer Ethnographie*, Vol. XXXVII (1939), 127–28.

unlikely that such a large proportion of the warriors were equipped with them. They were not captured pieces but were given only to important warriors and chiefs throughout the nineteenth century. Villasur carried with him, among other weapons, a few short swords as presents for friendly Indians who were willing to serve as guides.[17]

A word should be added about the hooplike objects carried by Figures 20 and 93. Such hoops, made of sticks, were trimmed with animal hooves to serve as rattles in various ceremonies. Such rattles were reserved for the medicine man, the priest, and the keeper of the sacred bundles. It would thus appear that these figures represent medicine men, who among the Plains nations were also frequently outstanding warriors. The Knife-Spear Society of the Chaui, Pitahauerat, and Kitkehahki Pawnees had four rattles fringed with crow and swan feathers.[18] All the Pawnee spear societies had at least two, and usually four, such rattles. Later, in the nineteenth century, they used large gourd rattles in their famous calumet ceremony. But for the Two-Lance Society are explicitly recorded four rattles made of buffalo hoofs, which could be hung on hoops.

As for the body paintings of the Indian attackers, it must be concluded that the painter, even though a participant in the expedition, could scarcely have seen Pawnee warriors—and certainly not at the massacre itself, which happened too quickly to allow for detailed observation. The painter simply adopted the body paintings of ceremonial dancers of his own people and of neighboring villages and transferred them to the enemies (see the section on the Katcinas in Chapter XVII below).

[17] "Declaration of Hurtado, Santa Fé, April 21, 1724," Thomas, *After Coronado*, 248.

[18] Murie, "Pawnee Indian Societies," American Museum of Natural History *Anthropological Papers*, Vol. XI (1914), 561.

XV

The Spanish Expedition Under Villasur

The first generally available report about the Villasur expedition was the comprehensive presentation by Villiers, based on contemporary, and often inaccurate documents.[1] From this account it appeared that the French did not participate in the attack but heard of it later either indirectly or from participants. Certain French accounts incorrectly report a total massacre. The attack could not have taken place in the camp of the Indian attackers, as Boisbriant writes,[2] for in that case the Spaniards would have known that no French were present. If they failed to recognize their opponents because they were under attack from ambush, then there would scarcely have been time for the fleeing Spaniards to determine who their attackers were. And since the Spaniards refused to provide their Indian allies with firearms, they may well have assumed that they had fallen into a trap laid by the Frenchmen for whom they were looking. It would also have been humiliating to admit that they had suffered such a disastrous defeat at the hands of Plains savages. When Spanish documents referring to this event were obtained,[3] it became clear that the Spaniards had indeed entertained this illusion. The camp, the herd of unsaddled horses, the horse guards, and the setting—the fork of a river in the grazing territory of buffaloes and antelopes—as well as the surprise attack and the approximate number of Spaniards and Indian defenders—every detail fitted so remarkably that the discrepancies in the appearance of the unidentified attackers was easily explained.

[1] Marc de Villiers, "Le Massacre de l'expédition Espagnole du Missouri (11 août 1720)," *Journal de la Société des Américanistes de Paris* (New Series), Vol. XIII (1921).

[2] *Ibid.*, 251.

[3] Thomas, *After Coronado*.

What had induced the Spaniards to penetrate through unfamiliar plains to the at that time little-known, remote Missouri River region?

The unexpected landing of La Salle in 1686 on the coast of Texas impelled the Spaniards to extend their domain northeastward to prevent the French from seizing the Mississippi River region. The resulting hostilities northeast of Santa Fe, coupled with those at the borders of Texas, Louisiana, and Florida, gave the New Mexico border of that time the international character of all Spanish frontier countries.

Along the Spanish frontier the danger of Indian invasion was a constant threat, particularly in New Mexico. There the enemies of the Pueblos were also the Spaniards' enemies. Just as the French in Canada saw themselves threatened by the Iroquois on account of their loyalty to the Algonquians, so the Spaniards in New Mexico had to defy the widespread Apache nation surrounding the Pueblo settlements. On the other hand, if the Pueblos, who suffered greatly under Spanish rule, had allied themselves with their frontier enemies, the province would have been lost to Spain.

At the beginning of the eighteenth century the Navahos raided the region from the northwest, while the Faraon Apaches periodically attacked from the east. Directly northeast of Santa Fe lived peaceful Apache groups, the Jicarillas and Carlanas, who lived in northeastern New Mexico and south of the Arkansas; farther east and north they were joined downstream by the Cuartelejo and Paloma Apaches.

At the beginning of the eighteenth century the Comanches sallied forth from the mountains of Colorado with their kinsmen, the Utes, and repeatedly invaded New Mexico, only to withdraw again into the mountains. As soon as they had attained their full strength, they endangered Spanish control of the province, and the Spaniards feared that the province, weakened by the attacks of the Apaches and Comanches, would become easy prey for the French. According to Thomas, that fear was well founded, because behind the Cuartelejos, along the Platte River, lived the powerful Pawnee tribes, who were allied with the French, although the alliance was of such a nature that they seldom gained possession of firearms. Moreover, they did not settle farther west than the lower Loup Fork.

In the seventeenth century Pawnees came to New Mexico only as prisoners of the Apaches, who sold them to the Spaniards as slaves, or as prisoners of the Navahos, who regularly made long trips to the territory of the Wichitas to fight the Pawnees or the French and take their plunder back to New Mexico for sale.

In 1697 the Navahos were thoroughly defeated by the French and Pawnees.[4] In 1698 they again moved eastward and in revenge destroyed three Pawnee camps and a refugium. In 1699 they appeared at the annual Spanish fair with slaves and booty. They told the startled Spaniards of the defeat that had taken place the year before and praised the bravery of the French, their skill in shooting, and their willingness to support their allies.[5]

In 1700 the Apaches reported in Taos that the French had destroyed a pueblo of the Jumanos, which caused great alarm in Santa Fe. An expedition was dispatched in 1702, and a Frenchman with the Jumanos was killed by the Spanish escort, which consisted of fifty-six Pecos Indians. But no defensive measures were undertaken until twenty years later, when the French appeared to threaten both Texas and New Mexico, this time from the Mississippi.

By then the Spaniards were fully occupied with other troubles. In August, 1680, the Indians of the various Pueblo tribes had finally taken courage and driven their oppressors from New Mexico. Four years after the reconquest in 1692, the Picuris and the people of Taos rebelled a second time and fled from Governor Vargas with their goods and cattle. Most of them were recaptured,

[4] These "Navahos" may actually have been a unit of Plains Apaches, for the Navahos had been living for centuries in the three-states corner of Arizona, New Mexico, and Utah. These mountain people, cattle breeders, weavers, and farmers, would scarcely have moved onto the Plains by the thousands, at the end of an unknown world. The Apaches, to whom the Navahos were related only linguistically, were rivals of the Pawnees for possession of the buffalo herds. George E. Hyde, the historian of the Apaches as well as of the Pawnees, expressed the opinion that these "Apache Navahos" were actually some other Apache group.

[5] Thomas, *After Coronado*, 14.

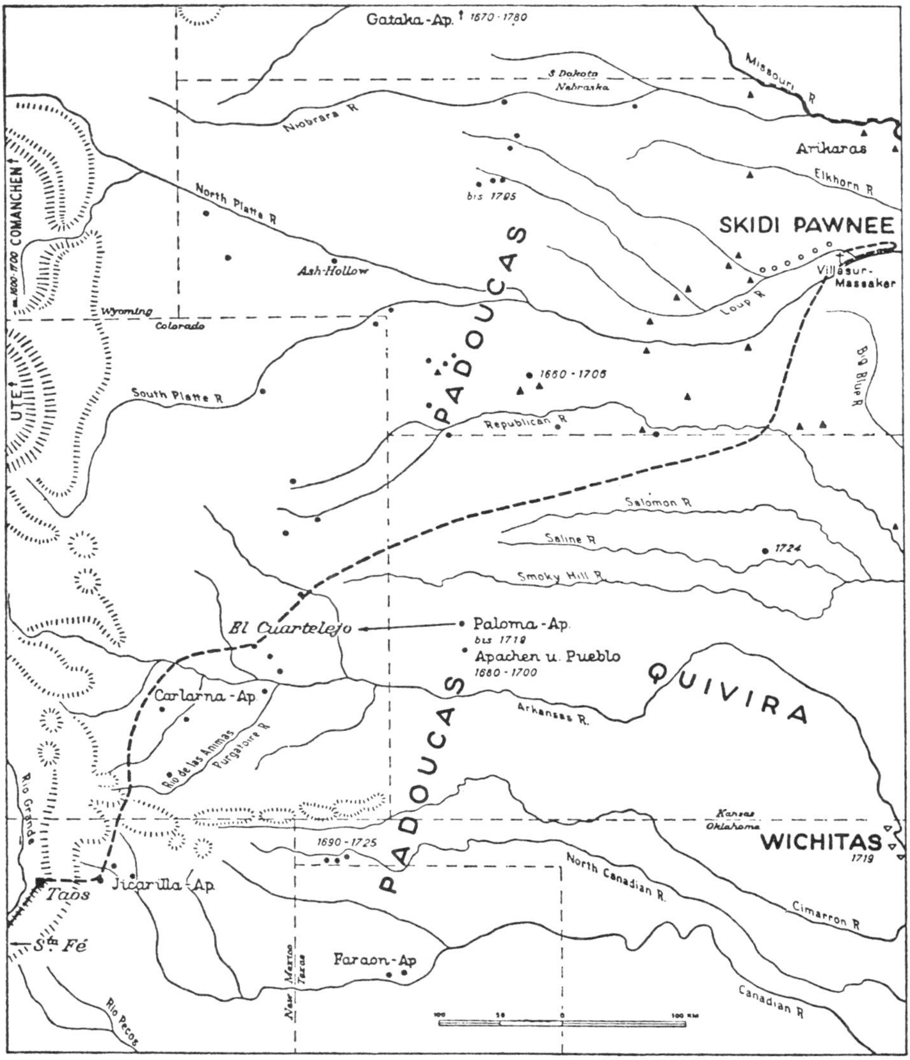

Settlements of the Padouca Apaches and the northern Pawnees about 1700.

● Villages of the Apaches (called Padoucas by the French).

▲ Settlements of the northern Pawnees between 1300 and 1725 (according to George E. Hyde).

● Skidi-Pawnees about 1700.

△ Wichitas, an alliance of Caddo tribes, relatives of the Pawnees.

- - - - The probable route of the Spanish expedition under Pedro de Villasur in the summer of 1720.

† Probable site of the massacre of the Villasur expedition.

— — — Present state boundaries.

Mountain ranges.

driven back through raging blizzards, and distributed as servants among the soldiers.

The Pueblos who had fled northeastward found refuge among the Cuartelejo Apaches but were made slaves by their hosts and in 1706 sent word to the Spaniards that they wanted to return. At once an expedition was dispatched, under Ulibarri,[6] guided by the Indian chief scout Naranjo, who functioned in all later expeditions as chief of scouts, helping Cuerbó achieve his successes. The French renegade Juan de l'Archévèque joined the expedition; he was at the time a trader in New Mexico and a survivor of the expedition of La Salle, in whose murder he evidently had a part.

The expedition was made up of twenty soldiers, twelve settlers, and one hundred enlisted Indians from various Pueblo tribes, a force considered sufficient to demonstrate Spanish power to the frontier nations over an area of many hundreds of miles. At length they reached the territory of the Cuartelejos, seminomads who lived in tents when they followed the buffalo but also planted maize, watermelons, pumpkins, and even wheat, and lived in wooden huts near their fields. Naturally the Cuartelejos did not want the sixty-two homesick Picuri slaves to leave. The Picuris, representatives of a higher culture, had been very useful to the Cuartelejos, especially in agriculture. However, the release of the slaves did not lead to hostilities; the Apaches even invited the Spaniards to go to war with them against the French and the Pawnees, from whom they had captured several shotguns, cloth, small short swords, iron axes, the foot of a gold-plated silver goblet, and two guns which were identified as French.[7] Ulibarri also learned that the Pawnees frequently stole Apache women and children and sold them to the French, just as the Apaches traded their Pawnee prisoners to the Spaniards. Shortly before, they had also killed a white man and confiscated his possessions. In the diary of the Ulibarri expedition rumors of the appearance of Frenchmen near the Rocky Mountains became more definite.

[6] "Juan de Ulibarri to El Cuartelejo, 1706," Thomas, *After Coronado*, 59–77; "Governor Cuerbó Reports the Return of the Picurís, 1706," *ibid.*, 77–80.

[7] "Declaration of Garduño, México, November 15, 1720," *ibid.*, 172–74.

Although the northern Mexican territories and in particular New Mexico Province were again and again subjected to the raids of the Navahos, eastern Apaches, Utes, and Comanches, and although the terror of these invasions was great, it must be said in defense of the Spaniards that they never used the notorious alternative of extermination employed by their Anglo-Saxon successors. In 1715 a larger expedition was sent out under Hurtado to punish the various Plains Apache tribes for their raids, which were mainly directed against the Taos and the Picuris and which they repeated over and over again in spite of the retaliatory expeditions of 1702, 1704, and 1712. Antonio Valverde Cosio is said to have driven them to the east in 1714,[8] which appears unlikely, however, since in the following spring they again carried out daring attacks on the pueblos of the Picuris and on Taos. For his expedition Hurtado enlisted, in addition to 37 soldiers and 18 settlers, 146 Indians from nine different pueblos.[9] Seventy-six of the Indians were equipped with guns, unlike the auxiliary Indian troops in Segesser II, who are pictured without them. The arming of the Ulibarri expedition Indians was probably kept secret, and a painting of a similar expedition five years later would certainly not reveal the arming of Indians. In addition to observing the stringent laws against doing so, the Spaniards were parsimonious with their weapons and saw to it that no good firearms fell into the hands of their allies, or even of Spanish settlers. An Indian fortunate enough to acquire an antiquated blunderbuss had to use pebbles for bullets. So scarce were firearms that many of the settlers themselves were forced to use bows.

The soldiers and settlers took 36 mules and 293 horses on the Hurtado expedition, as well as an undetermined number of riding horses and pack animals, which are not mentioned in the muster roll. On August 30, 1715, they finally started out, their immediate goals being to recapture a herd of horses stolen by the Picuris and

[8] A. F. Bandelier, "Expedition of Pedro de Villasur from Santa Fé, New Mexico, to the Banks of the Platte River," *Contributions to the History of the Southwestern Portion of the United States* (Cambridge, 1890), 183.

[9] "Diary of the Campaign of Juan Páez Hurtado Against the Faraon Apache, 1715," in Thomas, *After Coronado*, 94.

to teach the Chipaynes, Limitas, Faraons, and Trementinas (all bands of Plains Apaches) a lesson. To avoid losing their way, the group followed the Canadian River. On the slopes of the mesas were stands of fir and yellow pine. But the region of the Plains Apaches for whom they were looking was supposed to lie far downstream in the northern corner of modern Texas near the present town of Amarillo. Finally, after eighteen days' travel, hampered by difficulty in finding pasture and water holes, the scout Naranjo confessed to his suspicious commander in chief that he was lost. The officer lost patience with the chief scout, who was blamed for all the misfortunes of the expedition and was given fifty lashes; the setting of this event was appropriately named Whipping Creek. Then the force started on the return journey, without having seen a single Faraon.

In Spanish reports of travels and expeditions in these regions the commanders reveal a surprising dependence upon subordinates and a lack of determination to pursue a goal to its conclusion, weaknesses that help explain the results of the expeditions that took place in 1719 and 1720.

In 1719, Governor Valverde launched a campaign against the Comanches, who were making ever more devastating raids against the Jicarilla Apaches. The Jicarillas were friendly toward the Spaniards, and their pleas for help had caused the missionary at Taos to ask Viceroy Valero for permission to convert them and protect them, a request that was favorably received in view of the advance of the French toward Texas.[10] The Spaniards hoped to use the Jicarillas as a buffer, and Governor Valverde was ordered to support the missionary in his efforts and to reconnoiter the position of the French outside New Mexico. It had been reported that the French had already set out for the mines at Santa Fe.

Valverde decided to wait until the following spring to carry out the scouting expedition. He believed that the planned campaign against the Comanches and Utes might provide some information about the French. A total of 60 garrison soldiers and 40 settlers and

[10] "Cruz to Valero [Taos, 1719]," *ibid.*, 137; "Valero to Cruz, México, September 3, 1719," *ibid.*, 139.

volunteers answered the call to join the expedition. As in the Hurtado expedition, many of the volunteers were so poor that they had to be provided with leather coats, powder, lead, flour, and horses. In Taos an additional 465 Indians enlisted. From the many small rural settlements of the Jicarillas, who had suffered heavy losses from the Comanches, more than 100 offered themselves as reinforcements.

The animals on the expedition amounted to about nine hundred head and some sheep. The scout Naranjo and Don Gerónimo, lieutenant governor of Taos, acted as interpreters. Only Chief Carlana and his people were able to follow the tracks of the Comanches. Finally they came upon a wide trail of horse tracks and marks of tipi poles. Valverde halted his forces and called a council of war, in which it was decided to desist from further pursuit, which promised almost immediate contact with the enemy after a thirty-day search. Carlana was later accused of having declared that the march would lead into a region of few springs that could not provide sufficient water for the men and animals.

The column turned aside, an act that the Comanches interpreted as flight. Even if the criticism of Valverde's political rival Martínez is discounted, it is clear that he wasted a rare opportunity, one which he was obligated to seize if for no other reason than to discharge an obligation to his trusting allies, the Jicarillas. The expedition turned down the Arkansas and moved to a region slightly east of the modern La Junta. On the left bank of the Arkansas they met a large force of Cuartelejos who lived farther north, Palomas, and Calchufines—altogether more than a thousand warriors, women, and children and about two hundred tipis. One of the Palomas had a gunshot wound which he claimed he had received in an engagement with the French in the most remote border territory of the Apaches. The Palomas had fled, leaving their land to the Pawnees. They also insisted that the French had built two large towns, each as large as Taos, in which they were living with Pawnees and Jumanos, whom they had provided with rifles and taught to shoot.

Thomas believed that the French had moved with the Pawnees to the fork of the North and South Platte rivers because he thought that the Palomas were domiciled north of the Cuartelejos (in 1795 this fork was still known as Padouca Fork). Even farther to the north, on the Niobrara, there were Pawnee villages (those of the Arikaras) only near the Missouri; the territory on the upper course of this river was occupied by Padoucas, as shown on John Mitchell's 1755 map.

The wounded Paloma warrior also told Valverde that he had received his wound in a fight with the Kansa Indians,[11] who were allied with some "white people." This statement clearly points eastward, for in 1723, according to Bourgmont, the Kansas were living "thirty hours" above the Padouca River, which was later renamed for them. Mitchell's map of 1755 also shows them located there. According to H. E. Bolton and George E. Hyde, the Palomas who had temporarily fled to the Cuartelejos are the same tribe.

In the east the Apaches were called Padoucas by the Caddoes, the Sioux, and the French, a name which the western Apaches along the Spanish frontier did not use. In Scott County, Kansas, south of the Smoky Hill River (the northern branch of the Kansas) there are ruins of a village which clearly connect the Apaches and the Padoucas. The village was known by the end of the nineteenth century. It included small Pueblo buildings and was considered to be an Apache village in which Pueblo Indians who had fled from New Mexico had sought refuge. The ruins were later excavated by W. R. Wedel, and it became evident that the supposed Apache remains were actually those of Padoucas. He determined that the Pueblo buildings actually had been built by Pueblo Indians and found pieces of Pueblo jars. Thus it was an Apache village to which Pueblos came to live, and at the same time a Padouca village. A French document written about 1700 on the Red River near the Texas border mentions a tribe which the Spaniards called Apaches but which was known among the French as Padoucas.[12] In a report from Spanish Louisiana in the year 1785, the Spanish authorities called Kiowa Apaches "Pados," the French traders' abbreviation

[11] "Valverde to Valero, Santa Fé, November 30, 1719," *ibid.*, 141–48.

[12] Pierre Margry (ed.), *Découvertes et établissements des Français dans l'Ouest et dans le Sud de l'Amérique Septentrionale (1614–1754)* (6 vols., Paris, 1879–88).

of *Padoucas*. Jacob Fowler, who met the Kiowa Apaches in 1821, called them Kioway-Padoucahs.[13]

These ruins in Kansas and Nebraska lie in the same territory that was occupied by the Padoucas in the eighteenth century, according to information from the Pawnee and Sioux Indians and from the French. Excavations showed that the inhabitants made pottery and cultivated the soil. When this fact was established, W. D. Strong, who believed that the Padoucas were Comanches, made a thorough investigation but found no evidence that the Comanches had ever made pottery or cultivated the soil. Thus it was finally established that the Padoucas were Apaches, the only tribe on the Western Plains who lived in villages and carried on agriculture in the eighteenth century.

The documents in Thomas offer proof that Comanches and Utes lived in the mountains of Colorado until after 1700, long after tribes living in the Plains had been known as Padoucas. In their first migration into the Plains the Comanches moved down the Arkansas into southeastern Colorado. About 1730 they drove the Apaches from the territory. Then they turned against the Utes and attacked them. About 1740 they attacked the Apaches at the headwaters of the Canadian, east of Taos. In 1757 large numbers of Comanches allied themselves with the southern Caddo tribes and drove the Lipan Apaches from the San Saba River, a western tributary of the Colorado in central Texas. But before 1770 the Comanches made no effort to establish themselves southward along the Arkansas and contented themselves with periodic raiding expeditions.

Governor Valverde questioned the strange Indians so carefully that they soon realized what interested him most and exaggerated the rumors about the French. Now Valverde believed that at last he had something concrete to report about the French. He took his leave, promising the disappointed Palomas help the next year, when he would drive the French out of their territory. Then he set out for home.

The news Valverde sent to Mexico at the end of November,

[13] George E. Hyde to the author.

1719,[14] did little to calm the fears of Viceroy Valero, who had heard from Madrid that France, Savoy, and England had declared war on Spain. He had been ordered to protect the coastlines carefully from enemy sailing vessels.[15] At the same time, Manuel San Juan de Santa Cruz, governor of Nueva Vizcaya, sent alarming news from Parral about the poor discipline of whole companies of military personnel, whose insufficient training and equipment made it unlikely that they could withstand well-trained troops. He urgently requested five hundred long-range guns, powder, lead, a gunsmith, and a drill sergeant.[16] Two weeks later he again urged the authorities to do something and reported that six hundred Frenchmen were only seventy hours' marching distance from Santa Fe and had opened hostilities against Indians friendly to the Spaniards. Now he needed a thousand long guns, a like number of bayonets and scabbards, five hundred pistols, and five hundred spears.[17]

As a result of these appeals for help a council of war was held in Mexico on January 2, 1720, and Valverde was ordered to establish a military post in El Cuartelejo manned by twenty-six soldiers and two or three missionaries who would convert the Indians and persuade them to cultivate the soil. The governor of Texas Province was urged to make a similar arrangement with the Indians of northern Texas in order to use them as a bulwark against a French invasion.

Valverde tried to convince his superiors that El Cuartelejo was much too far from Santa Fe (nearly 350 miles) and in too barren a region for him to be able to accomplish anything effective there. He proposed to set up the post at La Jicarilla, which was only forty hours east of Taos and which had sufficient water, forest, and game, as well as a population inclined to be receptive to Christianity. He announced that he would call a council of war in Santa Fe to learn the views of the experienced notables of the city. At the same time he announced that when the time was right he or his lieutenant general would reconnoiter the French settlements.

14 "Valverde to Valero, Santa Fé, November 30, 1719," Thomas, *After Coronado*, 141–45.

15 "Durán to Valero, Madrid, January 30, 1719," *ibid.*, 140.

16 "Cruz to Valero, Parral, November 30, 1719," *ibid.*, 151–54.

17 "Cruz to Valero, Parral, December 11, 1719," *ibid.*, 146–48.

A second council of war, on June 2, 1720, heard the opinions of Naranjo, Captain Miguel Tenorio (the alcalde of Taos), the French renegade L'Archévèque, and four officers, experienced men indeed, who shared the views of their superior and also considered a garrison of twenty-five soldiers (who were to be transferred from Santa Fe) too small for La Jicarilla, threatened as it was by Comanches and Faraons.[18]

The French, for their part, possessed only one western trading post which they had acquired in a very unpolitical manner. In 1705 a band of Natchitoches went to the French for assistance after a bad harvest. Not until 1712 did they return to their old homeland, where St. Denis established a trading post for them about ninety miles above the confluence of the Red River and the Mississippi, and in 1713 added a garrison to protect them from Spanish attack.[19] For over one hundred years Natchitoches remained an important trading post and transit point in the traffic with the West. In the same year St. Denis appeared in San Juan Bautista, on the Río Grande. His arrival greatly alarmed the Spaniards, who hurriedly occupied Texas.

After the June, 1720, council of war, Valverde sent his subordinate, Pedro de Villasur (who had been left in charge at Santa Fe the previous year while Valverde pursued the Comanches), on an expedition to the northeast to ascertain the French position. Accompanying Villasur were forty-five Spaniards, sixty Pueblo Indians, and a Spanish priest, a small force considering that the French were expected to be quite near and there was the possibility, even probability, of a clash with them.[20]

Villasur left Santa Fe about the middle of June, 1720. Some of his soldiers had participated in the expeditions of Ulibarri, Hurtado, and Valverde. L'Archévèque, now a well-to-do merchant, went along as interpreter, taking with him ten horses and six pack

18 "Council of War, Santa Fé, June 2, 1720," *ibid.*, 156–60.

19 In spite of their friendly relations with the French, the Natchitoches dwindled away and after 1805 were absorbed by other tribes of the Caddo alliance.

20 "Martínez to Valero [México, 1720]," Thomas, *After Coronado*, 182.

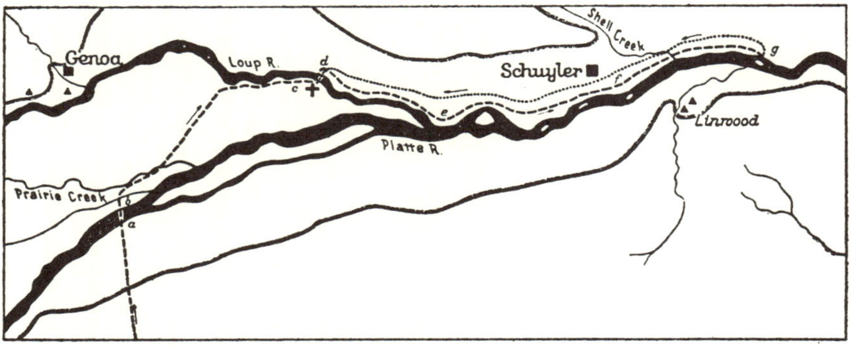

The Villasur expedition: the route of the last days, reconstructed on the basis of the last page of the diary.

▲	Indian villages.	*a*:	Tuesday, August 6, 1720, and Wednesday, August 7
■	Present-day towns.	*b*:	Wednesday and Thursday, August 8 (morning)
	Rocky banks.	*c*:	Thursday, August 8 (evening)
---	Route of the expedition.	*c, d, e*:	Friday, August 9
······	Probable return route.	*e, f,* or *g*:	Saturday, August 10
		f or *g*:	Sunday, August 11
		f or *g*:	Return march, Monday, August 12
		cross, *c*:	Massacre, Tuesday, August 13 (morning)

animals.[21] Only three settlers took part in the expedition. Valverde, who Martínez claimed had become rich by manipulating the soldiers' pay and by appropriating cultivated Indian land, did not equip the settlers with leather armor or horses.[22]

According to the testimony of survivors of the expedition, Villasur took maize, short swords, knives, sombereros, and half a muleload of tobacco as peace offerings for the Indian chiefs of the Jicarillas, the Carlanas, and the Cuartelejos. In his personal baggage this descendant of Castilian nobility had silver dishes, cups, and

21 Bandelier, "Expedition of Pedro de Villasur," *Contributions to the History of the Southwestern Portion of the United States*, 194.

22 "Martínez to Valero [México, 1720]," Thomas, *After Coronado*, 179.

spoons, a silver candlestick, an inkwell, writing paper, quills, and a saltcellar.[23]

It is not certain exactly which route they took, but doubtless Naranjo led them along the old trail by way of Taos to the Jicarillas' territory, thence to the Carlanas' lands, where they crossed the Arkansas on rafts, finally reaching El Cuartelejo.[24]

It can be assumed that the Palomas, who had been driven from their land by the Pawnees and Kansas the year before, were anxiously awaiting the Spaniards' arrival to attack their enemies. Thomas was of the opinion that the Palomas had lived north of the Cuartelejos, because Bandelier placed the massacre of the expedition at the junction of the North and South Platte rivers. If that were correct, Pawnees would have been living in the region, but, as pointed out earlier, the region was still occupied by Plains Apaches. The Palomas had been attacked in 1719 by Pawnees and Jumanos living east of them on the Arkansas, in the present Oklahoma. Yet Villasur permitted the Apaches to lead him on into Kansas. I suspect that Villasur had good reason for this, because from the statements of the Palomas, he had come to the conclusion that the French were not with the nearby Pawnees, their personal foes, but with the more northern Pawnees.

When the expedition arrived at a shallow river with many islands, which Martínez called the Pawnee River,[25] Villasur realized that they had traveled an estimated three hundred leagues without finding a sign of the French (an estimate which led Thomas to place the scene of the battle at the fork of the North and South Platte rivers).

When one considers that the Spaniards were traveling with a tribe of Apaches, one can understand that the Spanish witnesses could easily have been mistaken about the direction of the march and the distances they covered. To travel with an Indian contingent could necessitate frequent changes in direction to pursue buffaloes and frequent halts to skin the animals and dry the meat. There

23 "Declaration of A. Aguilar, Santa Fé, April 21, 1724," *ibid.*, 249.

24 "Declaration of Alva, Santa Fé, April 3, 1724," *ibid.*, 255.

25 "Declaration of Martínez, México, November 13, 1720," *ibid.*, 172.

could also be frequent side trips to visit tribal kinsmen. And there would be endless conferences between the confused and alarmed Spanish officers and the Apache chiefs. Traveling in this manner, no one could calculate distances and directions exactly.[26]

The only extant written record made during the expedition is a portion of a diary kept by Corporal Felipe de Tamariz, which was found among the Opatas after the massacre and was first printed in 1921 by Villiers in French. A translation of Villiers' version appears below:

> The tracks which we noticed led us through a region in which we suspected a war party which, to all appearances, was not very far away from some village. After the lieutenant general had called together all the active officers and those who were placed at his disposal, as well as the colonists, he told them that a savage had reported to him that he had found some maize and leaves of fresh sand cherries, evidently the remains of a meal of a group of warriors who had passed there a short time earlier. He then reflected on the distance we had covered and which in our estimation amounted to three hundred leagues. Then he considered whether we should wait for orders from the viceroy in New Spain, who had sent forth this expedition, to attempt to find out, with the help of the savage nations, whether any Frenchmen had settled in this region or whether we, because we had up to now found no indication which would have convinced us of this, should continue our search, starting with the nation of the Pawnees, the only ones who would be able to shed light on where we could contact them. On the council were Captain Tomás Olguín, Aide-de-Camp José Domínguez, Ensign Bernardo Casillas, Captains Miguel Thenorio de Alva, Alonzo Real de Aguilar, and Pedro Luján, Corporals José Griego and Lorenzo Rodríguez, Captain Cristóbal de la Serna, and Captain Juan de l'Archévèque; the last two are settlers. All were of the opinion that they should search for the Pawnees to learn the truth from them whether or not the Apaches had deceived us—the detachment should therefore cross to the other bank of the river and carry out all proper movements to reach the goal which they had set for themselves.

[26] George E. Hyde, *Indians of the High Plains* (Norman, 1959), 75.

In keeping with this decision the lieutenant general ordered a few of the savages to look for the ford of the river so that the detachment could cross to the other bank. After the noonday meal we began to ferry the baggage across on ladders and on the backs of the savages. It was not possible to get it across any other way. The large number of islands in this river make it impossible to use Indian canoes. And because the day was not long enough to transport everything across, the camp was divided by the river the following night; too, we did not want to ask our savages to wade the river at night, because it was very cold.

Wednesday, the seventh of August. At dawn the rest of the baggage and of our men were brought across from the other side of the Jesús María River. This was not accomplished without great effort, but finally we were all united again at noon.

Thursday, August 8. We left the river Jesús María and followed the trail of the Pawnees. The servant of Captain Serna had boasted that he knew it well, but he became lost and returned to the camp. He was sent out a second time escorted by Captain Narvanno [Naranjo], four corporals, and two soldiers. A servant of Captain Serna, a Pawnee by birth, said that he remembered, although he had been very young when he left, that the village of his kinsmen was located on the bank of a river north of here. Our soldiers were ordered to verify this statement. At the same time they were ordered, as soon as they had come near the village, to let the savage speak alone with his compatriots so that he could tell them that they need not be afraid, that we, the Spaniards, were their friends. In case they found no one in the village, they were to advance only far enough that they could be back in camp on the same day or the following night.

After we had left the Jesús María River, we tried to follow the tracks which we had found and which we believed were those of the Pawnees. A league from this river we found a large creek which we had to cross. Because its water was very warm, we believed that it was a tributary of the river which flowed from the west to the east. Then we marched into a plain, always following the tracks of those who had gone ahead of us. After covering a league, we discovered a great many trees and met one of our savages from the detachment of Captain Narrans [Naranjo]. He had been ordered to wait for us to tell us that we should follow the creek. He himself was following the tracks of those ahead of him, since they had not found anyone in the villages. We reached the bank of the creek, but because it was impossible to cross it with our arms, we were forced to march along the creek and take the same route as Captain Narrans. We had covered three leagues to get to this creek and had marched three more before reaching a plain. There we stopped, so that those who came after us should not lose their way. At the same time, two savages of Captain Narrans appeared to tell the lieutenant general that he should not worry if he did not return to the camp the following night, that he was following the tracks of the Pawnees, who evidently could not be far ahead of him, and that the main body of the troops should keep on advancing, because he was planning to catch up with them soon.

Friday, August 9. The army was ready to start when we saw at a distance of more than a league someone galloping toward us. We were in front and soon learned that they were some of our people who had been out scouting. They told us that they had found the Pawnees eight leagues from here, on the other side of the creek which we were following, in a campground where they were singing and dancing as was the custom of the savages. There seemed to be a large number of them. They had not considered it wise to approach them for fear of startling them in the night.

At this news, the order was at once given to cross to the other side of the creek. This was accomplished with such good luck that nothing got wet, although the water came up to the girths of the mules. We marched for three leagues along the creek, and when we stopped we were five leagues from the Indians, according to the judgment of those who had brought us the report. As soon as we had set up camp, the lieutenant general sent the savage of Captain Serna to his compatriots to speak to them, to assure them of our friendship and good will toward them, and that we were taking these measures to inform them, to show them our good will and our sincerity. Although the lieutenant general wanted to send two soldiers with this savage as an escort to prevent him from being attacked by his compatriots, the savage said that he had nothing to fear and that it would be better if he were alone, for if the soldiers were accompanying him, they might think that there was treachery and deception in what he was proposing to them. That was considered wise, and the savage left at about 11 o'clock in the morning to see this nation. May God and the Blessed Virgin grant him success! The general named the creek San Laurentius. The Jesús María River meets this creek here at the place where we are, so that if we had not already crossed it, we could not do so.

At six o'clock in the evening we saw François Sistaca, which is the name of the savage of Don Cristóbal de la Serna, coming back at a gallop. He told the lieutenant general and all of us that he had searched for the band which they had seen dancing the previous night but had not found them and had therefore followed the creek. Then he had seen them pass by on the other side where there was a village and many people. After he stopped on the bank of the creek and dismounted, he called to the people, who were crossing the creek, and made the usual signs of friendship and peace among savages, whereupon several savages came to him, among them four who preceded the others with tomahawks in their hand, but without bow and arrows, shouting all the time. After they had come as close as a stone's throw, he became frightened and waved his hat as though he were motioning to people behind him to come forward. Then he mounted his horse and rode at top speed the eight leagues without stopping until he reached the safety of the camp.

Saturday the tenth of this month, the festival of the glorious Martin, the Spanish Saint Laurentius. The army marched along the river to meet this band; we discovered on the other side of the creek a village consisting of a number of houses and people who went across the creek by a ford from one bank to the other always calling out to each other. We could hear them, since only the creek was separating us, as mentioned above, and made the sign of peace and friendship. Twenty-five or thirty savages came to the other bank to talk to our people. We could easily hear what they said, the savage of Don Cristóbal de la Serna, who recognized the language of his nation, told the lieutenant general that they wanted peace and that he should go over to them.

They made signs looking toward the sun, which meant that the Spaniards and they could not confer that day.[27] The savage of

[27] The Indians were evidently a hunting party of Pawnee Mahas who were retreating from the Spaniards to entice them to follow them to the Otos. The Pawnee Mahas' religion was founded on the worship of certain stars, and their main villages were always laid out in the direction of those stars. The Spaniards prob-

> Don Cristóbal de la Serna decided at once to cross the creek despite the fear which he had suffered the day before. The army stopped opposite the village, and the savage took off his clothes to swim across with the consent of his master. The lieutenant general admonished him to tell his nation that he had come to meet them without any intention of doing them any harm at all, as they could easily see since he was coming openly without using any ruse of war, as he could easily have when he heard that they were dancing and singing when he was only two leagues away from them. They could therefore negotiate with him in all confidence about the peace and the good understanding that should exist between them and us as brothers and subjects of the same king. The lieutenant general also gave the savage tobacco to take to them, which is the usual confirmation of this type of negotiation. . . .[28]

The excerpt quoted above is all that remains of the Villasur diary. Where had the Spaniards found this contingent of Indians? The site can probably never be determined with complete certainty. On September 25, 1924, a three-man expedition sponsored by the Nebraska Historical Society went to the valley of the Loup and Platte which had been for centuries the home of the Pawnee Mahas. The purpose of the expedition was to find the place where the Spaniards had crossed the river, described by the diarist as having a large number of islands and where, on an 1842 map, the main trail of the Pawnees from the southwest reached the Platte River, toward the lower end of Grand Island. But up to the junction of the Loup, the Platte is filled with islands. Moreover, the Spaniards spent Friday night, August 9, at the junction of the Jesús María (Platte) River and the San Laurentius (the Loup, according to Sheldon), "so that if we had not already crossed it, we could not do so."

If this last statement is correct, then the crossing point must have been the Platte, perhaps at the present-day village of Silver

---

ably interpreted such signs in their own way, and in my opinion their interpretation was not necessarily the correct one.

[28] Translated from Villiers, "Le Massacre de l'expédition Espagnole du Missouri," *Journal de la Société des Americanistes de Paris* (New Series), Vol. XIII (1921), 246–49.

Creek, where today a bridge spans the river. If that was the crossing point, the writer of the diary failed to mention Silver Creek—which would be understandable because the terrain is flat, and the creek flows parallel to the Platte and very close to it, so that it could be mistaken for one of the channels into which the Platte is divided until it reaches the Loup, from which it receives a sufficient amount of water to fill the bed. From the ford to the first creek, Prairie Creek, the distance does not amount to a Spanish league, unless the expedition proceeded northeast, in which case the subsequent statements of the diarist fit exactly.

Thomas' assumption that the meeting place was the junction of the North and South Platte rivers is incorrect, not only for historical reasons but also for topographical ones, because the two branches are scarcely four and one-half miles apart for nearly fifty miles above the fork, which does not agree with the diarist's description of the region. Moreover, the North Platte is wider than the South Platte and carries more water; the diarist would not have called it a creek and tributary of the Jesús María, the southern of the two rivers, which consists of small channels. Only west of the present-day village of Ogallala does the distance between the North and South Platte widen. Neither Pawnees who were living here nor a hunting party could have been encountered here at that time. Thus the meeting place must have been farther east.

The French references to the Spanish Expedition in Charlevoix, Dumont, and Le Page du Pratz are filled with contradictions, exaggerations, and otherwise unbelievable details that do not speak well for the judgment of the colonists, traders, soldiers, hunters, and priests of that time and region. However, the statement by Boisbriant, the commander of the Kaskaskias outpost (a short distance below the junction of the Missouri and the Mississippi), that Oto Indians attacked the Spaniards by surprise when they came within fifteen leagues of their village can be accepted as correct.[29] This Oto village lay on the south bank of the Platte and on the west bank[30] of Salt Creek, which flows from the southwest into the

[29] *Ibid.*, 251.

[30] Mitchell's 1755 map shows the location of the village to be on the east bank of Salt Creek.

Platte, where today the village of Yutan is located. The Otos lived there from about 1700 to 1739. In the summer they hunted in a wide area west and south of the village. Fifteen leagues west of the village is the Loup Fork.

Later travelers found these tribes still living in the same regions. Truteau wrote in 1794:

> Twelve leagues from [the Platte's] mouth lives the nation of the Octatas [Otos], good warriors and good hunters; twenty-five leagues farther upstream [an exaggerated distance when one takes into consideration the large bend in the Platte; at the time of the Villasur expedition only the Pawnee Mahas lived on the Loup and the Platte, all other Pawnee tribes being farther south]; is the village of the Grand Panis [Pawnees], cowardly and inferior hunters; thirty leagues from there, on a river which flows into the Platte, live the Pawnee Mahas, good warriors and hunters.[31]

Of course, they were first of all hunters and not warriors, in spite of their agriculture, which was the responsibility of the women. The Loup River was named for the French form of their name—Pani Loup—and they lived on that river until they resettled elsewhere after 1870. Though Truteau did not know the Loup River by that name, it is obvious that he was referring to it. From the point where the Loup flows into the Platte—that is, scarcely farther away from the Missouri than the Chaui Pawnees were living after about 1770—the rest of their settlements were scattered about sixty miles westward, to the junction of the North Fork of the Loup, and the Loup, so that Blackman could report that from Columbus (located at the junction with the Platte) to a point twenty miles west of Fullerson the Loup River region abounded in ruins of Indian villages, many of them dating to a time before 1720. Here lived the Pawnees, or, more precisely, the Pawnee Loup.[32]

Charlevoix, who traveled at least as far as the Missouri and knew Boisbriant personally, claimed that the Indians who massacred

[31] "Journal of Jean Baptiste Truteau on the Upper Missouri, 1794/95," *American Historical Review*, Vol. XIX (1913–14), 306.

[32] E. E. Blackman, *Nebraska History*, Vol. VII (1924), 95.

the Spaniards were Octatas. A mining engineer named Lallemand said the same thing in a letter dated April 5, 1721. But neither the Otos nor the seminomadic tribes were in their permanent earth-lodge villages at this time of year, but were away on buffalo hunts with families, tipis, and baggage; the Otos were evidently to the west, upstream of the Platte, close to the Loup junction. The tracks which the Spanish followed between the Loup and Platte might have been those of the Pawnees through whose territory they were traveling—the Pawnees who some Frenchmen, such as Bienville, the governor of Louisiana, asserted had played an important role in the massacre.[33]

In the extant portion of the diary it is stated that the first Indian camp the expedition encountered was located five leagues below the junction of the two rivers; that would have been approximately south of the present town of Schuyler. On the day after the dance the Indians moved three leagues farther, probably between the present Rogers and North Bend. Here was the ford, and their village (probably their summer camp) lay on the southern bank of the Jesús María, east of the present city of Linwood, an early-day Indian territory, as excavations proved. Martínez claims that the camp was on an island; close to the southern bank of the river is an island large enough to have accommodated such a camp.[34]

According to the French statements, all of which were based on hearsay, the Spaniards were enticed into this camp and attacked there. But the reports of the survivors prove that this is not correct. On October 5, 1720, Boisbriant wrote that all the nations on the Missouri made peace with the Pawnee Mahas, but they absolutely refused to do so with the Padoucas. He added that the Otos and the Kansas were at war with them and captured 250 slaves and

[33] Margry, *Mémoires et Documents pour servir à l'histoire des origines françaises des pays d'outremer*, VI, 450.

[34] "Martínez to Valero [México, 1720]," Thomas, *After Coronado*, 183: "They arrived on the banks of a very full coursing river which has an island in the middle of it where there is a very large settlement of Indians of the Pawnee nation."

killed 20 of the Spaniards who were in the village where the prisoners were taken.[35]

Either several events and rumors are mixed up in this account, or the Paloma Apaches, who led the Spaniards eastward, suffered the same fate as their white protectors. The former alternative is probably the correct one. The Apaches were very likely not mounted, just as their opponents were not. On the journey the whites and the Indians marched separately from each other, and at night they made separate camps. Perhaps the Palomas kept better watch and escaped in the night, for which they cannot be blamed, when one considers that their avengers and protectors did not dare enter the strangers' camp and finally even retreated some distance away. It could also be that the reference to the "war with the Padoucas" is to the battles of 1719, when the Palomas fled to the Cuartelejos, who tried to return to their homeland as the Spaniards' guides. Boisbriant's letter continues:

> This news was brought to Sieur Boisbriant by four Frenchmen whom he had permitted to go to buy horses from the Pawnee-ouessas [Wichitas]. Before the arrival of these Frenchmen, this nation had also destroyed a Padouca village. They had carried away a hundred slaves, whom they roasted to death unmercifully, day after day. Our Frenchmen ransomed four or five of them and thus saved them from the fiery death, but their generosity was badly repaid. The rascals ran away shortly afterward and took along the clothes of their liberators.

On November 22, 1720, Boisbriant wrote:

> The Spaniards came, 250 in number, accompanied by the Padouca nation, to establish a settlement on the Missouri. On their way they destroyed five nations. (Father Charlevoix reports that two of them were groups of the Octatatas.) After such a splendid victory, the commander believed that he was strong enough to resist any attack. He sent part of his forces back with the slaves they had taken in the villages and advanced fifteen leagues to meet the

35 Letter from Kaskaskias, in Villiers, "Le Massacre de l'expédition Espagnole du Missouri," *Journal de la Société des Américanistes de Paris* (New Series), Vol. XIII (1921).

> Otoptatas. His plan was to exterminate this nation. He still had 60 Spaniards and 150 Padoucas. The Otoptatas, informed of the Spaniards' advance by the Pawnee Mahas, came to meet them. They pretended to be Pawnee Mahas, which was easy for them since they spoke the language like their own.

Subsequent assertions become even more incredible. It was claimed that the Otoptatas spent the night with the Spaniards. The Otoptatas alleged that there were Frenchmen with the Pawnees whom they could easily capture. The Padoucas fled, but on the next day the expedition halted so that the Indians could show their new friends an Iroquois dance, for which they even borrowed the Spaniards' spears. During the dance they fell upon the Spaniards and killed them. Then follow more such absurdities.

If the Spaniards had exterminated five tribes, they would have doomed their reconnaissance mission, for survivors would surely have spread the news of the advancing enemy and prevented any peaceful approach. Valverde reports no such an action to the viceroy of New Spain, and his political enemy, Martínez, makes no mention of it in his enumeration of the mistakes Villasur was supposed to have made.

Only the assertion that the Otoptatas had attacked the Spaniards together with the Pawnee Mahas and perhaps a small hunting party of Missouris deserves credence. Scarcely anything else can be determined from the testimony of survivors, whose reports are for the most part very short.

It is probably that the Pawnee Mahas saw the Spaniards first, for they lived west of the Otos, who hunted south of the lower Platte. Captain Serna's servant was not permitted to return to the Spaniards because he would have told them that the strangers were not members of his nation. The hunters were probably Otos who summoned all the Pawnees within reach for help in order not to face the Spaniards alone. If in the battle volleys of gunfire were directed at the Spaniards, making them believe that they were being attacked by Frenchmen, that would indicate the presence of Otos, who lived much closer to the French than the Pawnees, carried on regular trade with them, and had obtained a rather large number of guns.

The most reliable information about the disaster was that given by Spaniards who had had a part in it and made their escape. On July 1, 1726, Yldefonso Rael de Aguilar made his statement in Santa Fe before Brigadier and Inspector General Pedro de Rivera.[36] The next day Felipe Tamariz made his report,[37] which was followed on July 5, 1726, by that of Antonio Valverde Cosio, governor of the province who in the meantime either had been dismissed or had not been reappointed.[38] On October 8, 1720, Valverde had sent a lengthy report about the fiasco to Viceroy Valero.[39] His messenger had been Tamariz, who had seemed to him to be the most trustworthy servant. On November 15, 1720, Tamariz had declared before the secretary of the Council of War in Mexico that he, a sergeant, had kept a diary which had been lost in the battle on August 13. On order of the authorities he rewrote it,[40] but that copy has also been lost.

In Mexico, Tamariz met Valverde's enemy, the former Governor of New Mexico, Captain Felix Martínez, who on November 13, 1720, had testified before the police magistrate and inspector-general of the army at the Royal Audiencia concerning political conditions in New Mexico.[41] After Martínez talked with Tamariz and received letters from the province, he wrote to the viceroy, making severe accusations against Valverde and a devastating criticism of Villasur's bungling leadership.[42] The details about the event can only have come from eyewitnesses; and perhaps the only one to whom Martínez spoke directly was Tamariz, who must have passed over in silence a number of points in his testimony before the author-

[36] "Testimony of Aguilar, Santa Fé, July 1, 1726," Thomas, *After Coronado*, 226–28.

[37] "Testimony of Tamariz, Santa Fé, July 2, 1726," *ibid.*, 228–30.

[38] "Confession of Valverde, Santa Fé, July 5, 1726," *ibid.*, 230–34.

[39] "Valverde to Valero, Santa Fé, October 8, 1720," *ibid.*, 162–67.

[40] "Declaration of Tamariz, México, November 15, 1720," *ibid.*, 174–75.

[41] "Declaration of Martínez, México, November 13, 1720," *ibid.*, 170–72.

[42] "Martínez to Valero [México, 1720]," *ibid.*, 177–87.

ities, in spite of being under oath, in order to avoid unpleasantness for himself.

When all these reports are studied together, the following information emerges. The servant of De la Serna, the Pawnee slave François Sistaca,[43] went across the river to talk to the Indians. It is odd that he decided to do so, since only the evening before he had fled from them in terror when they advanced toward him. It is not impossible that he made a secret agreement with them to deliver the Spaniards into their hands.

The large settlement of Pawnees on an island in the midst of the river mentioned earlier could scarcely have been a permanent earth-lodge village, because such strange buildings would surely have been mentioned by the Spanish witnesses. Opposite the western point of this island, Skull Creek flows from the southwest into the Platte. About 1800 approximately five and a half miles upstream was a Grand Pawnee village, parts of which, according to Wedel, may have belonged to a much earlier period.[44] The discovery of native artifacts indicate the existence of a Pawnee village between 1600 and 1700 twelve and a half miles west-northwest of the island, less than two miles north of the town of Schuyler on the foremost spur of the hill that separates the valley of the Platte and Shell Creek. Probably it was from this village that the inhabitants fled to the island, since it offered better protection of the river's swift current at that point. Moreover, a camp there might divert the attention of the strangers from their village, which had not yet been discovered by the Spaniards.

Sistaca was to distribute some knives and tobacco among the chiefs and take the opportunity to spy out the camp and ascertain the attitude of the inhabitants. He swam across but did not return. In his stead came at least one Indian (according to Valverde and Tamariz, several Indians) carrying a white flag on a stick. The

[43] Perhaps from the Pawnee words *Chais (Chaui)*, which means "man" or "Pawnee," and *taka*, which means "white"—thus white man or white Pawnee, which would indicate that Sistaca had been taken from the Chaui Pawnees who were living still farther south at that time.

[44] Waldo R. Wedel, *An Introduction to Pawnee Archaeology*, Bureau of American Ethnology *Bulletin No. 112* (Washington, 1925), 30 n. 55.

Spaniards could not understand what the Indians were saying. Valverde was sure only that they wanted to find out how many Spaniards there were in the party. The Spaniards took the flag from the emissary and gave him another one of white material with a letter in French which Villasur had his interpreter l'Archévèque write to the French leader whom he supposed to be with the Pawnees.

The next day another Indian appeared with a different flag of ragged linen and demanded that they exchange it for the one the Indian had brought the previous day. He also gave the commander a yellowed piece of paper (as answer?) on which something was written that no one could read. According to Martínez, this act showed "not only the bad intentions and contempt with which they regarded us, but that all was a piece of cunning to take the measure of the command and to attack it when they could not resist them."[45]

But Villasur gave the emissary another letter, this one written in Spanish, and in addition ink, paper, and a quill, because he thought the Frenchmen whom he believed to be with the Indians might lack writing materials. According to Valverde's statement they waited two days for an answer, but then were afraid that the Indians planned treachery—the correct conclusion, as it turned out.

Aguilar reported that Sistaca appeared on the far bank of the river in the midst of other Indians. The Spaniards called to him asking him why he did not return, whether there were any "Spaniards" in camp (meaning white men—in this case Frenchmen), and what was to be expected from the Indians. Sistaca answered that the Indians were well intentioned but that he did not know whether there were any "Spaniards" among them and that they would not permit him to return.[46] The water must have been very low, exposing broad strips of the banks; otherwise, they would not have been able to hear each other across the river, for at its narrowest point the river bed is nearly two thousand feet wide.

One important circumstance is not mentioned in any of the extant reports, as though none of the Spaniards had been concerned about it. The East Apaches who accompanied the expedition were

[45] "Martínez to Valero [México, 1720]," Thomas, *After Coronado*, 184.

[46] "Testimony of Aguilar, Santa Fé, July 1, 1726," *ibid.*, 227.

the enemies of the Pawnees and the Kansas, had been driven from their homeland by them, and had threatened to return with the Spaniards, who would avenge them. This hostility toward the Apaches, (here called Padoucas), on the one hand, and the alliance of the Spaniards with them, on the other hand, were ample reasons for the distrust of the eastern tribes and for their attempt to put off the Spaniards until they had called up sufficient reinforcements and circumstances were favorable to overwhelm the strangers or at least to get rid of them. The fact that the Spaniards either ignored or discounted the enmity among the tribes lends weight to subsequent criticism of Valverde and Villasur.

The Indians' delaying tactics finally impelled Villasur to convene a council of war attended by the most experienced men on the expedition—probably the same one listed in the diary. Villasur proposed crossing the river to survey the situation personally and to obtain information about the Frenchmen, but the council advised against it, pointing out to him the recklessness of such an undertaking and the dangers to which they would be exposed on the other side of the river. Moreover, the high waters would make the crossing dangerous. Later the Spaniards found a fording place and then made preparations to cross the river. The Pawnees surprised three Indians[47] belonging to the expedition who had swum across the river to bathe. The Pawnees seized one of them and led him away, while the two quicker ones escaped. This event proved the evil intentions of the Pawnees, and the council was reconvened. This time the members decided to turn back and give up the undertaking, because there seemed little hope of success and the Pawnees had clearly revealed their ill will.

The next day, August 12, the entire expedition moved without stopping nearly thirty miles up the Platte and, from the fork, up the Loup, which they had crossed four days earlier. They now crossed to the south bank of the river, where they halted at four o'clock in the afternoon, probably just west of the modern town of Columbus, or slightly south of it, nearer the confluence. According to Martínez:

47 "Testimony of Tamariz, Santa Fé, July 2, 1726," *ibid.*, 229.

> The master of the camp, Tomás Olguín, recommended that, since the retreat had begun, he should continue it, because the enemy was near and the spot in which he had ordered camp made was not fit to resist the enemy. Villasur replied to him that was fear and that there they were going to stop. He answered that he had never known fear and spoke only what appeared wise to him. Notwithstanding, the chief maintained his opinion, encamping in very thick grass higher than the stature of a man. From there he sent the horses to pasture, leaving the men on foot and without the least kind of sentinel for the enemy, who went to bed to sleep with as much insouciance as if they were in their homes.[48]

Valverde, however, insisted that Villasur had posted guards and had taken every precaution for the safety of the camp before he retired to his tent and had, moreover, given orders that he was to be informed about any suspicious events.

Shortly after nightfall several of Aguilar's comrades heard a dog barking and the noises of people crossing the river. According to Aguilar, the commander was informed about it, and he gave orders to alert the horse guards and sent out some Indians to find out what was going on along the river. They seem to have learned nothing, for they declared that all was quiet. Valverde, on the other hand, asserted that the report about the approach of the enemy had been made to the quartermaster, Olguín, by a corporal and that Olguín had considered the report fictitious and evidence of cowardice on the part of the head of the squad, for he did not report it to Villasur, who, Valverde insisted, would have done something to avert the disaster.[49]

This assertion need not be taken too seriously. Valverde, whom the authorities in Mexico City had expected to lead the expedition, had no choice but to defend his subordinate. In his report of October 8, 1720, Valverde gives details about what happened the next morn-

48 "Martínez to Valero [México, 1720]," ibid., 184. In Martínez' view every mistake made by Villasur reflected upon Valverde.

49 "Valverde to Rivera [Santa Fé, 1726]," *ibid.*, 223; Charles Wilson Hackett, *Pichardo's Treatise on the Limits of Louisiana and Texas* (Austin, 1931, 1934), I, II. The latter mentions (pp. 208–10) that Valverde named nine witnesses who testified in his favor, but their statements have never come to light.

ing, August 14, details which he probably learned from the survivors.

It can never be known whether the Indians who had followed the Spaniards from the Platte were the only ones who attacked them. There was a Pawnee village less than twenty miles west of the Spanish camp (four miles southwest of the present town of Genoa and one mile north of the Loup River) on a high mesa with an excellent view of the Loup Valley. The inhabitants could have been summoned from the village or nearby hunting grounds as reinforcements. Indeed, from their vantage point they might have been the first to catch sight of the Spaniards.[50]

At daybreak on August 13, Villasur ordered the horses brought to the camp and the animals used to catch them unsaddled. The Spaniards were again full of confidence, for the sun was rising and the time at which the Indians customarily attacked from ambush, shortly before actual dawn, had passed.

But now Sistaca was with his fellow countrymen, and Sistaca was well acquainted with the customs of the Spaniards and knew when they were most vulnerable to attack. The men in camp were busily packing utensils, dishes, and sleeping gear and tying baggage when a volley of musket fire crashed among them accompanied by a hail of arrows. (Valverde reported that two hundred Frenchmen had fired, supported by a countless number of Pawnee allies,[51] but Tamariz declared later that he did not know who the attackers were,[52] which must be interpreted as an admission that there were few if any whites among the attackers.) The attack took place at the very moment when the horse guards dismounted to saddle the rid-

[50] Although no systematic excavations have been made in this village, discoveries have been made of pieces of pottery, broken and discarded stone implements, worn-out bone awls and hoes, ornaments, scrapers, very beautiful arrowheads, and four-edged flint knives. However, no skeletons of horses have been found. Wedel claimed that this village was historically and ethnically related to the one at Schuyler, as indicated by the pottery found at both sites, and therefore might have been inhabited about 1720, though according to an aged chief, it was abandoned by 1770. (Wedel, *An Introduction to Pawnee Archaeology*, 40 n. 99.)

[51] "Valverde to Valero, Santa Fé, October 8, 1720," Thomas, *After Coronado*, 165.

[52] Declaration of Tamariz, Santa Fé, April 22, 1724," *ibid.*, 251.

ing horses. The gunfire and the shouts of the attackers threw the riding horses into a stampede. The Spaniards had no time to fire a shot and scarcely time to draw a knife. From the smoke and dust could be heard the voices of a few Spaniards who were surrounded, whereupon a corporal of the guards, who had mounted their horses again, led three riders through the ring of enemies, thus permitting seven of the surrounded men to break through, two of them badly wounded by bullets and arrows. One was Aguilar, who had nine serious wounds and had lost his braid to a brave. The corporal and one of his fellow riders paid with their lives for their courage in opening the gap.

Tamariz helped the guards catch some of the stampeding horses, although they could scarcely see for the clouds of smoke and dust. Moments later they were attacked by a large force whom they beat back three times. The number of attackers grew so rapidly that the guards had time to free only three badly wounded comrades who had been able to break out of the camp. Then, with the Indian allies who had all but alone held off the enemy, they withdrew and led the remnant of the horse herd to safety.

Left dead or dying in the tall grass were the chaplain, Father Juan Mínguez; the Commander in chief, Pedro de Villasur; Adjutant General José Domínguez; Master of the Camp Tomás Olguín; Captain Cristóbal de la Serna, Captain Miguel Tenorio, Captain Pedro Luxán, Lieutenant of the Presidio Bernardo Casillas; Corporal José Griego; Corporal Lorenzo Rodríguez; Manuel de Silva; Pedro Segura; Lorenzo Segura; Juan de l'Archévèque; Diego Velásquez; Ignacio de Aviles; José Fernandez; Simón de Córdova; Francisco Gonzales; Francisco de Tapia; Francisco Perea; Bernardo Madrid; Pedro de Agüero; Nicholas Girón; Domingo Romero; Luís Ortis; Juan Gallegas; Ramón de Medina; Antonio de Herrera; Domingo Trujillo; Juan Río de Rojas; Pedro Lugo; José Naranjo; Juan de Lira; Pedro de Mendizábal; and eleven Indian allies,[53] most of them probably from Pecos, Taos, and other pueblos, as in other expeditions.

53 "Martínez to Valero [México, 1720]," *ibid.*, 186; Hackett, *Pichardo's Treatise*, I, 199.

Of the thirty-five dead mentioned by name, the following had participated in Hurtado's expedition against the Faraon Apaches in 1715: Domínguez, Silva, Casillas, Griego, Rodríguez, Córdova, Trujillo, Ortis, Herrera, L'Archévèque, and Naranjo.[54] Rojas, Lugo, Lira, and Mendizábal were probably Valverde's four servants, who have already been mentioned.[55]

Commander Yldefonso Rael de Aguilar, a settler, escaped from the ambush. Aguilar listed as other survivors Corporal Felipe Tamariz, and the following soldiers: Manuel Teniente de Alva, Matheas Madrid, Joseph Mares, Joachín Sánchez, Jacinto Perea, Juan Antonio Barrios, Antonio de Armenta, José de Santiesteban, Melchior Rodríguez, and Diego Tafoya.[56] In addition to the twelve Spanish survivors were forty-nine of the sixty Pueblos. In his list of survivors Aguilar omitted Lieutenant Francisco Montes Vigil and Diego Arias de Quiros, who testified at Santa Fe as participants in the expedition who had escaped. Thus a total of sixty-three men survived.

Valverde wrote to Viceroy Valero:

> Although the enemy had the victory and all the supplies and provisions of war, they did not get out very cheaply because, according to what I am told, some of them died with their chief, so the escaped ones affirm. These on their return had the good fortune of finding refuge among the Indians of the Apache tribe [in El Cuartelejo] who came out to meet them with great tenderness, giving signs of much sympathy on account of the misfortune of those who were left dead. It must be wondered at that they, being heathen and seeing our men so weakened in health and strength, did not attempt to take away the horses they had with them; otherwise, more than those who perished in the encounter would have been lost. They not only did not do this, but kept them in their company with much kindness for two days, supporting and succoring them with their poor provisions. Their excellent conduct did not stop there, but they all offered to take revenge, manifesting a great de-

54 "Hurtado's Review of Forces and Equipment, Picuríes Pueblo," Thomas, *After Coronado*, 90–93.

55 "Valverde to Valero, Santa Fé, October 8, 1720," *ibid.*, 165.

56 "Testimony of Aguilar, Santa Fé, July 1, 1726," *ibid.*, 228.

sire that the Spaniards return to those frontiers in order that, allied together, they could make war effectively on the French and Pawnees.[57]

The survivors were back in Santa Fe by September 6, only twenty-four days later (including the days of rest spent with the Apaches)—actually a little less time than that taken on the march eastward, which had lasted from the middle of June until August 10.

Martínez could not restrain himself from giving his opinion:

> . . . it is the saddest, the most lamentable, and the most fatal event that has happened in New Mexico since the time of its conquest. . . . in the villa of Santa Fe, thirty-two widows and many orphaned children, whose tears reach the sky, mourn the poor ability of the governor; pray God for his punishment, and await the remedy of your justice.[58]

The province had actually lost a third of its best-trained and most experienced soldiers. In the letter which he gave Tamariz to take to Mexico, Valverde asked for thirty to forty soldiers to replace them.

So much for the reconstruction of the known events of the Villasur massacre. Now to a comparison with the scene shown on Segesser II.

The ground is bare; the tall grass described in Martínez' account could not be drawn in, for it would have hidden the human figures, and the painting is first and foremost a presentation of human beings engaged in mortal combat. To compensate, the artist filled the few gaps—mainly near the edges of the painting and between the horse guards and the battlefield—with shrubs which, geographically out of place, were borrowed from the artist's homeland.

In the left third of the picture are two rivers meeting just above the center of the painting, flowing to the left. According to the Spanish documents, the viewer is looking from north to south,

[57] "Valverde to Valero, Santa Fé, October 8, 1720," *ibid.*, 165–66.

[58] "Martínez to Valero [México, 1720]," *ibid.*, 184–85.

the lower edge of the picture being north. The lower river, the closer to the viewer, is taken to be the Loup and the one farther away, for the Platte. The tongue of land formed by the two is wooded, as indicated by a row of tree trunks, which are omitted on the north side of the peninsula (the lower side of the picture), so that the view of the figures is not obstructed. As late as 1923, a photograph of this region[59] shows a stand of trees along the bank up to the confluence of the two rivers, which explains Tamariz' remark in his diary that the river could not be crossed at this point.[60]

The trees shown in Segesser II might logically be considered part of the backdrop, especially since they do not appear to represent any specific botanical species. The most common species along the rivers and creeks of the western plains was the cottonwood tree, which grew to a large size in its native state. In the absence of evidence to the contrary, it seems reasonable to assume that it was this tree which the painter was depicting.

The rivers shown in the painting are narrow, to take up no more space than necessary. The river closer to the viewer is so deep that the two Indian attackers wading through it must hold their weapons and packs above their heads to keep them dry. However, the battle must have taken place about six miles upstream, in a plain about three to four miles wide, not far from the ford. In the painting the junction thus has pictorial rather than specific geographical significance.

A little to the right of the center of the picture is the Spaniards' camp, bordered from the northwest to the northeast corners by two conical tents, one with a saddle roof, and by another conical tipi, and on the east and on the south sides, by what appear to be saddles and saddlebags. In the southwest corner stands an Indian tipi (possibly the lodging of Naranjo, who held the rank of "captain-major of

[59] *Nebraska History*, Vol. VI (1923), 16.

[60] In 1823 Paul Wilhelm, Duke of Wuerttemberg, found it impossible to cross the Platte below the junction of the Loup and the Platte: it was so deep and swift at this point that the members of the party had to move upstream a few miles near a large island, where they found a place to ford. (*Erste Reise nach dem Noerdlichen Amerika in den Jahren 1822 bis 1824*, 369.)

war."[61] Its shape and construction show it to be a Plains Apache tipi, like those shown in Segesser I. Toward the west the camp is open.

In Segesser II the attackers are shown hurrying up from the left after having waded through the river (Loup) in the foreground. They have already encircled the Spaniards. A few more attackers are running up from the right. This advance is fiction; the painter took liberties in his presentation, either for artistic reasons or because it would have been shameful to show that the Spaniards had been surrounded long before the attack was launched. Actually, the encirclement probably began soon after midnight. The first volley must also have come off so well that the Spaniards believed that it was fired by regular troops. They were not accustomed to facing an enemy of equal rank, or one better armed than they, and they lost their heads.

If the painter took part in the engagement, then he exaggerates when he shows French soldiers penetrating the interior of the camp advancing to the very muzzles of the Spanish guns. This would appear to be proof of French participation, if it were not known that they had nothing to do with the massacre. The details of the soldiers wearing conical hats would also appear to be convincing. One of them, wounded or killed, is shown being dragged from the firing line by a wrist by an Indian ally. Another lies on his back under the hoofs of the horse of a guard who is counterattacking. The two hats, which were drawn very carefully, must be early grenadier hats, which were originally made of wool and cloth and later of sheet metal. But what the painter knew about the French he did not learn from the Villasur massacre—perhaps he had studied pictures of them. Of the red attackers he probably saw only the few who visited the Spanish camp between the tenth and thirteenth of August. He may have seen Pawnee prisoners brought to Santa Fe by Apaches. Those whom he unquestionably knew were the Spaniards, whose faces in Segesser II impress one as being portraits in miniature.

On the east side of the scene a round-leaved bush indicates a

61 "Valverde to Valero, Santa Fé, October 8, 1720," Thomas, *After Coronado*, 165.

possible place where the attackers might have taken cover. In front of the bush are two riders being dragged from their horses and slain with arrow and tomahawk. This scene reminds one of Valverde's mention of the brave corporal of the cavalry who with three others broke through the circle of attackers to free those still alive among the encircled men, and lost his life doing so.

There seems to be no doubt that Figure 138 is the commanding officer, Lieutenant-General Pedro de Villasur, who is lying just below the dead horse, visible above the upper edge of the saddle-roofed tent. He can be identified by the gold-and-silver decorations across his tunic. He, too, is dead; to indicate his importance, the upper part of his body has been raised and his head supported by something resembling a footstool. Before him, armed with shield and carbine, as though protecting the corpse, is his adjutant, José Domínguez (Figure 139). It cannot be anybody else, for the lower left corner of his uniform coat has decorations similar to Villasur's. Domínguez, who went to war against the Apaches in 1715 as Hurtado's adjutant, died here, after thirty-eight years in the service of his king. At one point in the Spanish documents it is mentioned that Villasur's personal attendant was killed with his master in front of his tent at the beginning of the attack; he must be the soldier (Figure 140) lying on his face underneath the horse, at Villasur's feet.

In the painting a special position is occupied by the Indian rider with the spear, standing stiffly in his big Mexican stirrups as he races to the camp (at the upper edge of the painting, above the line of enemy skirmishers). No other Indian rider is shown with iron stirrups. Can this be a memorial to Naranjo, the senior Indian scout?

The well-known trader L'Archévèque must also be shown in the picture. Between the square defended by the Spaniards and the head of the dead horse, near Villasur, is a prominent figure who seems to be an elderly, experienced fighter. To identify him as L'Archévèque is an assumption, but one that is not without reason, for, to judge by his equipment, he appears to be the best-equipped participant in the expedition.

It might be more rewarding to attempt to identify the corporal with the spontoon (Figure 165), breaking through in front of the horse guards and followed by a mounted Pueblo Indian. Valverde is the only one who mentions the "fearless corporal of the cavalry" who paid with his life for his brave deed of liberation. If Valverde is to be believed, then two corporals were ordered to bring in the horses, for Tamariz declares that on the fatal day he was in charge of a group of horse guards whom he helped to recapture the stampeding horses and that the guards were attacked and three times drove the attackers back, having just enough time to help three of their comrades who had fled from the camp to mount their horses before being forced to retreat, which they only succeeded in doing because the attackers were on foot. These two riders at the upper right of the picture are probably the nameless corporal and an Indian companion, chasing their enemies ahead of them and galloping over a (fictional) fallen French grenadier to enable several Spaniards to escape. The corporal may have been José Griego or Lorenzo Rodríguez, both of whom were former members of Hurtado's army. He might also be the other main witness, Valverde's trusted messenger, Felipe Tamariz. He is the only one in the picture who carries a three-pointed spontoon, as a sign of rank, for it was the typical weapon of corporals of the period.

Figure 142, the Spaniard lying on his back beside the dark tent and beset by three attackers could be the severely wounded Yldefonso Rael de Aguilar, who survived the massacre.

There can be no question about the identity of the priest hastening toward the camp. This is Father Juan Mínguez, who is shown in the painting in an especially prominent place outside the camp, although he was surely in the camp, where he died.[62] Father Mínguez, a Franciscan, had had a long service in New Mexico. In 1705 he was stationed in Santa Fe; in 1706, in Zuñi; and later, in the missions of Nambé, Santa Cruz, and Santa Clara.

The Indian walking in front of the priest is armed with bow and spear and carries two quivers filled with arrows. Obviously he

[62] Dumont de Montigny's assertion that Father Mínguez was spared by the Indians because of his strange habit (*Mémoires historiques sur la Louisiane* [Paris, 1753], II, 287), is most unlikely, since the priest was never heard of again.

is the priest's escort. This man is very carefully drawn and set apart. The calm with which he opens the way for the priest, although surrounded by attackers, indicates that he probably represents a specific person. Besides Naranjo, whom we presume to be the rider with the heavy spurs, no other Indian is listed by name. It is possible that the painter created a memorial for himself in this self-portrait.

At the right side of the painting are seen the horse guards, who have surrounded the herd of horses. Four of the men are Spaniards; four are Indians. A fifth Indian has turned away from the battle to try to stop the stampeding animals. The distance between the horse herd and the battle must be greater than the picture shows.

Manuel Teniente de Alva, a survivor, reported that the Spaniards' stock of trading goods was not opened until they reached the Carlana Apaches, among whom they distributed some of the goods in exchange for guides across the plains. De Alva was in a position to know, for he was in a sense "manager of the stores."[63] Only the Indian pursuing the herd of horses and one of the horse guards in front wear long braids hanging down their backs. All the other "Spanish" Indians wear their hair in knots, probably with the ends turned in. When one examines the figures closely, it appears that the Indian with the braid is the only Indian guard equipped with the leather coat worn by the soldiers in northern Mexico. Only a distinguished warrior would be honored in such fashion by the Spaniards. His braid indicates that he was not a Pueblo; he could be the Apache Chief Carlana himself, who had guided Valverde against the Comanches in 1719. He was among those who escaped the Villasur massacre, for Governor Bustamante visited him in November, 1724, in his territory.[64] He is not mentioned in the extant pages of Tamariz' diary, but his presence must be assumed, and it is likely that he was among the horse guards, because they were among the survivors.

These identifications are, of course, tentative; only Mínguez and Villasur can be identified with certainty.

[63] "Declaration of Alva, Santa Fé, April 23, 1724," Thomas, *After Coronado*, 254–55.

[64] "Diary of Governor Bustamante, November 17–27, 1724," *ibid.*, 197.

The thirty-seven Frenchmen shown in Segesser II are pure fiction. Martinez seems to have been the only Spaniard who realized that no French soldiers participated in the massacre. On November 13, 1720, he testified before the auditor general in Mexico: "If [the attackers] had been French, they would not have killed so many, but would have managed to make them prisoners and taken the horses which they lacked."[65] A note by the editor states that it was a bad inference, for the French would have killed everybody as they themselves would surely have been killed and therefore had come secretly, hiding themselves as much as they could from the Spaniards. Tamariz himself had to admit that he did not know who had attacked the expedition; yet he, being mounted, had probably had the best view of the action. But he knew that the French were to be blamed and therefore he could not flatly deny their presence.

In Segesser II thirty-seven riflemen are shown attacking the Spaniards, but it seems certain that there were not that many present, since the Pawnees had no guns at that time and the Otos had only a few and surely not new ones. But the Spanish settlers had obsolete models of small gauge; it was therefore a subtle reproach to the Spanish authorities to depict the attackers equipped with formidable guns.

If hundreds of close-cropped Indians had taken part in the battle, then one would have to multiply correspondingly the two dozen swords and three dozen tomahawks in the painting, every fourth man then brandishing a sword and every third one a tomahawk—all this in a region that is more than 600 miles by river removed from the nearest small French post, which itself is hundreds of miles from the settlements. The large number of weapons shown in the picture would illustrate in Mexico how much better off the friends of the French were.

How little the survivors saw of their attackers is indicated by the details of the attackers' headbands, shown with the ends hanging down. Such headbands were never reported among the Pawnees in later accounts and pictures. They were probably so depicted by the painter, who mistook wampum strings hanging down from the up-

65 "Declaration of Martínez, México, November 13, 1720," *ibid.*, 171–72.

per part of the ear as the ends of the headbands. The Pawnees, Otos, and neighboring tribes wore such strings throughout the nineteenth century, as shown in contemporary illustrations. Their close-cropped heads were more carefully presented, although the tribes left a small section of hair uncropped, which the painter evidently did not see or was unable to reproduce. It is true that these Indians fought naked except for moccasins. There are two or three travelers who report that the Pawnees were naked in summer. Murray, who visited them in 1835, says that most of them were naked except for belt and breechcloth;[66] Lieutenant Wilkinson, a member of Pike's expedition to New Mexico in 1806, made the same assertion and mentioned in addition white, yellow, and black body painting.[67] On September 24, 1806, Pike made specific mention in his diary of the Pawnees who arrived in the evening after sunset in the camp of the soldiers and brought buffalo meat: "Only a few had breechclouts; most of them were wrapped in buffalo robes but were otherwise completely naked."[68]

The booty taken from the Spaniards' camp after the massacre was scattered far and wide. Yet two hundred years later a good many objects were found in the region surrounding the battle. Not far from the point where Looking Glass Creek flows into the Loup, near the present town of Monroe, are the ruins of a Pawnee village. There, about 1914, about a mile north of the Loup, were excavated many small brass disks similar to those used in 1720 in Spanish armor. In 1904 near Monroe old Spanish coins were found in a hole dug for a post for a house. About 1890 a French settler found parts of a bridle and the crest of a helmet said to be of Spanish origin below the prairie island opposite Clarks, near the old Chaui village. At Genoa, the seat of the agency of the later Pawnee Maha reservation, were found a brass chain of Spanish workmanship and three small brass plates like those described above.[69] The discovery of these items, which Blackman suspected of having belonged to mem-

66 Charles A. Murray, *Travels in North America* (London, 1839), I, 255.

67 *Nebraska History Magazine*, Vol. X, No. 3 (1927), 172, 176, 247.

68 *Ibid.*

69 *Nebraska History*, Vol. VII, No. 3 (1924), 95.

bers of the Spanish expedition, convinced him that the massacre had taken place near this village, on Looking Glass Creek, which for other reasons seems unlikely.

That the massacre occurred near the Loup and the Platte seems proved by the report of a white man who had married a Pawnee woman and had learned from her that the girls of her village, near Genoa, always found bullets when they went swimming and diving in the river. The woman had also heard that shields, knives, and swords had been found in the area in earlier times. From time to time schoolboys from Genoa found guns, armor, and shot pouches, which they traded for tobacco at a drugstore in the little town.[70]

Some of the booty was scattered much farther soon after the event, if one gives credence to a story that the priest was spared. Dumont mentions Missouri Indians, who can only be Otos. It should be mentioned that the Missouris lived nearer the French posts and claimed, as bearers of the news, all the glory for the massacre for themselves, although they played little, if any, part in the affair, and at most provided only a few riflemen.

According to Dumont's report, the Spaniards camped in the village of the Missouris, who claimed to be Osages because the Spaniards disclosed to them that they intended to destroy the Missouris and then found a Spanish settlement in their land. Why they invented such a fantastic story can never be known.

Here is Dumont's account of the battle:

> At dawn the savages, who were divided into several bands, fell upon the Spaniards, who were taken unawares, and in less than a quarter of an hour the whole force was killed. Nobody escaped the slaughter except the priest, whom these barbarians spared on account of his strange habit. At the same time they seized all goods and objects of value in the camp.
>
> The Spaniards had taken along some horses, as mentioned earlier, but because the savages did not know their use, they amused themselves with having this Jacobin, whom they kept and made their slave, mount one of the horses. The priest provided them with this amusement almost daily for the five or six months he remained

[70] *Ibid.*, 96.

in their village without any of them venturing to try it, too. Becoming tired of his slavery, [the priest] considered the lack of daring among these savages as a chance offered to him by Providence to recover his freedom. In secret he collected as many provisions as possible and as seemed necessary for his plan. Then he selected the best horse, mounted it, and after he had made a few rounds on the track before the savages, who were completely absorbed by his manoeuvers, he gave his horse both spurs and disappeared from their eyes in the direction of Mexico, which, no doubt, he reached.

Some time later, a band of the very same Missouris went to the Illinois to offer the calumet to the French general who commanded this post. He was Sieur [Dugué] de Boisbriant, who was not a little surprised at the visit these savages paid him, to see some of them clad in vestments, others with surplices, and one who had a paten hung around his neck or a chalice in his hand. After he had them explain to him their strange attire, he bought the sacerdotal vestments and the sacred vessels which these barbarians were desecrating. He also obtained from them [a map] which they had found among the Spaniards' baggage. He at once sent it to the general in command of the country [Bienville] with all the details of this adventure. He was the one through whom we have the details I have just described.[71]

Le Page du Pratz repeats the story about the priest, adding some exaggerations and embellishments of his own.[72] He mentions particularly the chalice and the crucifix which the chaplain is shown holding in his hands, but it is unlikely that he had reliable information about such details.

Other accounts are even less believable. The Jesuit priest Charlevoix mentions two chaplains, "one of whom was killed right away, the other being able to escape to the Missouris" (in which case, of course, this tribe could not have taken part in the fight). Since there was only one priest, Mínguez, with the expedition, this report has all the earmarks of idle rumor.

According to a letter from Boisbriant dated November 22, 1720, the Otos had captured Father Mínguez and had promised to bring

[71] Dumont de Montigny, *Mémoires historiques sur la Louisiane*, II, 287–89.
[72] Le Page du Pratz, *Histoire de la Louisiane* (1758), II, 245–51.

him to the commander but had had to turn back to Kaskaskias to defend their village from a reported attack. This report, too, can be dismissed as fabrication.

Some of the captured items were scattered even farther from the site of battle. Father Charlevoix wrote in a letter dated July 21, 1721, from the fort at Michilimackinac on the strait between Lake Michigan and Lake Huron:

> The other day the chiefs of the two nations [Sakis, or Sauks, and Otchagras, or Winnebagos] offered me a Catalonian pistol, a pair of Spanish shoes, and a drug, which seemed to me to be a salve of some sort, all of which had been obtained from an Aiouez [Iowa]. . . .
>
> About two years ago, it is said, Spaniards came from New Mexico with the intention of penetrating as far as the Illinois to drive out the French, whose advance to the Missouri had filled them with the utmost alarm.

Then Father Charlevoix gives his version of the massacre, according to which the Spaniards had slaughtered the inhabitants of two villages of Octatatas (Otos), after which the inhabitants of a third Oto village, informed about the slaughter, had lured them into an ambush or, while they were in a drunken sleep, had attacked and killed them. After repeating the tale of the second chaplain, Charlevoix states (quite correctly) that the savages only wanted to curry favor with the French through these rumors

> by spreading the report that they had performed a great service for us with the defeat of the Spanish: Everything that they brought me came from the booty of the priest who had been killed. They had also found a prayer book on his person, which I did not see; it was no doubt his breviary. I bought the pistol; the shoes were not worth anything, and the savage did not want to part with the salve since he was convinced it was a panacea for every evil.

This is quite clearly the author's personal experience, and must be accepted as a fact. But he also mentions an additional dispersion of the booty, this time in the opposite direction to an even greater distance, to Biloxi, east of the mouth of the Mississippi on the Gulf of Mexico. He writes in his letter from Cap François on September 6, 1722:

> At the end of the month an inhabitant of Illinois arrived in Biloxi who had undertaken a business trip to the Missouri. He reported that he and one or two other Frenchmen had gone as far as to the Otos who, as I wrote you, had annihilated the Spaniards in 1719. They were well received and realized for the goods which they had brought to them seven or eight hundred silver francs, part of the money in coins and part in silver bars. A few of these savages accompanied them as far as Illinois and assured M. de Boisbriant that the Spaniards, from whom they had taken this silver, had taken it from a mine which was not far from the place where they had met them, and offered to lead the Frenchmen there, an offer the commandant accepted. Only time will show whether these savages spoke more honestly than so many others who have tried for so long to draw the French to them through the allurement of mines of which as yet not one has been found. As a footnote he added: One has never heard speak of this mine ever since.[73]

This letter seems to prove that it was Otos who destroyed the Spaniards and that no Frenchmen took part in the massacre (although the Mexican authorities refused to believe it as late as 1727); otherwise, they would have taken the silver themselves. The francs were, no doubt, Spanish coins. As for the bars of silver, the rumor about them was probably circulated to persuade bankers in Paris to put up money for the operation of American mines. France was seized by a frenzy for easy money, a frenzy which ended in a great financial crash. Either the letter quoted above or the rumor about the bars of silver became known in Mexico, where it came to be believed that the Spaniards, rather than mining the silver on the way, had taken the bars from Santa Fe to carry on illicit trade with the French.

In April, 1724, Bustamante, the new governor of New Mexico, carried out an investigation of the rumor because it had been asserted that the inhabitants of New Mexico had bought goods from the

[73] Pierre de Charlevoix, *Journal d'un Voyage, fait par ordre du Roi dans l'Amérique Septentrionale* (Paris, 1744), III, 293–94.

Frenchmen of the Louisiana colony for twelve thousand pesos. This great crime had to be punished severely, and at the same time an investigation had to be made to determine whether Villasur had taken along silver and money on his own initiative or by order of Valverde to carry on trade with the French. Of the ten declarations made under oath, five were made by distinguished colonists, and five by survivors of the expedition. All declared that Villasur had not taken along any silver, but only some dishes for his personal use. The only French goods to be found in the province were merely the guns of buffalo-hunting tribes who appeared occasionally for peaceful barter and who had captured these weapons from the Pawnees. Nothing had been traded with the French. They did not see them, nor did they know where they lived. Every year they came to the royal stores in Chihuahua and Parral to buy clothes and other necessary supplies.[74]

If what the French traders in Biloxi reported about the Otos is true—that a considerable amount of coined money had been found among the Indians—it casts a shadow on Villasur's character. But there could have been honorable reasons that moved him to take money on the expedition. Certainly he had no plans to carry on trade with them: the distance to their trading posts was much too great.

In 1727, Bustamante reported to Mexico City that the rumors were increasing. Among the rumors was one that six Frenchmen had joined the Cuartelejo Apaches and that five had joined the Palomas, Cuartelejos, and Carlanas in their search for the Comanches to seek revenge for their rapacious and bloody raids.[75] However, the auditor and probably the viceroy as well were no longer frightened by alarming reports from the northern border and decided that they could save the expenses of a scouting expedition, saying that there was no war as there had been in 1720 and that, as the New Mexicans declared, the French were coming only to trade with the savages for goods, muskets, and other weapons, or to help one of the tribes against another. After all, they were living mainly

[74] Thomas, *After Coronado*, 246–55.

[75] "Bustamante to Casa Fuerte, Santa Fé, April 30, 1727," *ibid.*, 257.

among the Pawnees, far from Santa Fe. In fact, the French lived far east of the Pawnees, on the Mississippi.

Since so much attention has been given here to the Villasur expedition, subsequent events should be summarized briefly. The appearance of the Spanish on the lower Platte had alarmed the French, just as the Spaniards had been alarmed by the rumors of French intrusion into their territory. Paris was wild with enthusiasm about the rumored discoveries of metals and precious stones in the Mississippi basin. In 1721, Dumont participated in an expedition to present-day Arkansas in search of a fabled rock of emerald.[76] The expedition members expected that any Pawnees they encountered would be hostile. Thus something had to be done to assure the good will of the tribes along the Missouri, where they suspected the rich mines to be, and also of the tribes who lived as far away as the northern border of Mexico.

In 1723 a colonial officer named Bourgmont, who had founded the small post on the Lower Missouri, was called upon to help win back the Padoucas (the Paloma Apaches), who were supposed to have made an agreement with the Spaniards.[77] He moved up the Missouri to a Kansa village, near the present Doniphan, Kansas. He sent French traders and Indians to the Padoucas, whereupon many Padouca chiefs and several whole groups moved close to the Missouri. A council was held in the Kansa village and the Kansa, Oto, Pawnee Maha, and Iowa tribes made peace with the Padoucas. Bourgmont then moved up the Kansas River and paid a visit at the main Padouca settlement (at present-day Salina).

He also accompanied the Kansas on a hunting expedition up the Kansas River and observed Otos hunting in the region to the north, but close enough that a few of them visited the Kansas' camp. In July and August of 1723 conditions were about the same as they had been in 1720 when Villasur appeared on the scene. The Kansas hunted on foot up the Kansas River, but not as far as the Big Blue. At that time the Kansas River was still called the Padouca River.

[76] Dumont de Montigny, *Mémoires historiques sur la Louisiane*, II, 67, 282.

[77] Bourgmont's expedition of 1723–24 is described in Margry, *Mémoires et Documents pour servir à l'histoire des origines françaises des pays d'outremer*, VI.

The Otos, who also hunted on foot, ranged west and south of their village, north of the Kansa tribe, in the region of a salt deposit and where the city of Lincoln is located today. The Pawnee Mahas hunted somewhere on the lower Platte, west or northwest of the Otos,[78] but not at the junction of the North and South Platte rivers. At that time these tribes had only a very few horses and therefore could not hunt far from their villages, regardless of the fact that it was Padouca territory which could at best be entered by war parties. It is out of the question that Pawnees or Otos moved there with an entire tent camp.

Thomas' conclusion that the Paloma Apaches lived near the fork of the North and South Platte rivers is contradicted by the Spanish documents. The Palomas were planting their grain on their rancherias in the spring of 1719, when the Jumanos and southern Pawnees came up from the Arkansas in eastern Oklahoma, attacked them with French guns, and drove them to El Cuartelejo. It is probable, but could only be proved by the lost diary, that the Palomas accompanied the Villasur expedition and also belonged to the Padoucas who were later visited by Bourgmont on the Kansas River in 1724.

Bourgmont's aim to entice the Padoucas away from the Spaniards and secure their services as guides for the French traders on their expeditions westward to New Mexico was evidently successful. A year after the negotiations, six Frenchmen appeared in El Cuartelejo with a large war party of Paloma, Cuartelejo, and Sierra Blanca Apaches to drive the Comanches out of the buffalo plains,[79] and, if possible, back into the Colorado mountains. The Palomas had dealings with Bourgmont's people in 1725 and brought them to New Mexico, as reported to the Spaniards by captured Comanches. Oddly enough, the Comanches who had been captured with the help of the French were full of praise for the newly arrived white men.

[78] It was Bourgmont who first called the Octatatas Hotos or Othos (Otos), by which name they have been known ever since.

[79] "Bustamante to Casa Fuerte, Santa Fé, April 30, 1727," Thomas, *After Coronado*, 256–58. In the letter the clothes and weapons of the French are carefully described according to the testimony of a Comanche woman who had been captured and sold to the Spaniards.

The Apaches seem to have played a suspicious role in these frontier hostilities. In 1719 they praised the Spaniards and asked them for help. In 1720 they led them eastward but ran away when the situation became dangerous. Then they cared for the Spaniards who survived the massacre and offered to go to war again as allies of the Spaniards against the French and Pawnees. But the Spaniards did not return, and nothing came of a promised military post. Even the Jicarillas were left unprotected and were forced to forsake their homeland and flee to Taos to escape the Comanches. On the other hand, the French helped the Palomas and related tribes in their efforts to obtain security from the better-armed tribes to the east. This fact became known to the Sierra Blancas and the Cuartelejos, who were defenseless against repeated attacks by Comanches from the mountainous Northwest. The Palomas brought Frenchmen to the tribes, and the whites not only offered immediate help against the Comanches but accompanied them at once on a punitive expedition.

To return once more to the Villasur expedition, the question remains unanswered why the Palomas failed to lead the Spaniards eastward into their country, between the Kansas and the Arkansas, but instead guided them northeast to the Pawnee Maha country on the lower Platte. In 1719 a small group of Frenchmen led by La Harpe and guided by the trader Du Tisné, had visited the southern Pawnees for a few days and had given them two guns in exchange. Du Tisné, starting out from the French settlement in Illinois, had crossed the territory of the Osages, who had robbed him of most of the guns he had intended to trade to the Pawnees. The Pawnees had already obtained six guns, which they treasured greatly. Finding the Pawnees very unfriendly, Du Tisné had left after a few days and returned to Illinois. This encounter took place in the fall, after the raid on the Paloma settlement. According to Du Tisné's report, the six guns were all the firearms the Pawnees and Jumanos owned. The French cities and forts among the southern Pawnees were pure invention on the part of the Apaches.

The Pawnees set out to test their new weapons on the Paloma Apaches, who were so terrified that they fled westward to faraway

El Cuartelejo. There Governor Valverde saw them, and the sight of a single Paloma with a gunshot wound was sufficient to throw the Spanish officials into a panic. Their questions confused the savages to the point that they claimed Frenchmen as well as Pawnees had attacked them.

In the twenty-four-page diary of Valverde's 1719 expedition against the Utes and Comanches it is stated that the shot had been fired by a Pawnee or Jumano.[80] Yet on November 30 of the same year Valverde wrote to Viceroy Valero that a member of the Kansa tribe had shot the Paloma with a French gun.[81]

Here may be found the solution to the question of the Villasur journey into Pawnee Maha territory. The Kansa Indians lived about seventy-five miles north of the mouth of the Kansas River, not far from the Missouri, and more east than north of the Palomas. The Palomas had also testified that the French had recently established two settlements beside a large river. Valverde must have come to the conclusion that this river was the one his scout Naranjo had named the Jesús María. The French never established a post on the Platte, of course, and not until many years later did they establish their first one on the Lower Missouri. If it was the Platte River that Naranjo saw, then it is understandable why Villasur went so far north. The Pawnee slave Sistaca must also have had a role in this matter. According to the fragment of Tamariz' diary, when they reached the Platte, Sistaca claimed to know the region and to have come from there. Thus he may have influenced the direction the expedition moved.

80 "Diary of the Campaign of Governor Antonio de Valverde Against the Ute and Comanche Indians, 1719," *ibid.*, 110-33.

81 "Valverde to Valero, Santa Fé, November 30, 1719," *ibid.*, 143.

XVI

The Indian Horsemen in the Spanish Party

A few of the sixteen Indian riders in Segesser II have definite Pueblo Indian characteristics, as exemplified by their long braids and the design of their bows and arrows. They are dressed almost exactly like their Spanish comrades-in-arms—in breeches and garters, long-sleeved shirts or jackets, and sleeveless leather knee-length armor. Among the horse guards only one figure wears this distinctive armor.

Seven of the sixteen "Spanish" Indians are mounted; of the seven, five are guarding the horses, and two are taking part in the battle. Most of the nine warriors fighting on foot are at exposed positions (which supports the assumption that the painter of Segesser II was an Indian). Of the Indians fighting on foot, only about half are wearing the sleeveless armor of their Spanish allies. In place of the Spanish breeches they wear long stockings or leggings (with or without garters), and light-colored shoes—probably soft-leather moccasins. Today the Indians in Taos and the Picuris, who live closest to the Plains, wear similar low-cut, hard-soled Plains moccasins.

It perhaps seems strange that these Indians have set up a green tipi in the Spaniards' camp, a tipi which appears to be exactly like those constructed by the Western Plains Indians, with which the painter of Segresser I was certainly familiar. Either they adopted it from the Eastern Apaches to use on the expedition, or it had been commandeered from the camp of the Cuartelejo and Paloma Apaches (the latter probably identical with the Kansas Padoucas) who accompanied the expedition and set up a camp nearby, from which they fled, however, at the first appearance of the Pawnees. But the Pueblos did not take along their clay lodges on longer hunting expeditions, but spent the nights in portable shelters like those of their eastern nomadic neighbors. There is no doubt that the Pueblos hunted buffalo at one time, as evidenced by the fact that their war shields are made of buffalo hide;[1] and they still perform buffalo dances in which the two chief performers wear buffalo heads with horns.

The buffalo dance is a most important ceremony and is supposed to guarantee a successful hunting season for any kind of game, even feathered game. It is held after the first snowfall and includes thirty-eight songs.[2] The buffaloes were at one time hunted in the Estancia Valley, and also in Colorado and Oklahoma. On these expeditions the hunters transported heavy equipment and the meat on travois,[3] exactly as did the Dakotas and the Cheyennes, who became known as first-rate buffalo-hunting nomads roaming on foot through the forests east of the Missouri. At that time, in the seventeenth century, the Río Grande Pueblos had long since begun sallying forth from their mountain valleys to hunt buffaloes which were moving east and north. Instead of dogs they had begun using donkeys and horses as beasts of burden to drag heavy loads, carried on frames made of poles, across the high plateaus and through passes and ravines.

The warriors' hair style is also Pueblo. Today both men and women still wear their hair long and wrapped with a band. There is no question that the Indian allies of the Spaniards were Pueblo. It is likely that one reason for their popularity as allies was their horsemanship. They were the first Indians north of Mexico to possess horses.

There are no extant records of Indian participants in either the Villasur or the Valverde expedition. There is, however, a record of the members of Hurtado's 1715 expedition against the Faraon Apaches. A total of 149 Pueblo Indians were assigned to Hurtado's troops. Half of them came from the Tewa settlements of San Juan,

[1] Personal information from Frances Densmore.

[2] Frances Densmore, *Music of Santo Domingo Pueblo, New Mexico* (Los Angeles, 1938), 143–66.

[3] Edward S. Curtis, *The North American Indian* (New York, 1926), XVI, 136.

Nambe, San Ildefonso, Santa Clara, Pojoaque, and Tesuque; one-third came from the Tiwa villages of Taos and Picuris; and the rest came from Pecos and thus belonged to the same linguistic group as the Tewas. Neither the Hopis in Arizona nor the Zuñis participated. Seventy-six of the Indian auxiliary contingent had guns; the weapons of the others were not mentioned.

The Pecos lived a little more than thirty miles northeast of Santa Fe on one of the upper tributaries of the Pecos River. Taos lies a little over fifty miles northeast of Santa Fe. Villasur went by way of Taos in the direction of El Cuartelejo, and it can therefore be assumed that he recruited most of the sixty Indian auxiliary troops in that pueblo.

The men of Taos wore their hair in long braids like other Pueblos. As mentioned earlier, the horse guards shown in Segesser II include only one Indian with braided hair who is wearing armor; this deliberate distinction must indicate that the Indian was one of high rank, possibly a chief from Taos. The report of the Council of War held in Santa Fe on November 9, 1723, mentions one Gerónimo Ylo, an Indian chief of the pueblo of Taos, as one of the interpreters in the negotiations with the chiefs of the Jicarilla Apaches.[4] In the muster roll of the 1715 expedition are listed thirty-six warriors (with guns!) under the command of their chief, Gerónimo,[5] who is probably the same man. He also took part in the Valverde expedition, probably leading several dozen Taos Indians, and it seems logical that he would have been asked to accompany Villasur. It may well be that Figure 186, the warrior with braids and leather armor, is he.

There were two small Pueblo nations whose warriors were often recruited for Spanish expeditions, those of Picuris and San Ildefonso. Picuris, a Tiwa pueblo like Taos, about forty miles north of Santa Fe, early became the seat of a Franciscan mission. In 1704 the Picuris fled to El Cuartelejo, where they intermarried with the Jicarilla Apaches. San Ildefonso, a Tewa pueblo near the east bank

[4] Thomas, *After Coronado*, 196.

[5] "Hurtado's Review of Forces and Equipment, Picuríes Pueblo," *ibid.*, 93.

of the Río Grande, about sixteen miles northwest of Santa Fe, was the seat of a Spanish mission by 1617. Thus both pueblos had a long history of subjugation by the Spaniards.

In 1853, more than 133 years after the ill-fated expedition, a German traveler, Balduin Moellhausen, a member of an American expedition looking for the best route for a railroad line to the Pacific, made the acquaintance of Pueblos. He visited one of their towns and learned much about them. He wrote:

> A more peaceful tribe of people than the Pueblo Indians . . . can scarcely be imagined. They are friendly and helpful toward strangers wherever they meet them, and they show the greatest hospitality to those who visit them in their towns and homes. . . . For a long time they have been in constant contact with the Mexicans and have adopted a good many of their customs and dress. Most of them have a good command of the Spanish language. Diligence and industriousness are two of their main virtues; they carry on agriculture and horticulture and occasionally undertake trips to the wildest Indians of the Plains to bring home pelts and hides which they trade as the white men do. This is also the reason why travelers who come close to the border of New Mexico frequently meet small caravans of Pueblo Indians driving their donkeys and mules with their loads across the plains at a quick pace.[6]

There are also good recent descriptions of the habits and religious beliefs of the nations who make up the Pueblo Indians. When one observes the heroic roles in which they are cast in Segesser II, it seems almost certain that the artist or artists of the skin paintings belonged to one of the Pueblo nations. Moreover, the artist must have been familiar with the Hopi katcinas, which the striped body paintings of Figures 158 and 159 and Figures 143, 151, and 183 closely resemble. Drawings of katcinas and the Segresser figures have a number of similarities: thirty-seven katcina figures have the same distinctive coloring of forearms and upper leg, nine show only the forearms painted, and twenty-one show the left forearm and right

[6] Balduin Moellhausen, *Wanderungen durch die Praerien und Wuesten des westlichen Nordamerika vom Mississippi nach den Kuesten der Suedsee* (Leipzig, 1860),143.

upper leg in one or two colors; eleven have a capelike painting, and six have special shoulder colors. The katcinas illustrated are Hopis, but some are derived from Zuñis, Tanos, and Navahos.[7] Oddly enough, the Indians so painted in Segesser II belong to the attacking force, not to the Pueblo defenders.

Even today among the Hopis the dancers representing the rain-god are painted in a similar manner. The upper part of the body is painted red, with special shoulder and neck painting; the forearms are painted with yellow stripes resembling cuffs. The painting of the lower part of the legs is partly covered by leggings.

It is truly amazing to discover body paintings shown in a work of art almost 250 years old still used on special festive occasions in the American Southwest. On June 9, 1968, I observed it on such an occasion at the Hopi pueblo Shipaulovi, on the Second Mesa.

[7] Fewkes, *Hopi Katcinas.*

XVII
Conclusion

Segesser II unquestionably originated in the territory of the Río Grande Pueblos. It was from that region that Villasur's ill-fated expedition started out across the uncharted prairies. For reasons discussed in earlier chapters, Segesser I must have originated in the same region and may have been the work of the same painter. However, a considerable interval of time elapsed between its execution and that of Segesser II.

Every effort was made to ascertain when and where the paintings were executed, but without success. Nor was it possible to identify the scene shown in Segesser I. During the search for clues to the background of the paintings, the following letter was received from Mrs. E. Boyd, curator of the Museum of International Folk Art at Santa Fe, in 1960:

> New Mexico was entirely a Franciscan province from its settlement in 1598 until the mission order was withdrawn gradually at the end of the eighteenth century. For lack of conventional materials, such as oil paints and artist's canvas, the Franciscans of talent painted many pictures on tanned buffalo hides, using transparent dyes for colors. These, in all cases, were pictures of the stories of the New Testament—such as the Crucifixion, the Virgin, Apostles, and various Saints. Although relatively few have survived, more are listed by name in eighteenth century church inventories here. In no case did these Franciscan paintings ever depict non-religious subjects although a few show small landscape details such as cactus, trees, a bridge, and European-style buildings in the distance as backgrounds. Of those which I have examined and recorded—about forty—only two suggest that they may have been painted by an Indian; the others have a rather consistent Ren-

aissance manner of drawing and composition and a definitely European source. The Franciscans made these for the purpose of graphic aids in the teaching of Christianity to their Indian wards since works of church art came from Mexico in far too small numbers. New Mexico was a very poor frontier or buffer province during its existence as a Spanish or Mexican possession.

On the other hand, the Jesuits who, as you know, were active in the Sonora (then a larger state than it is now) and Baja California until their expulsion, were consistently scientific in their recording of natural phenomena as well as of the manners and customs of the many strange countries and their inhabitants where they were stationed. In addition to their written journals and reports, which were often copied and read aloud to the inmates of Jesuit training schools in Europe, they collected many types of specimens and, when possible, made or had made pictorial matter to augment their writings.

Your photographs fall very clearly into the eighteenth-century period of painting on buffalo hides in northern Mexico and New Mexico. The baroque borders, simulating carved and gilden wooden frames, are much like those of our painted skins here. Because religious pictures painted on animal skins were disapproved of by the secular bishops who visited from Mexico as early as 1820, and were more severely disapproved by the French Bishop Lamy who came to make a new diocese at Santa Fe, New Mexico, in 1851, most of the skins were cut up and used for patching of wool sacks, book bindings, and so on. In the Sonora and Southern Arizona, where Jesuit paintings on skins must have been as usual, although of more informative subjects than religious images, the destruction of missions by Apaches throughout the eighteenth and much of the nineteenth centuries seems to have accounted for their disappearance.[1] In addition the taking over of their missions by Franciscans

[1] According to Bernard Fontana, curator of the Arizona State Museum, Tucson, in the Pima region of southern Arizona many documents and religious paintings have been preserved from the period of Spanish domination. Friar Luis Baldonado, of the Mission of San Xavier del Bac in Arizona, reported that there was no record of skin paintings among the Pima missions but that there was evidence of such paintings in the following missions in New Mexico: San Ildefonso, Nambe, Tesuque, Santo Domingo, Picuris, Isleta, Santa Cruz, Zía, Laguna, Acoma, Zuñi, and Pecos, and in Santa Fé, where there are today five large paintings on buffalo skins.

may have been responsible for the further disappearance of such paintings. It is therefore most fortunate that the two paintings you write of were sent to the Segesser family in Switzerland, where they have been preserved.

I cannot share the conclusion that Jesuits produced the skin paintings. If the Jesuits were engaged in such pursuits, why did Father Philipp never mention them, particularly since he often wrote at length about trifles? Neither in his correspondence with his family nor in his "Relación" did he mention such works. Even if they had been engaged in painting, what connection would the Jesuits have had with the Villasur expedition? Too, if there were any contacts with the Franciscans in New Mexico, they must have been of a rather strained nature.

For political reasons only, Valverde might have been interested in a pictorial presentation of the massacre—and the inclusion of a large number of Frenchmen among the attackers, for it was he who was held responsible for the disaster. Painted by an eyewitness, such a work would lend authenticity to the claim that the French had participated and might help exonerate him. Valverde's term as governor of the province ended in 1722. For four years he lived at El Paso, where he commanded the military post and managed his nearby estates. It was not until 1726 that he was finally summoned to Santa Fe by Brigadier General Pedro de Rivera to testify at an investigation of the expedition.[2] In 1727 he was ordered to pay 50 pesos for masses for the fallen soldiers and to pay 150 pesos to the church, but was otherwise acquitted.

If Segesser II was painted upon Valverde's order, then he must also have ordered the expedition depicted in Segesser I, for it seems evident that the two wall hangings belong together. Since his land holdings lay in a region which was surrounded by the Suma territory, it is likely that he employed members of the Suma mission for military purposes. In that case, Segesser I might represent an episode of the punitive expedition of the year 1714, which Valverde led personally. In this case the horsemen could have been Sumas,

[2] "Writ of Rivera, El Paso, May 13, 1726," Thomas, *After Coronado*, 220–21; "Notification to Valverde, El Paso, May 13, 1726," *ibid.*, 221–22.

rather than Tarascans, though the horsemen's headdresses would seem to make it unlikely.

Valverde had been in the royal service since 1693 and had participated under Vargas in the reconquest of New Mexico. He was with the troops which had come up from the south for the recovery of the province. How long this presumbably south Mexican Indian militia was used in Santa Fe or in the garrisons of El Paso and Parral is not known. If they were withdrawn rather early, then the shaved heads of the horsemen in Segesser I make it appear that they were Sumas, unless the painting originated as early as the turn of the century—that is, at a time when outside Indians were used to guard the natives. On the other hand, El Paso, which lay in the territory of the Sumas, was the starting point of the reconquest. Thus only the headdress of the horsemen, which would indicate southern Mexican Indians, gives rise to doubts about the presence of Sumas on Segresser I.

How Father Philipp gained possession of the paintings remains unexplained, but it is only half as far from El Paso to Ures as from Santa Fe. A report about the Sumas by Valverde is preserved in the Palacio Municipal in Parral, Chihuahua.[3] He must have been well acquainted with them, for he had taken from them his extensive landholdings and the land of the mission, which, of course, were the best lands. The Indians who had been robbed of their stores of seed and their land had been forced to withdraw into the mountains and become thieves. Valverde obtained rich harvests of grapes, wheat, corn, beans, and so forth. He further profited by overcharging the soldiers for the provisions he sold them and by employing them as farm hands, drivers, and shepherds for his large herds of cattle.[4]

The fact that Valverde resided in El Paso before and during his term of office as governor (1716–1722) does not necessarily indicate that Segesser II did not originate in Santa Fe, for the painter must surely have known the participants in the battle he

[3] Sauer, *The Road to Cíbola*, 87.

[4] According to the letter from Martínez (who had been replaced by him in office in 1716) to Viceroy Valero, included in a notebook entitled Document XX, 1719–1729. The letter was written in 1720.

depicted. Valverde could have had it painted there and could have taken it with him later. Valverde was born in 1672. In 1758, when Father Philipp sent the skin paintings to Europe, he would have been eighty-six years old. If he was dead at that time, an heir might have passed them on.

Since no Mexican sources are available to me that might support the theory that the skin paintings were made at the request of Valverde, it would be equally plausible to conclude that the surviving members of the expedition commissioned the painting as a memorial to their fallen comrades and to themselves. That being the case, Segesser II could have originated after Valverde's departure from Santa Fe. But then Segesser I could hardly have any connection with him.

For all the above-mentioned theories there are good reasons as well as valid doubts. In the absence of any corroborative evidence, of course, such hypotheses are in the end merely conjectures. The only facts about which there can be no doubt are that Segesser I represents a punitive expedition against Apaches and that Segesser II represents the Villasur massacre.

XVIII
Epilogue

The Villasur expedition can be placed in a larger frame. A century later, in 1806, Villasur's expedition was repeated by Lieutenant Don Facundo Malgares (or Melgares). Indeed, the expedition could be called "Villasur Two." But there was an important difference between the two expeditions: the second one was to a certain extent successful.

The Spaniards had not forgotten who had ambushed Villasur's party. After the Americans purchased Louisiana from the French in 1803, the Spaniards feared that the Indian tribes who had fought the Spaniards in 1720 would attach themselves to the new rulers of the Plains. Therefore, they got in touch with Joseph Gervais, a trader among the Platte Indians. In 1803 this man turned up in Santa Fe with a party of Pawnees, and in 1804 he and his Pawnees paid a second visit to the Spanish settlements. But Gervais then apparently went over to the Americans. The alarmed officials ordered a military force to proceed to the Pawnee villages in the fall of 1804 to make an alliance with that tribe. With their usual bad luck, the Spanish troops met a large force of Indians on the Arkansas River, were defeated in the battle that ensued, and had to return home without visiting the Pawnees.[1]

General James Wilkinson (whom George Hyde called an "archplotter") at St. Louis made secret plans for an invasion of New Mexico. Old French traders persuaded him that for such a purpose he first needed to win over the Comanches, a task which could be accomplished through the Pawnees. So Wilkinson sent

[1] Caso-Calvo in *Tabeau's Narrative of Loisel's Expedition to the Upper Missouri* (ed. by Annie Heloise Abel), (Norman, 1939), 240; Cox, "Opening the Santa Fé Trail," *Missouri Historical Review* (October, 1930).

Lieutenant Zebulon Montgomery Pike to visit both tribes. "Thus the Pawnees, without knowing anything about it, had suddenly become very important to many white men in St. Louis and Santa Fe who were busily hatching plots and counterplots."[2]

In a three-page footnote to his journal entry of September 25, 1806, Pike wrote that Spanish emissaries in St. Louis told the Mexican authorities about his expedition toward the Southwest, whereupon a counterexpedition was planned. Pike wrote:

> The [Spanish] expedition was then determined on, and had three objects in view: viz.—
>
> 1st. To descend the Red river, in order, if he met our expedition, to intercept and turn us back, . . . or to make them prisoners of war.
>
> 2d. To explore and examine all the internal parts of the country from the frontiers of the province of New Mexico to the Missouri, between the La Platte [and Kansas rivers].
>
> 3d. To visit the Tetaus [Ietans], Pawnees republic, Grand Pawnees; Pawnee Mahaws and Kans. To the head chief of each of those nations: the commanding [Spanish] officer bore flags, a commission; grand medal, and four mules; and with all of whom he had to renew the chains of ancient amity which was said to have existed between their father, his most Catholic majesty, and his children the red people.
>
> The commanding officer also bore positive orders to oblige all parties or persons in the above specified countries, either to retire from them into the acknowledged territories of the United States, or to make prisoners of them and conduct them into the province of N. Mexico. Lieut. Don Facundo Malgares, the officer selected from the five internal provinces, to command this expedition, was an European, (his uncle, was one of the royal judges of the kingdom of New Spain) and had distinguished himself in several long expeditions against the Apaches and other Indian nations, with whom the Spaniards were at war: added to these circumstances, he was a man of immense fortune, and generous in its disposal, almost to profusion: possessed a liberal education, high sense of honor, and a disposition formed for military enterprise. This officer

[2] George E. Hyde, *The Pawnee Indians* (Denver, 1951), 100.

> marched from the province of Biscay with 100 dragoons of the regular service, and at Santa Fe (the place where the expedition was fitted out from) he was joined by 500 of the mounted militia of that provinced, armed . . . and compleately equipt with ammunition &c. for six months; each man leading with them (by order) two horses and one mule, the whole number of their beasts were two thousand and seventy five. The descended the Red river [probably the Río Ojo, the Cimarron] 233 leagues, met the grand bands of the Tetaus; held councils with them, then struck off N.E. and crossed the country to the Arkansaw, where lieut. Malgares left 240 of his men with the lame and tired horses, whilst he proceeded on with the rest to the Pawnee republic; there he was met by the chiefs and warriors of the Grand Pawnees; held councils with the two nations, and presented them the flags, medals, &c. . . . He did not proceed on to the execution of his mission with the Pawnee Mahaws [Otos] and the Kans, as he represented to me, from the poverty of their horses, and the discontent of his own men, but as I conceive, from the suspicion and discontent which began to arise between the Spaniards and the Indians. The former wishing to avenge the death of Villineuve [Villasur] and party, whilst the latter possessed all the suspicions of conscious villainy deserving punishment.[3]

From the Arkansas, Malgares marched north to the Kitkehahki village on the south bank of the Republican River, between the present towns of Red Cloud and Guide Rock, Nebraska. The chiefs of the Grand Pawnees had come there from the Platte to meet the Spaniards. In a great council Malgares presented Spanish medals, flags, and commissions to the chiefs. He then proposed a joint expedition against the Skidi Pawnees; but although the Kitkehahkis were at war with that tribe and the Grand Pawnees felt none too friendly toward them, the chiefs refused to join forces with Malgares. Their attitude hastened his departure, for instead of going on, as ordered, to visit the Kansas, Otos, and other tribes, he hurriedly withdrew to his camp south of the Arkansas.[4]

[3] *The Journals of Zebulon Montgomery Pike, with Letters and Related Documents* (ed. by Donald Jackson, Norman, 1966), I, 323–25.

[4] Statements made by George E. Hyde after consulting available reports of the period, which he discussed with me.

Shortly after Malgares had left the Pawnee village, Lieutenant Pike arrived with a score of soldiers of the First Infantry, coming from the Osage villages. Having succeeded in frightening the Spaniards, the Pawnees attempted to do the same thing to the Americans but failed. The display of three hundred mounted warriors made no impression on Pike, and he and his handful of infantrymen resisted the attempts of the Pawnees to rob and intimidate them.

Pike wrote about this point that in the village of Sharitarish or White Wolf, chief of the Kitkehahkis, were several Spanish flags; and on the occasion of the meeting with Pike one of the flags was placed over the door of the chief's lodge. It is interesting to speculate what the Indian chief must have thought when the American with his twenty infantrymen demanded that the flag of the rich and mighty Spaniards be lowered. But it was done, and the American flag was hoisted in its place.

Pike proceeded westward, whereas Malgares with his command went 233 leagues down the Red River in search of Pike. Mistakenly thinking that he was at the source of the Red River, Pike entered the upper Río Grande Valley, where he and his men, hungry and ragged, were taken prisoner by the Spaniards on February 20, 1807. It was Malgares who escorted Pike from Santa Fe to Chihuahua. The two erstwhile enemies became good friends on the way, and both men were regretful when Pike was handed over to another Spanish officer to be led back to American territory.

Thus ended the quasi repetition of Villasur's expedition nearly a century later.

One final remark may be added in explanation of the fact that the painter of Segesser II drew the guns of the "French" soldiers, which he had probably never seen, in such enormous sizes. Pike wrote that at the mustering of a regiment of Militia at Chihuahua about twenty-five men were armed with muskets and lances; fifty with bows, arrows, and lances; and the rest either with lances or with bows and arrows. If that was the situation in the rich province of Chihuahua nearly a century later, how miserable the arms situation must have been in Santa Fe in Villasur's time!

Index